Alexis Soyer

A Shilling Cookery for the People

Embracing an entirely new system of plain cookery and domestic economy

Alexis Soyer

A Shilling Cookery for the People
Embracing an entirely new system of plain cookery and domestic economy

ISBN/EAN: 9783744785167

Printed in Europe, USA, Canada, Australia, Japan

Cover: Foto ©Lupo / pixelio.de

More available books at **www.hansebooks.com**

A

SHILLING COOKERY

FOR

THE PEOPLE:

EMBRACING

AN ENTIRELY NEW SYSTEM OF PLAIN COOKERY
AND DOMESTIC ECONOMY.

By ALEXIS SOYER,
AUTHOR OF "THE MODERN HOUSEWIFE,"
ETC. ETC.

"Religion feeds the soul, Education the mind, Food the body."
SOYER's *History of Food.*

Two Hundred and Second Thousand.

LONDON:
ROUTLEDGE, WARNE, AND ROUTLEDGE,
FARRINGDON STREET.
NEW YORK: 56, WALKER STREET.
1860.
[*The Author of this Work reserves the right of translating it.*]

LONDON :
SAVILL AND EDWARDS, PRINTERS, CHANDOS STREET,
COVENT GARDEN.

PREFACE

TO THE 110TH THOUSAND.

It is with the most profound gratitude that I have once more to thank the British public for their extraordinary and ever increasing patronage; extraordinary is indeed the only word applicable to the success of this my last work, which has actually attained its hundred and tenth thousand in less than four months.

In this, the last edition of 10,000 copies, completing the above wonderful number, I have been induced by some friends to make my appearance at the head of the work as I am now in my ninth lustre. The majority of those friends being ladies, and making it a point of honour never to refuse anything in my power to those charming members of society, I immediately went to my friend, Mr. Hogg, the eminent photographer of West Strand, who in a few seconds produced a facsimile of

Yours most gratefully and devotedly,

A. SOYER in the year 1854

CONTENTS.

CONTENTS.

IMPORTANT OBSERVATIONS.

First, most of the receipts, having been especially written for the various ordinary kitchen utensils, some of them may appear to the reader to be repetitions, which is not the case, as the same food may be used, yet each process will differ one from the other, from having been cooked in a different manner.

Secondly, to obviate the reading of two or three receipts to be able to execute one, I have made each receipt in itself as complete as possible, as regards seasoning and proportion, and the few references I unavoidably make will, after a little practice, become familiar to my readers.

Many of the receipts may appear to you rather lengthy, but I want to draw your attention to the fact, that they are more than receipts—indeed, I may call them plain lessons, some containing a number of receipts in one.

In some cookery books many receipts are explained in few lines, which at first sight gives to the thing the appearance of simplicity; but when acted on by the uninitiated are found totally impracticable.

By my plan my readers may read and prepare the contents of two or three lines at a time, so that when they get at the end of a lesson, their dish will be found well seasoned and properly cooked.

INTRODUCTORY LETTERS.

DEAR ELOISE,

MORE than a year has now elapsed since I wrote to you, with a promise that I would send you such receipts as should be of use to the artisan, mechanic, and cottager. The time has, however, passed so quickly, that I was not aware of its hasty flight, until I took up the last edition of our "Housewife." But still, dearest, I must say I have not lost any time; for you will find that my letters, which have conveyed my receipts from time to time, have been dated from almost every county in the United Kingdom.

In the course of my peregrinations, I have made a point of visiting the cottages and abodes of the industrious classes generally, and have also closely examined the peculiarities and manners which distinguish each county, as well as the different kinds of labour; and I have viewed with pleasure the exertions made by philanthropic individuals to improve the morals of the labouring class, and render their dwellings more comfortable. But still I have found a great want of knowledge in that one object which produces almost as much comfort as all the rest put together, viz., the means of making the most of that food which the great Architect of the Heavens has so bountifully spread before us on the face of the globe.

Those who visit these humble abodes to inculcate the divine precepts of the Saviour of mankind, do but half the great work, unless they at the same time show how those things which the Almighty has created as food for man can be employed towards his nourishment.

In some of my letters, my dear friend, I think I have sent you a description of some scenes I witnessed in the course of my rambles, especially in Ireland, resulting from a want of knowledge, all of which bears a moral; and what a high feeling of delight and satisfaction it will be to us, should we find that the result of our labour is crowned with success, in ameliorating the conditions of these classes; for believe me, I was right when I stated that the morals of a people greatly depend on their food and wherever the home of an individual, in whatever class of society he may move, is made comfortable and happy, the more moral and religious will that person be.

DEAREST HORTENSE,

I highly approve of your plan; it is time that it was put into action. I am fearful that our friends, the public, to whom we promised, some four years since, a work like the present, will have become impatient; but they will be gainers by the delay, as by your visits to the various parts of the United Kingdom, you have obtained that insight into the domestic arrangements of the class of persons for whom it is intended, that could not be obtained by any other means.

Your new plan of writing a series of receipts peculiarly adapted for such humble utensils as the gridiron, frying-pan, iron pan, and black pot, is at once original, and cannot fail of being very effective; for no matter how humble or poor the dwelling, one of those faithful servants are sure to be found at its post; and I do not doubt but that, under your tuition, they will prove of greater value to the public at large than they hitherto have been.

If a person, after purchasing this work for a shilling, had to lay out five or six more in kitchen utensils before he could cook by it, it would be a great drawback on its worth; but by your happy and simple style, you have so successfully avoided all complicated matters in its pages, that nothing will be requisite but the aforesaid simple kitchen implements to bring it into action.

I also perceive, with pleasure, that you have not omitted the slightest article of cheap food of any description, which, with the numerous receipts you give for dressing the same, must prove a great blessing to many, and only require to be introduced to the notice of the public to form a part of their daily diet.

It is to be regretted that men of science do not interest themselves more than they do on a subject of such vast magnitude as this; for I feel confident that the food of a country might be increased at least one-third, if the culinary science was properly developed, instead of its being slighted as it is now. I myself think it worthy the attention of a peer of the realm; for, as you justly observe, the morals of a country greatly depend on the

production and preparation of its food, and most heartily
do I re-echo your sentiments.

My dearest Friend,

You are right. Cookery, in our era,
has been thought beneath the attention of men of science;
and yet, was there ever a political, commercial, or even a
domestic event, but what always has been, and always will
be, celebrated either by a banquet or a dinner? And pray,
who is answerable for the comfort and conviviality of the
guests of such festivals but the cook, who has been in-
trusted with such important duties? The selection of good
and proper beverages will, of course, greatly assist the
cook's endeavours; but these may be purchased months,
or even years, before you require them, which would of
course give you an ample chance of remedying any error;
while a dinner is the creation of a day and the success of
a moment. Therefore you will perceive that nothing more
disposes the heart to amicable feeling and friendly trans-
actions, than a dinner well conceived and artistically
prepared.

In ancient times, a cook, especially if a man, was looked
upon as a distinguished member of society; while now he
is, in the opinion of almost every one, a mere menial.

Still there are a few who highly appreciate the knowledge he possesses, especially in the higher circles, who
have classified cookery as a high art. For example, let
us see what one of the greatest chemists of the day

(Liebig) says on this imperishable subject, in his valuable work, "The Chemistry of Food," that

" Among all the arts known to man there is none which enjoys a juster appreciation, and the products of which are more universally admired, than that which is concerned in the preparation of our food. Led by an instinct, which has almost reached the dignity of conscious knowledge, as the unerring guide, and by the sense of taste, which protects the health, the experienced cook, with respect to the choice, the admixture, and the preparation of food, has made acquisitions surpassing all that chemical and physiological science have done in regard to the doctrine or theory of nutrition. In soup and meat sauces, he imitates the gastric juice; and by the cheese which closes the banquet, he assists the action of the dissolved epithelium of the stomach. The table, supplied with dishes, appears to the observer like a machine, the parts of which are harmoniously fitted together, and so arranged that, when brought into action, a maximum of effect may be obtained by the theory of them. The able culinary artist accompanies the sanguineous matter with those which promote the process of solution and sanguification, in due proportion; he avoids all kinds of unnecessary stimuli, such as do not act in restoring the equilibrium; and he provides the due nourishment for the child or the weak old man, as well as for the strong of both sexes."

Such is the high eulogium paid to culinary science by that learned man; and perhaps there is no one more able of appreciating its value than him. Therefore I do not yet despair of seeing the day when that science, like others, will have its qualified professors. I now close our labours for the present, and wait with anxiety the first proof, which on receiving I will immediately correct and forward to you.

COOKERY FOR THE PEOPLE.

SOUPS, IN IRON SAUCEPAN,
OR STEWPAN.

SIMPLIFIED STOCK FOR SOUPS, GRAVIES, AND PLAIN SAUCES.

ELOISE,—Perhaps you are not aware of the reason why the great majority of people in this country are opposed to, and even accused of not liking, soup; the simple reason is, that every receipt described in most Cookery Books, is so complicated and expensive, that they cannot afford either the money, time, or attention, to prepare it. I will therefore endeavour, in this little book, to obviate that difficulty, by simplifying the receipts, and reduce it to a system alike quick, nutritious, wholesome, and economical; and thus soup may form a part of the daily fare of every dinner table.

Please pay particular attention to the following receipt, for when you are perfect in it, and can make it quick and well, almost every sort of soup can be made from it, and it will often be referred to in different sauces and dishes.

1. *Stock for Clear Soup. First Lesson.*—Cut two pounds of knuckle or scrag of veal into small pieces, place them in the iron pot or stewpan, with two ounces of salt butter or dripping, two ounces of n bacon cut small, three teaspoonfuls of salt, half a spoonful of pepper, a gill of water, three middle-sized, or six ounces of, onions sliced. Put on the fire; when boiling, stir round with a spoon for about ten minutes, or until it forms a whitish thick gravy at the bottom, or gets rather dry, then add five pints of hot or cold water; when boiling, let it simmer gently for three quarters of an hour, skim it well, pass it through a sieve, and it will be found clear and ready for use for the following soups. Only one third of this quantity need be made.

B

In case bacon or ham cannot be obtained, use half a pound more meat and a little more salt.

The meat not being overstewed, will be found excellent eaten plain, or with parsley and butter, or any sauce.

2. *Second Lesson.*—Proceed exactly as No. 1. Add two cloves and about two ounces of carrot, and the same of turnip, leeks, celery, or a quarter of a pound of one of them, if you cannot get the variety. To add more zest to the flavour, add the smallest quantity of thyme, winter savory, or a bay leaf. You are, no doubt, aware that at present, in most market towns, an assorted lot of vegetables may be obtained at one penny per plate, and sometimes at one halfpenny. This second lesson is very important, as it gives you the key whereby you may vary the flavour of every kind of soup.

Note. This broth is of a nice white colour, and should it be required to look like sherry wine, add sufficient colouring, (see No. 453), or half a burnt onion when it is making: these in most large cities are now becoming common, and may be procured at the grocers, at the cost of eightpence the pound. They will go a great way, and if kept in a dry place will last for years.

3. *Brown Gravies.*—The following is very good for brown sauce, and also for every kind of roast meat, game, or poultry; and a gill of it may be used to give a colour to any kind of broth, instead of colouring or burnt onions. As there is a little difficulty to make it properly, it should only be done on particular occasions.

Grease the bottom of the pot with about two ounces of fat, butter, or dripping; cut four onions in thick slices crossways, lay them on the bottom, and place over them three pounds of leg or shin of beef, or clod and sticking; cut it slantway in pieces, chop the bone, then add two teaspoonfuls of salt, half a spoonful of pepper; set it on the fire until it begins to hiss, which indicates that all the moisture is dispersed; reduce the heat of the fire by throwing ashes on the top; put on the pan with the cover over. Let the onions stew until quite brown, but not burnt, and the fat is as clear as oil, which you will easily perceive by holding the pan or pot on one side, the contents of which will be smoking hot, and stick to the bottom, though not burning, immediately add five pints of cold water; when boiling, skim and simmer one hour; pass through the sieve, and put by till wanted. It will keep for many days in winter, and also in summer, by boiling it every other day, with the addition of half a gill of water added to it now and then.

4. *Lesson No. 2.*—The remains of roast or boiled meat, game, poultry, &c., may be added, cut up, and the bones broken, using only half the quantity of meat. The meat may be taken out and served separate, with a mustard or any sharp sauce.

The addition of cloves (say four), a little mace, carrots, turnips, and celery, and a few sweet herbs, will vary the flavour of the gravy.

5. *Clear Vegetable Soup, Lesson No. 1.*—Cut in small dice, two-thirds of carrots and turnips, and one-third of onions, leeks, and celery, altogether about half a pound ; wash them well, drain, put into pan or iron pot, two ounces of butter or dripping, and a teaspoonful of sugar; put on the fire, stir often; when no moisture is to be seen add three pints of broth No. 1, simmer and skim, until the carrots are tender, and serve. If all the above vegetables cannot be obtained at the same time, use the same weight of either. Be careful that you remove the fat from all clear soup. All clear vegetable soup, when done, ought to partake of a brownish colour.

6. *Lesson No. 2.*—The addition of a few green peas, when in season, also small pieces of brocoli, a cauliflower, or a few Brussels sprouts, previously boiled, makes an improvement in the above. A little chervil and tarragon render it both pleasant and refreshing.

7. *Clear Turnip, Lesson No. 3.*—Peel and cut in large dice half a pound of turnips, put in pan with butter or fat, and a little sugar ; proceed as above, Lesson No. 1, add the broth, simmer skim, and serve. It will not require so long doing as No. 1. Give it a nice brown colour. If turnips are either streaky or spongy, they will not do.

8. *Jerusalem Artichokes.*—Wash, peel, cut in dice, and fry as above; when nothing but the clear fat is seen in the pan, and they are sufficiently done, add the broth. A few minutes will cook them.

9. *Carrot Soup.*—For carrots proceed as above, and simmer till tender ; they take twice as long as the artichokes doing.

10. *Vermicelli and Macaroni.*—Pray, Eloise, why should not the workman and mechanic partake of these wholesome and nutritious articles of food, which have now, in consequence of those restrictive laws on provisions having been repealed, become so plentiful and cheap? It only requires to know how to cook them, in order that they should become as favourite a food in these northern climes, as they are in the southern.* Boil three pints of the broth No. 1, break into it a quarter of a pound of vermicelli or macaroni; boil till tender, and serve. Macaroni takes twice as long as vermicelli doing.

Or, the macaroni can be boiled separate, and kept in salt and water for some days, and used as required for soups and made dishes.

11. *Rice.*—Wash well two ounces of common Bengal rice; boil it gently in three pints of broth; when tender, serve.

12. *Tapioca and Semolina.*—In case of illness, two ounces of tapioca or semolina may be used instead.

13. *White Soup with Meat.*—When the broth No. 1 is done, skim off the fat, put the meat in the tureen, then put into a basin two ounces of flour, mix gently with half a pint of milk, a half teaspoonful of salt, and a quarter ditto of pepper; add to the broth by degrees; boil it ten minutes, and keep stirring; skim and serve with the meat. Fried or toasted bread cut in dice may be added.

14. *Good White Mock Turtle Soup* may be easily and cheaply made thus:—Purchase a calf's head; if large, use one half for a day's dinner; cook as receipt No. 87; take the remains of that, if any, with the other half, and remove the bone; cut the meat into square pieces; add it in proportion of one pound of meat to every four quarts of broth of No. 1; mix some flour and milk, as above, and add it to it, and half a teaspoonful of cayenne pepper, and four cloves; let it simmer on the fire for one hour, tie up six sprigs of savory, same of thyme, which put into the soup, and remove when serving. The juice of half a lemon is an improvement, just before serving, as well as a drop of

---

* Macaroni is now selling in London at fivepence per pound, and makes four pounds of food when boiled, as No. 463.

wine, if handy. If required brown, add three tablespoonfuls of colouring; and use water or broth for thickening, instead of milk. The water in which the calf's head is boiled may be kept, and added to the stock. This soup will keep for a long time if boiled occasionally, and a little water added; it should never be covered, or fermentation will commence; it should be occasionally stirred until cold. Strong stocks are more likely to turn sour than thin ones, more particularly if they have vegetables and flour in them; to prevent which, when this soup is kept in a basin, leave the mouth exposed to the air.

15. *Cow-heel.*—Another very cheap and nutritious soup may be made by an ox-foot or cow-heel; having bought them cleaned and partly boiled, stew them till tender, remove the meat from the bone, cut them into nice pieces, and proceed as for mock-turtle.

16. *White Soup, with Vegetables, &c.*—Having cut and fried the same quantity of vegetables as No. 1, add them to the white soup, free from meat as No. 13; simmer and skim off the fat. Two ounces of vermicelli, macaroni, rice, &c., previously boiled, can be used in the same way.

17. *Purée, or Thick Vegetable Soups.—Green Pea.*—Put a quart of large green peas, when cheap, in the pot or pan, with two ounces of butter or fat, and the same of lean bacon cut small, a middling-sized onion, little mint, two teaspoonfuls of salt, one of sugar, half the same of pepper, a gill of water; set on slow fire, stir now and then, or until no more moisture remains on the bottom of the pan; add two or three tablespoonfuls of flour, stir round quick, and break the peas against the side of the pan with a wooden spoon; moisten with a quart of milk and a quart of water, simmer twenty minutes, or more if old peas, and serve.

This, by leaving out the bacon, becomes *Meagre Soup.* Fried bread, in small dice, is a good accompaniment.

If you have any broth (No. 1), use it instead of the milk and water.

By passing the peas through a hair sieve, which is done by breaking and pressing them with the back of the spoon, an inviting purée is produced; after which warm up, and serve.

18. *Pumpkin Soup* is a very favourite dish in many parts o

France, especially with the juveniles; and when in season, there
is not a school, college, hospital, convent, or monastery, where
it is not made; a proof that it must be very wholesome.   In
this country, whose climate will not allow its arriving at the
same size as on the Continent, the *Vegetable Marrow*, the
American Butter Squash, and the *Mammoth Gourd*, will
replace them.

Cut about two pounds of the flesh of the pumpkin or gourd
into large dice, put it into your pan, with three ounces of salt
butter or fat; add two teaspoonfuls of salt, the same of sugar, a
little pepper, and half a pint of water; set on the fire, and stew
gently for twenty minutes.   When in pulp, add two tablespoonfuls of flour, stir round, and moisten with three pints of
either milk, skim-milk, or water, boil ten minutes longer, and
serve with fried or toasted bread, cut in dice.

19. *Meagre Soups.*—This soup is on the list of meagre soups,
a word used by the Catholics for dishes partaken of in Lent,
but which is not understood in England; the word having the
meaning, want of strength.   But this soup, and many others in
the same category, are well worthy the attention of the middle
classes of this country, it being only meagre in name, and not
in fact, as it possesses a large quantity of farinaceous matter;
bread being also served with it.

20. *Vegetable Marrow.*—Peel, and take out the inside, if
seeded, cut in slices about two pounds; put in saucepan on the
fire, with a quarter of a pound of butter or fat; add two teaspoonfuls of salt, one of sugar, and one quarter of the same of
pepper, a gill of water, and one onion sliced; stew gently until
in pulp, then add two tablespoonfuls of flour, and proceed as for
pumpkin soup.

21. *Turnip Soup.*—Use two and a half pounds of good
turnips, and proceed as above.

22. *Red Carrot Soup.*—Scrape gently, and cut in very thin
slices two pounds of carrots; put them in the saucepan or pot with
two onions sliced, two ounces of ham cut small, two cloves, a
little thyme, salt, pepper, sugar, as above, half a pint of water,
simmer gently forty minutes, then add three tablespoonfuls of
flour, and two quarts of broth (No. 1), or use milk, or even water.

It is much better passed through a hair sieve, after which warm up again and serve.

White Carrot.—Proceed as for the red.

The Swede, Parsnip, Red and White Beet.—Proceed as for carrot.

23. *New Spring and Autumn Soup.*—A most refreshing and exquisite soup. At the end of the London season, when the markets are full of everything, and few to partake of them, this soup can be made as a bonne bouche:—

Wash, dry, and cut up four cabbage lettuces, and one coss ditto, a handful of sorrel, a little tarragon and chervil, and two or three small cucumbers peeled and sliced; put into a saucepan a quarter of a pound of butter, then set in the vegetables; put on a slow fire, and stir often, until there is no liquid remaining; add two tablespoonfuls of flour, mix well, and moisten with two quarts of broth (No. 1) or water, and set it to boil; when boiling, add a pint of green peas, two teaspoonfuls of powdered sugar, a little pepper and salt; when the peas are tender, serve. If you use water, increase the quantity of seasoning.

New Cock-a-Leekie.

Ma chère Amie,—With all due respect to Scotch cookery, I will always give the preference, in the way of soup, to their cock-a-leekie, even before their inimitable hodge-podge. Having a very old friend, from the neighbourhood of Dundee, who used to praise my cock-a-leekie, when on a visit to St. John's Wood, I thought I would give him the same treat here, and on looking over my frugal store and garden of Camellia Cottage, I found I had all that was required, barring the bird; but, with a little perseverance and ingenuity, I succeeded in producing a very nice soup, although it wanted the principal ingredient, so that it deceived not only my husband, but my friend from the other side of the Tweed. Here is the receipt:

24.—I bought two pounds of veal cutlet, and cut it into pieces, like the flesh from the breast of a fowl, and put them in the pan with a quarter of a pound of butter, the same of lean bacon, three cloves, two good onions sliced, two teaspoonfuls of salt, one of sugar, half a one of pepper, a gill of water; set it on the fire, turn it over until forming a white glaze at the bottom, add to it five pints of water, simmer half an hour, pass through a sieve, save the best pieces of the veal. In the meantime blanch two pounds of leeks, free from the top green part, for ten minutes, in a gallon of water, and drain them; then boil the stock and half the leeks together, till almost in a pulp, then add the other half of the leeks and the meat, also eighteen good fresh French plums; simmer half an hour, and serve.

I must observe that my friend praised it very much for having put in the flesh of the fowl only, as he thought, and not the whole carcase, which is the way they serve it in Scotland; an exceedingly inconvenient way, as everybody expects a piece of the fowl, and you often tear it to pieces in serving.

25. *Simplified Hodge-Podge.*—Cut two pounds of fresh scrag of mutton into small pieces, which put into a stewpan, with three quarts of cold water, and a tablespoonful of salt, one ditto of sugar, half a ditto of pepper; set it on the fire; when boiling, place it at the side to simmer for one hour; keep it skimmed; well wash a large carrot, two turnips, two onions, and six small cabbage lettuces; cut them up, and place in the pot, and simmer till done. *A pint* of green peas, if in season, may be added. A carrot grated is an improvement. If in winter, use cabbage instead of lettuce. Serve the meat with it.

26. *Various Meat Soups.*—*Giblet.*—These should be procured ready cleaned, but if not, they must be scalded; when done, cut them into about twelve pieces, wash them well, and dry in a cloth; put into a pan a quarter of a pound of butter or dripping, set it on the fire, melt it, then add four ounces of flour, stir continually until it begins to brown, add two ounces of lean bacon, and two onions or leeks sliced, fry a few minutes longer, put in the giblets, fry gently for ten minutes, stirring now and then, pour over two quarts of water, stir till boiling, and set it to simmer; then add two teaspoonfuls of salt, half one of pepper one of sugar, three cloves, a little thyme, bay leaf, and about a quarter of a pound of celery well washed and cut up small; continue simmering until the giblets are tender, remove the fat, and serve. A wineglass of sherry and a little cayenne may be added. A pound of beef or veal is, of course, a great improvement. This receipt is for the giblets of a middle-sized turkey.

27. *Hare Soup.*

MY DEAR ELOISE,—Since the alteration in our circumstances I have learnt to practise the most rigid economy, which you will remark in this receipt. When I buy a hare, as I sometimes do, for two shillings, skinning it myself, and selling the skin for fourpence, I save all the blood in a pie-dish, take out the heart and liver, removing the gall; I then cut the hare into two, across the back, close to the last ribs, and cut this part into pieces, using it for soup, and the hindpart I keep for roasting the following day.

28. *Hare Soup.*—I then proceed as for giblet soup, only using half a pound of either veal, beef, or mutton, cut into dice, and put in the pot with the hare. Fifteen minutes before serving, I mix the blood with the heart and liver, which I have chopped fine, and boil it up ten minutes; skim and serve. The addition of a little brown sugar and a glass of port wine is an improvement: if no wine, a little stout or porter will improve it. It ought to be of a dark brown colour, for which use colouring.

29. *Ox Tail.*—Cut them at the joints, and proceed as for giblets, adding one pint more water for two small tails, and simmer half an hour longer, or till done. This should be of a brown colour. Vegetables cut into dice may be added. Serve when tender: some will take double the time cooking, according to size.

30. *Ox Cheek.*—Boil half a large cheek for twenty minutes in two quarts of water, to set it; take it out, cut it into thin slices, or small pieces, and then proceed exactly as for giblets. Serve when tender.

31. *Simplified Mulligatawny, quickly done. Lesson* 1.— Cut in small dice two pounds of leg of veal, no bone, then put in the pan with two ounces of salt butter, two teaspoonfuls of salt, a quarter that of pepper, a quarter of a pound of onions sliced, and a wine-glass of water. Put it in the pan and place on the fire, stir it about until nearly dry; two ounces of bacon or ham is an improvement; then add a good teaspoonful and a half of curry-powder, four of flour, and one of brown sugar; moisten with five pints of water, simmer for an hour or a little longer, skim, and serve. Half a pound of rice, as No. 455, may be served either with it or separate.

Lesson 2.—To the above may be added a small apple, cut in thin slices, also any other meat may be used, instead of veal, and a little bunch of aromatic herbs; the meat·to remain in the soup.

32. *New Mutton Broth.*—Cut two pounds of the scrag, or any other lean part of mutton, in ten or twelve pieces, put in a pan with two ounces of fat, two teaspoonfuls of salt, half of pepper, a gill of water, two middle-sized onions, a good teacupful of pearl barley. Set it on the fire, stir round until it is reduced, moisten with five pints of water, boil, and skim, simmer two hours; and serve.

33. *Potato Soup.*—Proceed as above, omit the barley, add two pounds of potatoes, peeled and cut in slices, put them in when the broth is boiling; simmer till in pulp, and serve. A few sprigs of parsley, or the flowers of four marigolds, is an improvement, and, at the same time, an agreeable change.

34. *Ox Tail Soup in Baking Pan.*—Divide two ox tails, wash them well in cold water, then put them in the pan, with three teaspoonfuls of salt, one of pepper, four cloves, a little thyme, if handy, two good onions; add three quarts of water, two tablespoonfuls of colouring; put on the cover, place it in a moderate oven for three hours to simmer, take off the fat, which save for use, and serve. Half a pound of any vegetable, mixed or not, cut in dice, can be added with advantage.

35. *Ox Cheek in Baking Pan.*—Get half a one ready boned, if not to be had, get the half head with the bone, in which case they should be broken small and put in the broth; but it gives more trouble than it is worth. The solid meat at threepence per pound is more economical. Wash it well, cut off the white part, put the cheek in the pan, and proceed exactly as above, only give it three or four hours to bake. A little mixed spice improves the flavour. Take the fat off, remove the meat, cut it into small pieces, put it into the tureen, and pour the broth over.

36. *Cheap Pea Soup.*—Put into the iron pot two ounces of dripping, one quarter of a pound of bacon, cut into dice, two good onions sliced; fry them gently until brownish, then add one large or two small turnips, the same of carrots, one leek, and one head of celery, all cut thin and slanting (if all these

cannot be obtained, use any of them, but about the same amount); fry for ten minutes more, and then add seven quarts of water; boil up, and add one pound and a half of split peas simmer for two or three hours, until reduced to a pulp, which depends on the quality of the pea, then add two tablespoonfuls of salt, one of sugar, one of dried mint; mix half a pound of flour smooth in a pint of water, stir it well; pour in the soup, boil thirty minutes, and serve.

37. *The above Meagre.*— Precisely as above, only oil or butter used instead of bacon or dripping : skim-milk could with advantage be used, in which case add three ounces of salt. Although this is entirely deprived of animal substances, yet the farinaceous ingredients, with the addition of bread, will act generously on the digestive organs, satisfying the heartiest eater.

GRIDIRON.

WITH this primitive utensil a great deal may be done in the way of cooking, but it requires care, or otherwise great loss of food and money will be sustained; a few minutes' constant attention, when the article is on the gridiron, will save at least twenty per cent., and the palate will feel more gratified.

I use two kinds of gridirons, each costing very little; one is of cast iron, to go on the fire, and the other is of iron wire, made double, to hang from the bar of the grate before the fire, made so as not to too much press the object cooked within it. The principal care in this, as in all kitchen utensils, is never to put them away dirty; always wiping the gridiron after it has been used, and again before you use it, and a place kept where it should be hung.

WHAT I CAN COOK WITH MY GRIDIRON.

Firstly, Fish, nearly all sorts, both dried and fresh, either whole or in pieces. I shall not begin with the king of the ocean, but with one of the most humble of its inhabitants, and which daily gratifies the palates of millions; it is—

The Plain Red Herring.—Though we have agreed to make use of every kind of eatable food, it is still important to point out the best quality first, for I must tell you, that the quality of herrings varies as much, if not more, than any other kind of food; the proper way of curing them being as important to know as the quality of the fiesh itself. This unassuming kind of fish, which we may venture to call the poor man's friend, ought to be chosen plump, though not too full of roe, as when they have large roes they are sure to be oily, and cannot have taken the salt properly; they feel softish to the touch, eat stringy, and sometimes decay, and emit a bad smell while cooking; these are unwholesome: but if hard and firm, the flesh reddish, the roe well set, and smell sweet, they are good. The only drawback is that they might be too salt, which cannot be avoided, only by cutting the back up, and soaking them in lukewarm water for a few hours, and when taken out well dried on a cloth, previous to their being cooked. But the way to ascertain if a herring is too salt, is to take the fish in the left hand, and pull out a few of the fins from the back, and taste; you may thus find out the quality and flavour. This plan is adopted by large dealers.

38. Wipe your herring; dry it well in a cloth: you may slightly split the back, or make a few incisions crossways; rub it with flour, or dress it plainly, by placing the herring on the gridiron about six inches over a clear fire, or before it; turn them often, and in five minutes they may be done, according to size.

Or, when it is done, mix a piece of butter with a little mustard together, and place inside of it, or rub it over. By opening the back, it will do much quicker; but to keep the essence in it, it should be done whole.

Or, butter and chopped parsley, and a little vinegar or lemon juice.

Or, butter and chopped fennel and onions, very fine.

Or, cut off the head, open it up the back with a knife, and remove the back bone of the herring; put in about one ounce of butter and chopped parsley, with a slight tint of onion. Fold two herrings together in some paper, so that the fat does not escape; broil gently for nearly twenty minutes, and serve. The butter is to be inclosed between the two herrings.

The same plan with a bloater and a fresh herring dressed together is first-rate.

39. *Fresh Herrings.*—These should be cleaned and scaled, the head removed, opened on the back, and the gut taken out. Make three slight incisions on each side, throw some pepper and

salt over it, broil for ten minutes, and serve plain, or with either plain melted butter or fish sauce.

Or, a little mixed pickle chopped fine, with melted butter, also makes a good sauce for herrings.

40. *Haddock.*—A fine Finnan haddock should be rubbed with butter, and plain broiled before the fire for ten minutes, or more if rather large, keeping it of a yellowish colour, and turning it occasionally. If very salt, steep it in water for one hour; beat the thick side down, and broil gently.

Another Way.—Cut a middling-sized haddock in six pieces, which wash in cold water, take them out, and place them either in a bason or pan, then pour over about a quart of boiling water, covering your bason or pan over, so that no steam can escape· after your haddock has steamed ten minutes, take it out, place on a dish, rub over with butter, sprinkle a little pepper over, and serve.

Sprats and pickled herrings can also be done this way, as likewise smoked salmon; you may vary the flavour of this simple dish, by adding either a little chives, thyme, winter savory, bayleaf, parsley, eschalots, or onions.

41. *Whitings, Fresh,* should be merely cleaned, cut on each side, rubbed over with salt, pepper, and flour, and broiled for seven to ten minutes. Serve with melted butter, or without, adding a little vinegar or lemon in the sauce.

42. *Mackerel.*—Cut off the point of the head, open it at the back, keep it open flat. Pepper and salt, and fennel, if handy; place it between the fish, broil gently for ten minutes, and serve with either melted butter, or parsley and butter, or black butter sauce. (See No. 425 A.)

43.—Cut as above, open it on the back, chop up a small piece of fat bacon, with some parsley, one eschalot, or a small onion; add a teaspoonful of vinegar; fill the inside with this stuffing. Close it again; tie it round with a string, broil very gently for twelve to fifteen minutes: it depends on the fire and size. Serve plain.

44.—Prepare it as above, and put it into a pie dish, with vinegar, salt, pepper, and slices of onion, for an hour, and broil as before.

45.—Get a tin baking dish, and put into it some chive, chopped fine, some parsley, salt, pepper, a little vinegar, and about one ounce of butter or lard: put the mackerel, cut open at the back, and divided in six pieces; place it on the gridiron, turn the pieces, and in about twenty minutes they are done. Serve it on the tin dish.   Onions may be used.

46.—It may be put into paper, like the herring, No. 38, and served without any sauce.

Small fresh-water fish, such as tench, pike, perch, barbel, &c., may be done like mackerel.

47. *Small Soles and Flounders* are very good when nicely broiled in the double gridiron before a clear fire; the time depends on the size and the state of the fire: they should be rubbed with salt, pepper, and flour.

48. *Salmon, Salted,* should be cut in small slices, of about one quarter of a pound each, slantways, rubbed with either butter or oil, and broiled gently.   Serve plain, or can be broiled, wrapped up in oil paper.

49. *Eels, Dried.*—Steep them in water and vinegar for twelve hours, rub them with butter, cut them into pieces four inches long; broil gently, and serve.   These are rather scarce, but very good thus.

50. *Eels, Fresh.*—Skin and cut them into lengths of four to five inches; broil gently for seven to ten minutes; have some parsley chopped fine, which mix with some butter, and put a little in each piece, and serve very hot.   They may also be egged and bread-crummed (see Fried Eels), or with plain sauce.

51. *Ling, Fresh.*—Take about a pound of ling, cut it into slices of about three-quarters of an inch thick, rub it with pepper and salt, and put it on the gridiron over a clear fire; in about ten minutes it will be done.   Serve it plain, or with a little melted butter and chopped parsley, lemon or vinegar, or with a little piece of the liver chopped up and boiled in the sauce.

Turbot, brill, hake, halibut, plaice, or cod, may be cooked the same way, either over or before the fire.

HOW TO BOIL ALL KINDS OF FISH, EITHER WHOLE OR IN SLICES.

GENERAL RECEIPTS.

IN all processes of cooking that which appears the simplest is generally the most neglected, or at best but carelessly done. Many persons, unacquainted with the subject, would imagine that the boiling of fish is so simple, that it merely requires to be put on the fire in a saucepan full of water, and let simmer or boil until it has lost its transparency, to be fit to eat. To those who are careless and extravagant, this process may answer very well; they know no better, and do not care to improve; but to the careful housewife, who wishes to make every penny go as far as possible, by retaining in every article of food she cooks the flavour and succulence it possesses (which is, in fact, the basis of economical and perfect cookery, no matter how simple it may be), the following simple receipt, if carefully followed, will greatly assist:—

First of all, let us remember that all large fish, with the skin whole, must be placed on the fire in cold water; if crimped, or cut in slices or pieces, in boiling water; if whole, it must not be covered with more than two or three inches of water, or the skin will crack, and not only spoil the appearance of the fish, but will diminish the gelatine and gluten it contains, and instead of eating firm and full of flavour, it will be soft and woolly, especially if overboiled.

For all kinds of fish, to every quart of water put two teaspoonfuls of salt; and if the fish be whole, as soon as it begins to boil, remove the cover on one side, and let simmer gently till quite done, calculating the time according to the size and quality, which vary so much, that it would be quite impossible to say, " Take a cod, turbot, or salmon, or any other fish weighing so many pounds, and boil so long;" for according to its quality, the process of cooking will act upon it, and therefore in all the following receipts we must make use of the word *about* with regard to time, but by all means do it rather over than under. If large fish, I generally try it by gently pushing a wooden skewer through the thickest part; if it goes in easily, it is done.

How to ascertain if Fish, whether boiled, stewed, or fried, is done. —If the bone sticks firm to the flesh, or the flesh to the bone, it is not done; by the same rule, if quite loose, and the flesh of the fish drops off the bone, it is overdone, and you lose some of its qualities. For fish in slices try the bone with your knife; if the flesh comes from it, it is done; or by placing the point of a knife between the flesh and the bone, and on raising it, if done, the knife will part it easily.

To boil fish whole, such as turbot, plaice, large soles, salmon, cod, trout, pike, or any such like fish, it is requisite to have a drainer at the bottom of the kettle, or you will be sure to break your fish to pieces; and as the cottage of a working man is seldom furnished with cooking utensils of this nature, let him cut his large fish in pieces, or boil only small ones; but as, no doubt, the middle classes of society will buy largely of this our last work, I think I am in duty bound, Eloise, to give the following receipt, which, without the foregoing explanation, might seem to you out of place.

52. *To boil Brill.*—Place your fish in the pan, letting it lay on the strainer; rub it over with six teaspoonfuls of salt—it will make it firmer, then add six pints of cold water, or enough to cover the fish; put your pan on the fire, and when it commences to boil, put the lid slightly on one side, and let simmer till done. A brill of about five or six pounds will be done in half an hour after boiling. When sufficiently cooked, lay hold of both ends of the drainer, lift your fish out, and let it lay on the top of the kettle for two or three minutes, then slip it on your dish on a napkin, and garnish round with parsley, if any. If your fish weighs from three to four pounds, it will take from twenty-five to thirty minutes doing on a moderate fire. Anchovy, shrimp, lobster, or lemon sauce, may be used.

53. *Turbot.* — Make two incisions with a knife across the back—it prevents the white skin on the top cracking; rub it with the juice of a lemon and salt previous to putting the water over; let it lay about three inches under water. A turbot of seven or eight pounds will take about three quarters of an hour doing, after the water commences boiling; one of fifteen pounds, one hour and thirty minutes. Serve with either of the above sauces, or cream sauce No. 424.

54. *Salmon.*—A salmon weighing ten pounds will take one hour gently simmering when the water commences boiling. Head and shoulders of six pounds, forty minutes; cod fish of the same weight as the salmon, fifteen minutes less; cod's head and shoulders, ten minutes less; conger eels, hake, ling, same time as cod. The liver and roe of any of the above-named fish are very good when boiled and served with them.

Gurnet, pike, barbel, and carp are boiled the same way. If

either the turbot, salmon, or cod is crimped, it will take less time to boil, and should be put in boiling water, timing it in proportion to the other fish that has been put in cold water.

55. *How to boil Sliced Fish.*—To every pint of water put a teaspoonful of salt; when boiling, add your fish, of whatever kind it may be, calculating that a pound of any sort of fish will take from fifteen to twenty minutes; but ascertain if the bone separates easily from the flesh, as described in the preceding directions. Halibut and sturgeon will take longer than any other fish, plaice less than any. Any fish cut in slices will always eat firmer and better if rubbed, previous to boiling, with the quantity of salt you otherwise put in the water; therefore boil the water plain, adding the fish and salt at the same time. Mackerel will take from fifteen to twenty minutes; trout and haddocks of the size of a mackerel, a little longer; herrings, from twelve to fifteen minutes; skate, a trifling time longer; adding a drop of vinegar in the water to any of the above fish is an improvement.

56. *New way of boiling Fish.*—The addition of a few herbs and vegetables in the water gives a very nice flavour to the fish. Add, according to taste, a little sliced onions, thyme, bayleaf, winter savory, carrots, celery, clove, mace, using whichever of these ingredients you can procure; it greatly improves skate, fresh haddocks, gurnet, &c. Fresh-water fish, which have no particular flavour, are preferable done thus, with the addition of a little vinegar. Choose whatever sauces you please for any of the above fish, from the series at No. 411.

57. *Salt Fish, Cod, Ling, and Cod-Sounds.* — Soak two pounds of salt fish for six hours, if not previously soaked, or according to the cure; put them in boiling water, in which some parsnips have been previously boiled. Twenty minutes, if the fish is thick, will be sufficient; and serve with egg-sauce No. 411. Proceed the same with cod-sounds.

Fresh-water Fish.—These are not much esteemed amongst the many, although some are excellent eating, and much in use on the continent.

58. *Tench* and *perch* must be well scaled and cleaned, and put into the pan with a pint of water and a teaspoonful of salt, one onion, sliced, three sprigs of thyme, bay-leaf, pepper, parsley,

C

celery, all in proportion; a wine-glass of vinegar. If they weigh one pound boil for half an hour, according to size. Serve with my fish-sauce.

59. *Eels* may be done as above, with a little scraped horse-radish, and served with parsley and butter. Pike and carp may be boiled in the same way. If no herbs or vegetables, boil in plain salt and water; but the above is a great improvement.

Fish in Oven, in Tin Dish.—A long square tin dish, like those for baking, may be used for this excellent mode of cooking fish, by which all the flavour and succulence of it is preserved. They may be had of all sizes, and at a very trifling expense.

60. *Lesson 1.*—Scale and clean a sole, dry it well, chop up half an ounce of onions rather small, put in the dish one ounce of either butter, dripping, or oil, and sprinkle a little chopped parsley and onions at the bottom; lay the sole over, season with pepper and salt; mix the remainder of the chopped onions and parsley with some bread crumbs, and cover the sole with them, adding three or four pieces of butter or fat over, and a wineglassful of either wine, ale, or broth, or even water underneath; put the dish in the oven or before the fire until done: a large sole will take about an hour. In case the oven is not hot enough to brown the top, put the shovel in the fire until it is red-hot, and hold over it. Serve in the tin. The oven is far better than the front of a fire.

Plaice may be done the same way, or cut in slices, only it takes longer doing.

61. *Whiting* are done the same way, but require a sharp oven, or they will turn watery. Weaver may be done in the same manner.

Conger Eels.—Cut four slices, half an inch thick, dry well, dip each piece into flour, and proceed precisely as for soles. A little grated horseradish and a little spice will vary the flavour.

62. *Lesson 2.*—*Codfish, Halibut, Ling, Hake, Sturgeon,* and *Haddock* may be done in the same way; and a little stuffing, No. 459, may be used for every one of them, especially cod-liver stuffing.

63. *Lesson 3.*—The remains of boiled fish may always be done in this way. A few spoonfuls of melted butter added over

any of the above fish, before the bread crumbs, makes a change ; it eats more delicate, and gives very little more trouble.

64. *Another Way.*—Place any of the above fish in the dish, omitting the onions, if not liked ; add a few herbs or chopped mushrooms instead ; and make the following—

65. *Sauce.*—Put in a pan a quarter of a pound of flour, moisten with a pint and a half of milk or skim-milk, add three parts of a teaspoonful of salt, the same of pepper, mix all smooth, add a little mixed spice, or two cloves, grated nutmeg, one onion cut in four, set on the fire, stir continually, and boil twenty minutes ; it must be rather thick ; take out the onions and cloves, add to the sauce four ounces of butter, mix it well, pour over the fish, and bake as above : a little parsley, chopped, and thrown over before sending to table, improves the appearance, and a little grated cheese thrown over previous to placing in the oven, gives a nice yellow look, and this will be much liked. The sauce can be made and kept for some days without spoiling. This sauce is nice with every kind of white fish. Bread-crumb may be put over the sauce before cooking. The remains of previously cooked fish may be dressed in this way.

66. *Halibut, Conger, Hake, and Ling* (*receipt for four pounds of fish*).—Season either of the above rather strong with two teaspoonfuls of salt, half the same of pepper, the same of ground ginger, and two teaspoonfuls of chopped onions. Put two ounces of fat in a deep tin pan, lay the fish on it, mix two ounces of flour with a pint of milk ; when smooth pour over the fish, bake for an hour, and serve.

67. *Plaice and large Gurnets.*—The flesh cut from the bone may be done as above. They all require to be well done. Any of the above dishes may be surrounded by a border of either mashed potatoes or boiled rice.

68. *In Oven.*—*Small Fish.*—Put in a deep pan four teaspoonfuls of onions chopped, half a pint of melted butter, a gill of vinegar ; lay over six pounds of any common fish, season over with two teaspoonfuls of salt, one of pepper ; place it in the oven for twenty minutes, then turn it, baste it with the sauce now and then ; dish it up, and pour sauce over, or serve in the pan ; if the sauce should be too thin, boil on the fire till it gets of a thickish substance.

69. *Mackerel in Pie Dish.*—Open two or three mackerel on the back, cut off the tail and head, rub the inside and outside with salt, pepper, and chopped parsley; mix in a bason half a pint of melted butter, No. 410, add to it a teaspoonful of chopped fennel and parsley, and a tablespoonful of vinegar; put the fish in the dish, pour the sauce over, and well bread-crumb it; put it in the oven for half an hour or more, and serve. The roe may be left in the fish, or chopped up and mixed with the sauce. Balls of cod-liver may be added.

70. *Pickled Mackerel, Plain Way.*—Cut two onions in thin slices, mix with salt and pepper and a little mixed spice or peppercorn; then have four mackerel ready, with the gills and gut removed, but not cut; put a little of the onions inside, and rub the outside with them; and then rub them with flour, put them in the dish, put in the remainder of the onions, add half a pint of vinegar and a gill of water; bake in a slow oven for one hour; use cold. They will keep a long time.

71. *Fresh Herrings, Sprats,* and *Smelts* may all be done the same way, only they require less time to bake. Any other kind of fish, if in small pieces, may be done this way, and is excellent in summer with salad. The flavour or the pickling may be improved by adding three cloves, two blades of mace, some peppercorns, a little garlic, and some sweet-herbs, according to taste.

FRIED FISH.

The great art in frying fish is, to have it free from grease, and in that state it is one of the most delicate descriptions of food that can be given to the invalid, and at the same time the most nourishing. The sudden immersion in the fat solidifies the albumen in the flesh of the fish, and renders it easy of digestion; the coating of bread-crumbs prevents the fat penetrating into the fish, and when eaten by the invalid, the skin should be removed, and only the white flesh partaken of.

The great point is to have plenty of fat in the pan, for it is not wasted, far from it. If it is kept at a proper degree of heat, in the same pan a sole may be fried, and at the same time an apple fritter neither will taste of the other, proving that the high degree of heat in the fat prevents the flavour of the object immersed in it escaping.

72. *Fried Sole.*—Put a pound or two of fat into a deep frying-pan; whilst it is getting hot, take a sole, of course cleaned, cut off the fins and tail, wipe it with a cloth, egg it, and cover with bread-crumbs all over, shake off the loose crumbs, and press it, and lay the sole in the fat, the white part, or belly, downwards; the fat must be at a proper heat, which is ascertained by throwing a pinch of crumb into it; if it hisses, it is ready; if it burns, it is over-done; if of a nice colour it will do. Turn it once while doing. A middle-sized sole will take ten minutes. Take it out, place it on a cloth; if any fat is on it, it will come off. Dish it on a napkin, on which it hardly ought to show a spot of grease. This receipt is applicable to all kinds of fish; but large round fish should not be fried whole, only the fillets, or thin slices. Whitings may be fried whole, like sole, and will take about ten minutes; flounders, about five or six minutes; smelts, gudgeons, four or five minutes. The last should be fried as few as possible at a time, and served crisp.

73. Large soles, plaice, cod, halibut, conger eels, ling, hake, weaver, should all be fried in fillets, or thin slices; the sole should be cut down the back bone; then run the knife under the flesh, close to the bone, and cut it off; thus each sole will make four fillets; or they may be cut across in pieces of three inches, with the bone in.

74. Plaice do in the same way, cut in pieces one inch wide. Cod should be filleted lengthways, or in slices. Hake, haddock, and gurnet, the same; halibut, ling, and conger eel, in very thin slices, that is, not more than half an inch thick. Salt should be sprinkled over them half an hour previous. All these should be egged and bread-crumbed, as described in sole. All fish cooked in this way are excellent cold, as a salad, in summer. Slices should be broken, or cut, for about a pound of fish, and put into a bowl, with two tablespoonfuls of vinegar, four of oil, half do. of chopped parsley, half a teaspoonful of salt, quarter do. of pepper. Toss it up well, that it may mix; it is very cooling, and makes a light supper. A little fresh salad, as lettuce, endive, &c., makes it still more so. Slices of cooked potatoes, lentils, and haricots, may be introduced.

75. *Fried Fish, Jewish Fashion.*

This is another excellent way of frying fish, which is constantly in use by the children of Israel, and I cannot recommend it too highly; so much so, that various kinds of fish which many people despise, are excellent cooked by this process; in eating them many persons are deceived, and would suppose them to be the most expensive of fish. The process is at once simple, effective, and economical; not that I would recommend it for invalids, as the process imbibes some of the fat, which, however palatable, would not do for the dyspeptic or invalid.

76. Proceed thus :—Cut one or two pounds of halibut in one piece, lay it in a dish, cover the top with a little salt, put some water in the dish, but not to cover the fish; let it remain thus for one hour. The water being below, causes the salt to penetrate into the fish. Take it out and dry it; cut out the bone, and the fins off; it is then in two pieces. Lay the pieces on the side, and divide them into slices half an inch thick; put into a frying pan, with a quarter of a pound of fat, lard, or dripping (the Jews use oil); then put two ounces of flour into a soup-plate, or basin, which mix with water, to form a smooth batter, not too thick. Dip the fish in it, that the pieces are well covered ; then have the fat, not too hot, put the pieces in it, and fry till a nice colour, turning them over. When done, take it out with a slice, let it drain, dish up, and serve. Any kind of sauce that is liked may be used with it; but plain, with a little salt and lemon, is excellent. This fish is often only threepence to fourpence per pound; it containing but little bone renders it very economical. It is excellent cold, and can be eaten with oil, vinegar, and cucumbers, in summer time, and is exceedingly cooling. An egg is an improvement in the batter.

The same fish as before mentioned as fit for frying, may be fried in this manner. Eels are excellent done so; the batter absorbs the oil which is in them.

Flounders may also be done in this way. A little salt should be sprinkled over before serving.

77. In some Jewish families all this kind of fish is fried in oil, and dipped in batter, as described above. In some families they dip the fish first in flour, and then in egg, and fry in oil. This plan is superior to that fried in fat or dripping, but more expensive,

Many of the above-mentioned families have stated days on which they fry, or stew their fish, which will keep good several days in summer, and I may almost say, weeks in winter; and being generally eaten cold, it saves them a deal of cooking. Still, I must say that there is nothing like a hot dinner.

THE THREE-LEGGED IRON POT.

INTRODUCTION.

DEAREST FRIEND,—You are aware that every cottage throughout the land has a peculiarity in cookery and cooking utensils, which nothing can alter. One of them has a great claim on our gratitude, which neither time nor place can erase. War, famine, epidemic, revolutions, which have from time to time shaken the foundation of mighty empires, has not caused a wrinkle to appear on his noble brow even in this miraculous age of discovery, which has created railways, steam, electricity, photography, and by the last powerful agent we are actually enabled to take the strongest fortifications without bloodshed.

Not even one of the miracles of the nineteenth century has affected his noble position one jot: he is a posterity in himself, and no throne ever has been, or ever will be, stronger than his.

In winter, when all nature is desolate, when hoary Frost spreads his white mantle over the myriads of defunct flowers, then this homely king rallies round him his subjects, to entertain, comfort, and feed them, and make them happy, even when nature has almost refused to humanity her powerful service. This mighty monarch, Eloise, is no other than the three-legged iron pot, who has done such good service for so many generations, and will continue to do so if properly treated by his subjects.

So much for his moral virtues; but let us see what he has been doing, and if we can make him do anything more, and that in accordance with the enlightenment of the nineteenth century. You will perhaps say, that it is dangerous to try to make any change in a government so well established. Not at all; my object is not to interfere with his noble position, and deprive him of his rights. On the contrary, I only wish to enrich his kingdom, which I am sure no sensible monarch can object to.

Now for the immortal *Pot-luck*. All these receipts are for one containing two gallons.

78. *Salt Beef.*—Put in a piece of six pounds, add four quarts of cold water; boil gently for three hours. One hour before serving, wash clean, and cut the roots away of two cabbages, which cut up in four pieces, and put in the pot with the meat. When done, drain the cabbage, and place round the beef on the dish, and serve. Leave the broth or liquor from the meat on the fire, put in two pounds of split peas, a little pepper and brown sugar; boil slowly till done, and put by, uncovered, for next day, to drink with the cold meat. If more salt and pepper is required, add it: if, on the contrary, it should be too salt, add more water and a pound of potatoes. Or skim-milk may be added, and about one pound of toasted bread, cut into dice, and put in the soup when serving; or half a pound of flour, mixed with a pint of water. Every part of salted beef may be boiled thus, using about four ounces of vegetables to every pound of meat, instead of cabbage. Turnip-tops, brocoli-sprouts, green kale, carrots, turnips, Swedes, parsnips, &c. &c., may be used. Suet dumpling may be served with it.

The pieces of beef generally salted are the brisket, edge bone, round, flank, skirt. The ribs, when salted, are very fine, and much more economical than when roasted. This receipt if adopted for a farm-house; but two pounds of beef, and the other things in proportion to be used for a small family. Rice may be used instead of peas.

79. *Salt Pork.*—Put four pounds of salt pork, either leg, loin, head, belly, or feet, into the pot with six quarts of water, and one pound of split peas. In one hour add four greens, cut small, or turnip-tops, leeks, parsnips, &c. &c., placed in a net, and boiled in the pot. When done, take them out, and keep warm. Mix half a pound of flour with one pint of water, and put in the pot, and stir it round. Boil for ten minutes, and serve the meat and soup separate, and vegetables round the meat. Pieces of bacon, knuckles of ham, cooked in the same way, are very nice, only they will take rather longer boiling. A teaspoonful of pepper may be added.

You will perceive, my friend, that I have already opened a large field for our old hero, adding in a few lines about twenty new subjects in the shape of receipts to his kingdom.

80. *Veal.*—The flesh of the calf being of that light nature,

requires more the process of roasting, or stewing, than of boiling, except for the purpose of making broth, for which purpose it is superior to any other kind of meat. The only part which is usually done so, is the knuckle, and if cooked in the following way, is not an expensive dish:—Get a knuckle of veal and a small knuckle of ham, weighing together about six pounds. Or in the absence of the ham, or bacon, two pounds of the belly of pork. Put this in the pot, and fill up with six quarts of water and four spoonfuls of salt, one of pepper, two carrots, cut in dice, two onions and two turnips. Boil gently for three hours, take out the meat and serve with mashed turnips, or potatoes. Plain, or parsley and butter over. The liquor boiled up with a pound of ground rice, mixed in a quart of cold water. Put in and boil for half an hour, and save for the next day's use. When boiled for next day, add any remains of the veal, cut small, and put in it, with a little milk, if handy. Whole rice, or peas, may be used. Four Swedish turnips may be boiled with the veal, and eaten with it, mashed up with pepper, salt, and butter. Vegetables may be omitted when scarce.

81. *Mutton.* — The leg, neck, breast, head, and feet, are most often boiled; sometimes the shoulder, when not too fat, is boiled, smothered in onions. Whichever joint it is, the pot must be filled with water, to which six teaspoonfuls of salt and one of pepper have been added. Put in the joint and ten peeled turnips. When either joint is done, take it out, and serve the turnips round. Parsley and butter, capers, or chopped gherkins, mixed with melted butter, may be served with boiled mutton.

Save the liquor for the next day, add to it half a pound of Scotch barley and a pound of any vegetables that may be in season. Boil for one hour, and serve with toasted bread. Or instead of barley, two pounds of potatoes, sliced, and boiled with the vegetables, make a nice soup. For every pound of this joint, let it cook fifteen minutes.

82. *Ham.*—A ham of about fourteen pounds will take about four hours, and ought to be boiled in a three-gallon pot. Put in the ham, and fill up with water: skim off the scum as it rises; if wanted to be eaten cold, allow it to get cold in the pot. If it is an old ham, it should be soaked for twelve hours previously. Some carrots, turnips, and other vegetables, may

be boiled, with also a bunch of sweet herbs, which will improve the flavour of the ham.   If the liquor is used for soup a couple of cow heels may be boiled with it, which may be eaten separately, or cut up in the soup, which should be strained.   Or, fry ten onions, sliced, until nearly brown; add to them half a pound of flour, stir well in, then add some of the liquor from the ham, until it is rather thick; put into a tureen, and pour more over it, and serve with slices of bread.   Or instead of onions, use cabbage or leeks.

As many cottagers kill their own pigs, and cure the hams and bacon, and often boil only half the ham at a time, the knuckle part should be boiled last, and the yellow fat, if any on it, should be cut away.

IMPORTANT OBSERVATIONS ON CURING HAMS AND BACON.

Tons of ham and bacon are yearly wasted throughout the country for want of proper attention and judgment, in allowing the fat to get rancid.   Instead of hanging them up, as is the custom, to a low ceiling, in every cottage or farmer's kitchen, the consequence of which is, that the continual heat turns the fat and flesh of such a quadruped as dry as a mummy, while, by the following simple rules, they would keep equally as long without undergoing this antique Egyptian process.

To prove to you the truth of my remarks—about six months ago, I was on a visit to our excellent friend, William Tucker, Esq., of Coriton Park, near Axminster, Devon, when all the neighbourhood was searched to get a couple of home-cured country hams; however, no such thing was to be found; every one of them bought were dried to chips.   The fat of the first one we operated on, when sawn in two, (for we could not cut it in the ordinary way,) was of a blackish yellow, and the meat of the same colour as rotten wood, only much harder.   Being anxious to see the person who had so effectively "preserved" this ham, a very natty, clean old woman was brought to me; and on showing her the bone, and asking her for the receipt, she said she did not know how it was done, but her son Thomas did, and she knew he would be glad to give me the receipt, to which proposition I strongly objected, at the same time writing down the following receipt, which she said her son would doubtless follow.

After you have pickled your ham or bacon for either winter or summer use, dry the moisture with a cloth, and hang it in your

kitchen for about three weeks, or until the outside begins to crystal-
lize; then remove it to your dairy, or any other dampish place, for a
few days; then place it in your kitchen again, and so on, backwards
and forwards, three or four times, till perfectly dry, and quite sound;
if any part should happen to get yellow and rancid, scrape it off,
rubbing the spot with a mixture of salt, pepper, and flour; but
be sure you don't keep it eighteen months, as it appears the old
woman's son did; so that, with all the indulgence of nature, who
allows us to preserve meat, by means of pickling it, for some considerable time, yet common sense tells us, that it will not last for
ever.   Ham, when well cured by experienced hands, can be kept
good for several years.   The fault I before mentioned, exists in every
county, not excepting Westmoreland and Yorkshire, which two latter,
being ham counties, of course the evil does not run to so great an
extent.   I daresay, Eloise, you will fancy this country conversation
rather too long to be pleasant.   You may be right, as far as its value
as reading for the drawing-room goes, but let me tell you again, that
if these simple plans were adopted, more than one hundred thousand
tons of meat would be saved throughout the kingdom yearly, and
made to feed man rather than wasted as it is at present.

LAMB.

I think I ought not to mention this innocent and playful little
animal, but on second consideration, and remembering that King
Alfred once sought shelter in a cottage, and it being possible that
from accident, or some other cause, that a cottager might find himself unexpectedly honoured by a guest, to whom he would like to
give a delicacy, which could not be done better in the elaborate
kitchens of the most wealthy, than in the old iron pot of the most
humble abode.

It is rare that lamb is partaken of by the labourer, as he requires
more strengthening nourishment for his hard-looking frame, which
can digest everything eatable, without the aid of medical science.
These delicacies are left to those who would give a great deal if they
could possess the good appetite and the organic mastication of a
labouring man.

83. *Boiled Leg of Lamb.*—Put six quarts of water into the pot,
with six teaspoonfuls of salt; when boiling put in the lamb, boil
slowly for one hour; remove the scum as it rises; serve it with
plain melted butter, or parsley and butter, or caper sauce; boiled
turnips or spinach.   The broth may be made into soup the
same as the mutton.

84. *Boiled Rabbit.*—Stuff a rabbit as No. 456; put in pot ten

or twelve large onions, with four quarts of water; boil them till
tender, then add the rabbit, simmering slowly for one hour, if
large; dish it up, keeping it warm; take out the onions, chop
them, and put into a pan or the pot with two ounces of butter,
half a teaspoonful of pepper, four of flour; mix all well to form
a purée, add a pint of milk, boil twenty minutes, stirring now
and then; pour over the rabbit and serve; little pieces of pickled
pork boiled with it is an improvement.   Use the broth as above.

85. *Our Christmas Dinner—Small Boiled Turkey.*—Put
into the pot four quarts of water, three teaspoonfuls of salt,
one of pepper, have the turkey ready stuffed, as No. 456; when
the water boils, put in the turkey, and four pieces of salt
pork or bacon, of about half a pound each, or whole, if you
prefer it; also add half a pound of onions, one of white
celery, six peppercorns, a bunch of sweet herbs; boil slowly
for one hour and a half, mix three ounces of flour with two
ounces of butter; melt it in a small pan, add a pint of the
liquor from the pot, and half a pint of milk, the onions and
celery taken out of the pot, and cut up and added to it; boil for
twenty minutes, until it is thickish; serve the turkey on a dish,
the bacon separate, and pour the sauce over the bird.

A turkey done in this way is delicious.   With the liquor, in
which you may add a little colouring, a vermicelli, rice, or clear
vegetable soup can be made; skim off the fat, and serve.

The above with a plum pudding boiled the day before, and
rewarmed in boiling water in the pot whilst eating the soup
and turkey, and the addition of potatoes, baked in the embers,
under the grate, is a very excellent dinner, and can all be done
with the black pot.

Fowls and *Chickens* may be done the same way, giving only
half-an-hour for chickens, and three quarters for fowls.

86. *A cheap Tripe Dinner.*—Sometimes the cuttings of tripe,
or pig's chitterlings, or even a cow-heel, can be had very cheap, in
which case they should be cut into square pieces; peel eight good
onions, and ten large potatoes, for every four pounds of the meat;
lay some of the potatoes at the bottom of the pot, season with salt
and pepper, then some of the tripe, then onions and potatoes,
until all is in; then mix a quarter of a pound of flour with three
quarts of water; mix smooth, and boil gently for two hours;

scum and serve. This will make enough food for a family of twelve, and cost about one shilling and sixpence.

87. *Calve's Head and Feet.*—If by any chance either of these articles are to be bought cheap, which is sometimes the case in London or any market town, cut the head open, take out the brains, put it in the pot with six teaspoonfuls ot salt, two of pepper, four onions, parsley, and a little thyme; put in six quarts of water, in which mix one quarter of a pound of flour; being placed, set it to boil gently, skim it occasionally, boil three hours; just before serving, add a wineglass of vinegar; serve with parsley and butter, alone, or with the brains, cleaned and boiled in it; sharp sauce, No. 420.

The feet may be boiled in the same way. The liquor makes an excellent soup for the next day, either thick or thin, and with or without vegetables, or purée of peas, carrots, turnips, &c., or mock turtle.

88. *Sheep's Head and Feet.*—Take two sheeps' heads and cut the same as calf's head, and put in pot, with half a pound of pearl barley, four spoonfuls of salt, one of pepper, two carrots, four onions, and four quarts of water; boil for about two hours, or until tender, and serve.

Four feet added to it improve the broth. The heads when cooked may be egged and bread-crumbed over, and then put in the oven to brown for fifteen to twenty minutes. Eat it either plain or with sharp sauce. Calves' head is very good done the same.

89. *Curry Fish.*—Put into the pot four onions and two apples, in thin slices, some bayleaf, thyme, or savory, with a quarter of a pound of fat or dripping, three tablespoonfuls of salt, one tablespoonful of sugar, and fry for fifteen minutes; then pour in three quarts of water and one pound of rice; boil till tender; add one tablespoonful of curry-powder, mixed in a little water; cut up six pounds of cheap fish the size of an egg; add to the above, and boil for twenty or thirty minutes, according to the kind of fish. If salt fish is used, omit the salt. If no herbs, do without, but always use what you can get.

90. *Savory Rice.*—Take six pounds of bones, broken small; boil in eight quarts of water for three hours, having added three

tablespoonfuls of salt, a bunch of thyme, bayleaf, and savory, if any. When done, pour it into an earthen pan, remove the bones; the fat will do for puddings; or put the fat or two ounces of dripping into the pot, with two onions cut thin, half a pound of either carrots, turnips, or celery, cut thin; two teaspoonfuls of sugar; put it on the fire for fifteen minutes, stirring it continually; add half a pound of oatmeal, and mix well; then pour over the stock that has come from the bones. Add one pound of rice previously washed; boil till tender, and serve. This will be found both cheap and nutritious.

91. *Rice Panada.*—Boil one pound of rice in four quarts of water; add one tablespoonful of powdered sugar, and two tablespoonfuls of salt. Mix with some cold water one pound of flour or oatmeal, so that it forms a thin paste; stir in three teaspoonfuls of curry powder, add all to the rice, boil for twenty minutes, and serve. A quarter of a pound of butter or dripping may be added. *Should it be preferred sweet,* use a quarter of a pound of treacle instead of curry. This will make ten pounds of solid food, and is good either hot or cold.

92. *Peas Panada.*—Cut a quarter of a pound of fat bacon, or pork, into small dice; put it in the pot with two onions, sliced, or leeks; fry for ten minutes; keep stirring; then add one and a quarter pound of split peas, two teaspoonfuls of salt, one of sugar, and one gallon of water. Boil till it becomes a purée, or pulp; then add sufficient oatmeal or flour to make it very thick; simmer twenty minutes; keep stirring it, and serve.

Indian meal may be used, but it must be soaked; the husk, which floats, removed, boiled for two hours, and then added to it. If there are no onions, use some sweet herbs.

This may be made sweet by omitting the bacon, and using a quarter of a pound of treacle, and when cold, may be cut to pieces, and given to children as food.

93. *Cheese Stirabout.*—Nearly fill the iron pot with water, throw in three table tablespoonsful of salt; when boiling, throw in by degrees some Indian meal,—the quantity depends on the quality; on an average, if the water is soft, one pound to every two quarts; that would be four pounds. When well stirred, remove the husk with a spoon, which floats on the top. Then throw in one pound of strong cheese, broken in pieces, or grated

Boil for twenty minutes, and serve. Or, put it on a greasy baking-tin, throw some more cheese on the top, put in the oven for twenty minutes, and serve. Or, allow it to get cold, cut in pieces, and fry.

94. *Indian Meal Poullenta.*—Boil the meal as above (it must be very thick), without the cheese; mind that it is stirred up a great deal, or it will catch to the bottom of the pot; pour some into a baking-dish well greased; cut some beef or pork, sausages, saveloys, or black puddings, into slices, and place them on it. Cover this over with some more meal from the pot; bake for twenty minutes, and serve.

This is an excellent and cheap dish, and well worthy the attention of all classes, now that flour has become so expensive; it is fit for the tables of the most wealthy, if a strong gravy is poured over it when served. This may be made sweet with either jam, treacle, or brown sugar.

95. *Another Way.*—For the above proportion, mince about two pounds of meat, as No. 156, or liver. Mix well, then let it get cold; cut and fry anyhow you like; of course omit saveloys and black-puddings when meat is used.

In France, ox-liver is used in soup, to flavour the broth, and many people eat it, fried or stewed. If it is in use in cooking in one country, why should we not give it a trial. The proverb says, "what is good for the goose is good for the gander," therefore what is good for our neighbours and allies cannot possibly be bad for us. An ox in France is uncommonly like an English one, and these quadrupeds are equally as particular in their selection of food as ours; and if the calves', pigs', sheep's, and lambs' liver is fit for the tables of the wealthy, why should not that of the ox be deemed good for human food.

It is our duty, Eloise, in this work, to bring every wholesome kind of cheap food to the notice of the poor, so that with a little exertion, they may live, and live well, with the few pence they earn, instead of living badly at times, and most extravagantly at others, and not to allow nourishing food to be wasted, as it is at present. In many parts, and even in Ireland, during the year of the famine, those who were starving would not partake of ox-liver. These are bought up in that country, put into casks, with salt, sent over to a sea-port in England; they are then subjected to a cold pressure, by which the liquid is extracted, which is used for adulterating an article in universal use; the remains are then dried in ovens, pounded, and sent back to Ireland to be made into snuff.

96. *Stewed Ox Heart and Liver.*—Wash the heart well; chop a few onions and sage, and mix with it a teaspoonful of salt, and a quarter of pepper. Put it in the heart, and lay it in the pan with the top part downwards. Cut one pound of suet in quarter of a pound pieces; also two pounds of ox liver, and a little bacon, if handy. Season with three teaspoonfuls of salt, one of pepper, four or five onions, three pounds of potatoes, and pour over three quarts of water. Place it in the oven for three hours, and it is done.

In this dish, dried pulse of any kind, previously soaked, may be used with advantage, such as the white harico bean, the dried Windsor bean, the lentil bean; all of which may be had in the winter time in great abundance; and it is to be regretted that there is not a large consumption in this country of pulse, as the crop does not rob the ground so much as the potato, and is considerably cheaper than flour. Dried yellow or green peas may be used.

They are a good article for a tradesman to keep in stock, as they do not deteriorate, like the potato, and only require to be known, to be equally as much esteemed as that root.

FRENCH POT AU FEU.

(*This may also be done in the iron saucepan, stewpan, or baking-pan.*)

I cannot expect that this truly national soup of France can be made to perfection, or done with so much care as in that country, therefore I have simplified it, and shall call it *The French Cottage Pot au Feu*, or French Soup.

97. Put a gallon of water in the pot, put four pounds of the buttock of beef, or shin, or five pounds of the thick part of the leg, three teaspoonfuls of salt, one of pepper, four onions, four leeks cut in pieces, two carrots, and two good-sized turnips, three cloves, one burnt onion, or three spoonfuls of colouring; set it on the fire; when beginning to scum, skim it, and place the pot on one side of the fire. Add now and then a drop of cold water; it will make it clear. Boil four hours. Bread sliced, put into the tureen, and pour the broth, with some of the vegetables, over: serve the meat separate, and the remaining vegetables round.

If this simple receipt is well attended to, you will find it a very good soup and bouilli. If you run short of any of the vegetables, make it good with others. If no burnt onions or colouring, the soup will be white, instead of a sherry colour; but still it will be good. In France they always put in half a pound of ox-liver to every four pounds of meat. I am sure they are too good judges, over the water, to spoil their soup; in fact, there the ox-liver costs as much as the meat — sixpence per pound — therefore it is not with a view of saving, but to make it better.

97A. *French Ragout of Mutton.*—Put in the pot a quarter of a pound of dripping : when hot, peel and cut twenty small turnips, or ten large ones, into pieces the size of a walnut; put them into the fat, and fry until brownish. Take them out, then put into the fat a quarter of a pound of flour; stir round until brown. You have prepared four pounds of scrag of mutton, cut in small pieces; put them in, and stir round; then add enough water to cover the meat; stir until boiling. When the mutton is nearly done, which you will find by trying it with a fork, add the turnips; season with three teaspoonfuls of salt, one of pepper, the same of brown sugar, and a little bit of scraped garlic, if handy. Any part of mutton may be used. Ragout of veal or lamb may be done in this manner.

The following receipts to be done in a middle-sized iron saucepan.

98. *Stewed Eels.*—Put into a saucepan a teaspoonful of chopped onions, half a pint of melted butter, No. 410, one teaspoonful of anchovy sauce, one of vinegar, and one teaspoonful of colouring. Cut up one pound of eels in pieces two inches long, rub them in a little flour and salt, put them in the pan, and stew for half an hour, and serve with some toasted bread round. A little ale or wine may be used instead of vinegar, and the sauce should be thick.

99. *Stewed Eels.* No. 2.—Cut them as above, dip in flour, and partly fry them in fat a few minutes, and stew them as above, and serve with toast.

100. *Eels Stewed White.* No. 3.—Cut up one pound, as before; put them in the pan with half a pint of milk and three-quarters of a teaspoonful of salt, half of pepper, half an onion, in slices, and some sprigs of parsley. Stew gently for twenty minutes; mix one ounce of butter with half an ounce of flour,

put in your stewpan in small pieces, stir round gently, boil for five minutes, or longer, if large, and serve. The juice of a lemon, or a little vinegar, is an improvement. Lampreys and weaver may be done the same.

101. *Cod's Hard Roe.*—Tie a cod's roe in a cloth, place in a pan two quarts of water and two teaspoonfuls of salt; put in the roe, boil gently for one hour, take it out, cut off as much as you require, put it in the dish, pour over parsley and butter, and serve. Or egg sauce, or plain, with a little butter and pepper. The remainder, when cold, may be cut into slices and semi-fried, as fish.

102. *Cod's Sounds, Melt, and Frill.*—Nothing is more delicate than this dish. Boil thirty minutes in boiling salt and water. Dish it up, pour thick egg sauce over, or fennel sauce, or black butter, No. 425A. The first-mentioned, if salted, rust be well soaked.

Truly, my dear Eloise, I cannot but return you my very best thanks for the incessant inquiries you make as to the state of my health.

You blame me in your last letter for having visited the small town of Castleford, as also the beautiful little village of Methway, while the cholera was raging in those places. Allow me to impress upon your mind that, first of all, I have no personal fear of the epidemic, and that I take a deal of interest in endeavouring to ascertain the cause, or partly so, of such an awful visitation, as my letter of the 25th of March, which has appeared in the public press, will partly explain the cause of this calamity.* In that letter I ought to have included Leeds, Hull, and Bradford, those immense towns of thick fog, wealth, manufacturers, charming habitations, palaces, bad drainage, and real black—not sea, but—river, which, for want of proper drainage, if not attended to, will always subject those places to such epidemics.

The working classes of the commercial districts of Yorkshire earn very good wages, though, at the same time, they work very hard; their ignorance in the science of cooking is deplorable, and, without boasting, Eloise, I must say that I have been of some service to these same people, in improving the condition of their homes, as three parts of the wives of this hard-working class are utterly devoid of any knowledge of domestic economy. Cookery to them is almost unknown; but I must say they are willing to learn, and I hope this

---

* See end of the book.

work will be the means of terminating that which I have so successfully begun.

Respecting my visiting prisons, hospitals, lunatic asylums, work-
houses; also the interior of mines, coalpits, &c. &c.; and though I
must admit that those localities do not show the brightest part of
the mirror of life, still, you must not fancy that these people are all
unhappy; on the contrary, they are as contented as I am, and not a
day passes but what I teach them something in my way, at the
same time learning many little things from them, and I think you
will own that my correspondence partakes more of a jovial than a
morose nature.

Such is my opinion of that large class of society, termed the
million, after nearly twelve months stay among them, throughout
the united queendom.

IMPORTANT REMARKS ON COD-LIVER OIL.

But now to a very important culinary, and I think medical discovery,
which I owe to my persevering visits to various public charities in the
towns through which I passed. This happened at Hull, about three
months ago, from which town, if you recollect, I forwarded you the
drawing of the Station Hotel, where I was staying—I call it the
Monument Hotel, being so large and beautiful. But to come back to
the question; one of the proprietors, Mr. Jordan, on my asking if I
could visit the infirmary, kindly proposed to conduct me there, and
introduce me to the governor, which was done to my entire satisfaction; and I must say that the sick are not better attended to in any
similar establishment I have visited in the country.

Being aware of the immense quantity of cod-liver oil taken by
delicate persons, now-a-days, and the great benefit derived from its
use, I asked the medical officer present his opinion of its efficacy.
"Nothing can be better," was his reply, "in many cases. But,"
said he, "many patients cannot take it, being of such an unpleasant
taste, more especially children, and as we in this establishment use
the second quality, from motives of economy, it is doubly unpleasant."
I myself tasted some, and must say that I found it anything but
relishing.

After bidding adieu to the doctor, I and my host left, and while
returning to my hotel, I thought that something could be done to
alter the present unpleasant way of administering it. Accordingly,
upon reaching home, I sent for the following:—

103. One pound of fresh cod-liver; I then peeled and steamed two
pounds of nice floury potatoes, then cut the liver in four pieces, placed
it over the potatoes, and then steamed them, letting the oil from the
liver fall on the potatoes; I then made some incisions in the liver
with a knife, to extract the remaining oil, afterwards dishing up

the liver, which was eaten with a little melted butter and anchovy sauce. The potatoes were served up with a little salt and pepper. Both dishes were found extremely good.

The following is another way of extracting the oil of a cod's liver, with the aid of that abundant article, rice.

104. *Rice and Cod Liver.*—Boil half a pound of rice in two quarts of water. When nearly done, remove three parts of the water; then put over your rice a pound of cod's liver, cut in large dice. Put the saucepan in a slow oven for about thirty minutes, by which time it will be nicely cooked. Then take the liver out, which serve as above directed. Stir the rice with a fork, and serve it; if allowed by a medical man, add a little salt and pepper. If no oven, cook the liver and rice on a very slow fire, for otherwise it would burn, and be unwholesome as food.

Of course you can easily see what a blessing such diet as this must be to a person incapable of taking the oil by itself, as, by mixing it with the food, it entirely loses that rancid quality for which it is proverbial.

105. *Tapioca and Cod Liver.*—Boil a quarter of a pound of tapioca till tender in two quarts of water; drain it in a cullender, then put it back in the pan; season with a little salt and pepper, add half a pint of milk, put over one pound of fresh cod liver, cut in eight pieces. Set your pan near the fire to simmer slowly for half an hour, or a little more, till your liver is quite cooked. Press on it with a spoon, so as to get as much oil into the tapioca as possible. After taking away the liver, mix the tapioca. If too thick, add a little milk, then boil it a few minutes; stir round, add a little salt and pepper, and serve. If you have a slow oven, use it in preference to the fire; but if you are without an oven, here is another good way of cooking it:

106. Put three inches depth of water in a largish pan; then put the pan containing the tapioca in the above-mentioned pan; let it simmer till quite done. It will take about an hour. By adopting this plan, all fear of burning is obviated; afterwards remove the liver, which serve as at No. 103.

107. Sago, or semolina, may be done the same way, and by adding an egg, it will make a delicate pudding; or by cutting the liver in small dice, you may add it to your pudding, putting in a little more milk to make it moist; then add a couple more

eggs, well beaten, and mix; putting it in a basin, previously well buttered; then let it simmer in a stewpan for half an hour, or till set; then turn it out on a dish; sauce with a little plain melted butter, anchovy, or parsley and butter.

A little stringent food, such as the above, will be found very refreshing, even to persons in good health.

108. Rice may be also turned to good account; and I do not see why, after having taken the liver out, and adding four tea-spoonfuls of sugar, two eggs, one ounce of butter, and a little lemon peel, it would not make a very good sweet pudding. Pour over it, when done, a little melted butter with a spoonful or sugar, some lemon juice, or wine; or treacle, for children.

109. *Cod Roe and Cod Liver.*—Buy a cod's liver and roe, cut open the skin which surrounds it; put the eggs in a basin, pour water over them, mashing them with your hand, to separate them, throwing away the water; add half a pound of salt, and a teaspoonful of pepper; let them soak all night, afterwards washing them well in two or three waters, leaving about a gill at the bottom; then put about two pounds of cod liver over it, cut in six or eight pieces, putting the stewpan either on a very slow fire, or in an oven, for one hour; then take out the liver, which serve as usual. Add about a gill of melted butter in the roe, when it will be ready.

110. Or for any one in health four hard-boiled eggs, chopped, may be added, or three raw ones instead, and make a pudding of it; pour it in, steam it in water till well set, then turn it out, and sauce over with any fish sauce you like. The hard roe of any fish may be dressed like this, especially the roe of sturgeons.

CARTHUSIAN OF MEAT AND VEGETABLES.

You will perhaps be surprised at the name I have given to this curious mixture of vegetable produce, but you will immediately perceive that I have taken it from those well known monks who took vows to partake of no animal food, something like our strict vegetarians of the present day; but those jolly old dogs in former days were obliged, at times, to break their vow; as, however, it could not be done openly, they were obliged to mask the object cooked in covering of vegetables, and thus cheated their oath and their own conscience.

Carthusian, or Chartreuse, in French cookery, means any article or food, such as meat, game, or poultry, so surrounded by vegetables, that even a vegetarian would be deceived with its appearance, while sitting at dinner, and would not find out his mistake until helped with some of the dishes.

111. *1st Lesson.*—If in winter, cut crossways, in four, a large savoy cabbage, or two small ones; take off a few of the outside green leaves; wash the cabbage well, then put on the fire either an iron pot, or a three-legged black pot; put in about three quarts of water; when boiling, add your cabbage, boil them for ten minutes, or a little longer, then drain them in a cullender or cloth, pressing out the water; cut away the stalk from each piece, then chop your cabbage, though not too fine, letting it weigh about two pounds; when thus prepared, which will be our proportion of vegetable to one pound of meat; previous to chopping them upon the board, season with one teaspoonful of salt, that is, if salt meat be used; two ditto if the meat be fresh; one teaspoonful of pepper at all times.

Suppose we select for this, our first lesson, three middling-sized pigs' tongues. You have put them to boil with your cabbage, then cut them through lengthways, then place at the bottom of your pan about an inch deep of cabbage, and half an inch round the inside of the pan, placing your meat in the centre, thus making the meat invisible to the eye when turned out of the pot; when filled, add a quarter of a pound of butter or dripping, two wineglasses of vinegar, if English, or one, if French, one gill of water; set it on a brick, placed in the oven, for two hours; then open your pan, and place over your cabbage a tea saucer; press out all the gravy in a cup, pass a knife round your pot, then put a dish over the mouth inside downwards, turn the pot or basin upside down, when your carthusian will turn out like a pudding: pour the gravy or bread crumb sauce over, and serve.

112. *2nd Lesson.*—The above may be done in pudding-basins, or in deep oval pie-dishes, and either baked slowly as above, or steamed as puddings, but as there will be no cover to it, put over a cover of pudding-paste (see No. 319); fix over as for pies or puddings, making several small holes in the paste, and only putting half the moisture in. When done, remove the paste, which put on the dish you intend to serve it in; press out the

gravy, turn your carthusian out on the paste, already laid on the dish; then proceed with the gravy as above described; red cabbage is also very good, but requires double the quantity of vinegar, and more pepper; proceed the same; they require boiling in water about thirty minutes, if at all large, and rather old, as they are at Christmas.

113. *3rd and General Lesson.*—Having given you the base or foundation in the above receipts on animal food, I will now in a few words describe the extraordinary variations that can be made with this favourite dish of the best judges of good cheer, —viz., the monastic fraternity of olden times.

Instead of the above, you may use pig's feet, cheek, pickled pork, bacon, ham, liver of all kinds, previously fried, or partly so, sausages, black-pudding, or salt beef, previously boiled and cut in slices, or any part of fresh meat previously roasted, any remains of poultry or game may be done the same by cutting them in slices; if, however, they have not been previously cooked, they will take two hours instead of one. Pigeons, partridges, and all kinds of small birds, may be put in rows, only they should be larded or stuffed previously.

This will give you an idea of the various ways in which this dish can be made, as far as animal food goes.

The following will, by omitting the meat, be applicable for vegetarians.

VEGETABLE PUDDING.

114. *4th and General Lesson for the Use of the Vegetarian.* —You must observe, Eloise, that the above receipts are all made with cabbage only. I have made them so, because, while travelling last winter, I found that every cottager grew cabbage, while no other vegetable was to be seen in his garden; but now that summer is here, I will give you the receipts in the way the monks used to make them; and, mind, they were all good cooks in those days. They always had a foundation of cabbage or greens, or some kind of Brussels sprouts, one pound of either of the above done as in the first receipt; then they added a pound of either boiled carrots, turnips, parsnips, beet-roots, artichokes, potatoes, leeks, celery, or onions; boil the pound of whatever you choose from the above till tender; chop

it with your cabbage; season, and proceed as with cabbage only.
Sprue-grass, cut small, or peas, may also be boiled and mixed,
out not chopped; a little sugar is an improvement to vegetables,
as it varies the flavour; use any aromatic herbs and spice you
choose, but always in proportion.

You may also, for a change, pour either a little white or
brown sauce over (see sauces), but observe that the vegetables
must always be kept firm enough to turn out as a pudding;
either serve in a pan: or, to save trouble, turn the whole into
a tureen, or in a large dish, that is, if for a large family, but the
proper way is as first described. In fact, there is no end to the
ingenuity which may be displayed in the variation of this dish;
and to the cottager, with his small plot of garden-ground,
wherein he can produce sufficient vegetables for his family, it is
one of great economy, besides being exceedingly conducive to
health at all times.

GENERAL IGNORANCE OF THE POOR IN COOKING.

Ox checks may be bought at present, cut from the bone, and very
fresh, at about twopence-halfpenny to threepence per pound, in
London. It is the most gelatinous food which the ox produces, and
contains a large amount of nourishment, as I have already mentioned
to you. The only drawback there is to it is the length of time it
requires to cook, and the general way in which it is done, being in
many cases prejudicial to its use. Frequently on my visits to the abodes
of the poor, while in London last winter, I have often seen this article
of food completely spoiled. On one occasion, I asked an old lady how
she cooked it. " Sure enough," said she, " by fire." " But, my dear
woman," I inquired, " how long do you cook it?" " Ah !" she
replied, " sometimes as long as an hour, and boiling like the very
deuce all the time, till the water will not stand it any longer."
" And pray," I asked, " what do you do with the water?" " Faith,
there is no water left, but only black muck at the bottom of the pot,
which I throw away," was her reply.

Therefore I am always of the same opinion, dearest Eloise, as
regards our long talked of scheme of opening a national school to
teach the poor how to cook their food, and make the most of it.
Some of the money spent on our new palace prisons would be much
better employed for this purpose, and would ultimately decrease the
parish rates.

But I am digressing from the conversation I had with this old
dame. When I found she was so ignorant, I asked her if I should

come and teach her how to cook, properly, an ox cheek. " No, faith," said she, " I have no money to throw away, not even enough to buy another." Sanguine as I always am upon my favourite theme, I offered to bring one with me, as a present, the following day, and gave her sixpence to buy some sand to clean her iron pot, which I found done on my arrival the following day; she having also purchased two pennyworth of coals out of the money. I then produced the ox cheek, and put it into the pot with four quarts of cold water, and four teaspoonfuls of salt, and some leaves of celery, which articles were given to her by a neighbouring greengrocer. Her fire was made up, and the pot was placed on it, until boiling, and then removed to the side of it, and skimmed. There I left it, and went round to pay my other visits.

At the end of three hours I returned, and, she having a large basin in the room, I put some crusts of bread in it, and poured the liquid from the pot into it, and the meat I placed on a dish, and sat down with the old dame, serving the soup out into cups with a beer jug, having nothing better, and, to her great surprise, cut the cheek easily with a very bad knife, it being so tender. After tasting it, and finding it very good, she said she would show her neighbours how to do it. I told her that, if she would do so, I would give her more like receipts, when she exclaimed, " Bless you, ma'am, do; I will do them as well as you, now I have seen you do it." In anticipation of sending them to her the next day, I was about to retire, wishing her goodbye. " Lor', ma'am," said she, " you would not go without taking a drop of the ' crature.' " To my astonishment, a small bottle was brought out of her pocket, and offered to me. From its strange smell, I was induced to taste it, and I feel confident, if it had been analyzed by the " Lancet," it would have proved to be real *blue ruin*, composed, as it was, of a mixture of vitriol, &c.

This opened to me the secret of the emaciated looks of the thousands of the inhabitants of these back alleys, and I could then account for the remainder of my change out of the sixpence. I, however, sent her the following receipts, of course omitting her favourite seasoning—gin.

Having sent her the receipts, as promised, on reconsideration, it occurred to me that the old lady might not be able to read. I was not mistaken, for on calling upon her, I found six elderly matrons and an old man holding council together, and trying to make out the writing. The latter was just sending for his grandson, who, he said, was a scholar, having been three months at a Sunday-school. My arrival set all to rights, at the same time it frightened three of the council away; but I begged the others to stop, and hear the receipts read, which they accordingly did, afterwards giving several copies away.

115. *1st Lesson.*—Rub an ox cheek (middle size, or half a large one) with four teaspoonfuls of salt and one of pepper; put it into the iron pot, with four quarts of cold water; set it on the fire to boil; remove it then to the side, and *simmer gently* for three hours after it begins to boil. Skim off the fat, which will do for puddings, and, at the expiration of the time, nearly three quarts of very strong gravy, in addition to the meat properly done and tender, will be found in the pot. A gill of colouring is an improvement to the look of the broth. A head of celery, or some leaves of it, or onions, &c., may be added in boiling. Put the head on a dish, and serve the soup separately, with bread in it.

116. *2nd Lesson.*—Or any small quantity of mixed vegetables may be used. They should all be cut into dice, and not peeled, but well cleaned, with the exception of the dried skin of the onion. One pound of rice, at the cost of twopence-halfpenny, when added, is a great improvement; or half-a-pint of split peas, or barley, or a pint of white haricot beans, or a pint of Indian meal soaked the over-night, or a little flour to make the gravy or broth thick. It may be varied in several ways; but the chief point is, when once boiled, simmer slowly till tender, which you may ascertain by piercing it with a fork; if it sticks to it, it is not sufficiently done. Sheep and lamb's head may be done the same way, but will only take one quarter of the time; season accordingly.

This receipt is applicable to all kinds of hard meat.

THE GRIDIRON AND FRYING-PAN.

The Results of their Rivalry in Domestic Cookery.

YOUR favourite utensil, the frying-pan, Eloise, is, without doubt, the most useful of all kitchen implements, and like a good-natured servant, is often imposed upon, and obliged to do all the work, while its companion, the gridiron, is quietly reposing in the chimney corner.

The following scene was witnessed by those two faithful servants, the other afternoon, in a domestic establishment, where the sly dog of a gridiron often laughs between its bars at the overworked frying-pan.

The husband, who is employed by a railway contractor, and a man who is what the world calls middling well off, and who has risen by his own exertions and abilities from a more humble position, arrives home, and asks his wife what he can have for dinner, the hour of her dinner, and that of the children, having long past. " What would you like to have, my dear?" was her question. "Anything you have." " Let's see! why—we have nothing, but I can get you a mutton chop, or steak." " Can I have nothing else; I am tired of chops and steaks." " Why, my dear, what can be better than a chop or a steak?" " Well, let me have a steak." " You had that yesterday, my dear: now, let me get you a chop. I always make it my duty to study your comfort; and as I have been reading, not long since, a medical work on diseases of the skin, written by Dr. Erasmus Wilson, in which he says that nothing is so wholesome as a change of food, since which time I have made a point of varying our bill of fare, as they call it in that useful work." " Very well, send for two chops." In about twenty minutes the servant returns, saying she could get no chops, but has got a nice piece of steak. " Very well. That will do as well, will it not, my dear?" to her husband, who is reading a periodical." " Yes; but how long will you keep me here before it is done?" " Not a minute, my love. Now, Jane, do that well on the gridiron." Jane descends, but quickly returns, saying, " Please, ma'am, the fire is not fit for broiling." " Well, fry it," is her answer. The husband, who hears it, exclaims, " Drat the frying-pan, it is always so greasy." " Then, my dear, how would you like to have it." " Not at all," was his reply, throwing down the paper, and exclaiming, " Bother the place, there is no getting any victuals properly cooked here. I must go to the cook-shop and have it." He seizes his hat, and slamming the door, makes his exit in a passion.

The mistress blames Jane, and begins to beat the child for having upset the milk on the toast. Jane kicks the cat, and gives warning. The night comes. There are no candles in the house. Jane is sent out for them, but does not return in proper time. The husband arrives, and finds all in darkness. They quarrel, and swear they must separate in order to " *live comfortably together.*" Jane comes home, and is ordered to pack up her boxes, in order to be off the first thing in the morning, by which time, however, their tempers have had time to cool, and Jane is accordingly reinstated in her former position.

Moral (not on fable, but on truth): A man disappointed in something to eat, consoles himself with something to drink. If he has no stimulus in wholesome food, he will have it in pernicious spirit. He is quarrelsome, scolds his wife, beats his children, frequents the dram-shop, and becomes what is called a bad husband. It is not altogether his fault, the dinner was not eatable, and he must have something to support him, which he foolishly finds in spirits; and thus, by the want of attention on the part of the wife, is made what he is. In no country in the world do the annals of police courts show such

scenes as are daily noticed in the public journals of London, which
the increase of punishment by a modern law has not yet succeeded in
putting down.

Before proceeding with the following receipt, it is advisable to
read the introduction of semi-fried steaks, and steaks in pan, page 56,
as it would be tautology to repeat it here.

IMPORTANT REMARKS ON STEAK AND RUMP STEAK.

Broiled Steaks and Rump Steak.—Previous to cooking a
steak, nurse your fire; it will well repay your trouble, and also
remember, in the morning, that you are obliged to dine that
very identical day, and no doubt you decide upon having a
steak for dinner, which is a very good thing, when the meat is
good and well cooked, also fix the hour you intend to dine, and
half an hour previous stir up the fire, clear away the ashes,
stir all dead cinders from the bottom, and in a few minutes you
will have a clear fire, fit for the use of the gridiron; and every
article you may submit to that process of cookery stands a
chance of being well done.　I herewith forward you the following
lesson :—

117. *First Lesson.*—For first quality of steak, the meat ought
to be well hung, and if cut nicely off the rump of a Scotch beast
will weigh from a pound and a quarter to a pound and a half,
that is, being three-quarters of an inch thick; if it should be
cut rather thicker in one part than another, beat it even with a
chopper; if of the above thickness, it should be placed about
five inches above the fire; if thicker, six inches; taking it as
an invariable rule, that the thicker the steak, the further in
proportion it must be from the fire.　The extra piece of fat
which accompanies it should be put on a little after the steak,
or it will be too much done.　Whilst doing, throw over some
pepper and salt, and turn it the moment the fat begins to drop:
the motive of constantly turning the steak is to keep the gravy
in.　Never put a fork into it to turn it, but use a pair of tongs
but if you have not any, place the fork in the fat and turn it.
When the steak is done, it will feel firm under the pressure of
the finger.

Second Lesson.—Sometimes it is impossible to broil over the fire, but easy to use a double gridiron, to broil in front. In such cases, the gridiron should never be opened until the steak is done; then the gravy will not be pressed out. If *carefully attended to*, this plan is as good as the other, but otherwise, it spoils the best of meat.

The time required for a nice tender rump steak, three-quarters of an inch thick, weighing a pound and a quarter, over or before a nice clear fire, is from twelve to fifteen minutes. If turned four times in that time, the gravy will remain in it, and if served immediately, on a hot dish (not too hot, to dry up the gravy), it will eat tender and juicy, and be fit for a member of the Rump Steak Club.

Third Lesson.—Some persons put a bit of butter on the dish, others ketchup, others sauces of various kinds; all these should be left to the party who partakes of it; it is the duty of the cook to send it up plainly, but properly seasoned with salt and pepper, unless otherwise ordered. Every pound of steak will require one and a half teaspoonfuls of salt, and a half of pepper.

But if required flavoured and seasoned to satisfy a *blasé* appetite, then the following should be adopted.

118. *Rump Steak with Eschalot.*—Chop up one eschalot very fine, mix it with a teaspoonful of salt and half of pepper, rub the steak all over with it, and press it in with a knife; place it over the fire as the above, cook and serve. If not required so strong, rub only the gridiron and the dish with eschalot.*

Rump Steak with Eschalot Butter.—Cut up two eschalots very fine, and mix it with half an ounce of butter, which spread over the under part of the steak when dishing up.

Rump Steak with Maitre d'Hôtel Butter. — When your steak is just done, rub it over with an ounce of prepared butter as No. 426.

Devilled Steak.—Mix in a plate two teaspoonfuls of salt, half

---

* If eschalot is required to be served up in the dish, or on separate plate, chop them up fine, as at No. 449, and serve two teaspoonsful to every pound of steak.

of cayenne, two of made mustard; place the steak on the fire; after the first turn spread half of the mixture on it, and dredge it with flour; do the same with the other side. Broil as above.

Curry Powder, mixed with mustard, or curry paste alone, can be rubbed over the same way.

119. *Wakefield Steak.*—Cut a steak one inch thick, score it on each side, crossways. Put into a tart dish two teaspoonfuls of salt, one of pepper, one of sugar, a teaspoonful of chopped tarragon, a tablespoonful of Soyer's relish, two tablespoonfuls of vinegar; put the steak in it for six hours; turn it now and then. This seasoning is called marinade. Previous to broiling, dredge it lightly with some flour, while doing, and serve with butter in very small pieces under the steak. At Wakefield they sometimes use the Warncliffe sauce.

Some raw potatoes cut into very thin slices, and nicely fried, served round it, renders it a dish fit for the greatest epicure. This dish proves that the inhabitants of Wakefield have not lost the culinary reputation they formerly possessed, and which they first acquired some four hundred years since, when the French queen and her suite came to reside there, and allowed them to quarter the *fleur-de-lis* in the arms of the town. Beef skirt and other pieces may be all done in the same way, allowing time to cook according to the quality and hardness of the pieces you dress.

120. *Mutton Chops.**—These may all be cooked and flavoured like the steaks, but in many cases garlic is used instead of eschalot, when preferred. Peel a clove of garlick, put it on the end of a fork, and rub both sides of the chop lightly with it. Chopped mushrooms are very good with broiled chops. Any fleshy part of the sheep may be broiled the same way.

121. *Mutton Chop.*—In my opinion, two chops out of a fine South Down, well hung, cut three quarters of an inch thick, leaving half an inch of fat round them, and broiled over a clear fire for ten minutes, turned four times, sprinkled with salt and pepper, served on a hot plate, one at a time, with a nice mealy potato, is as good, as wholesome, and nutritious a dinner as can be partaken of. One and a half teaspoonful of salt and a half of pepper to a pound of chops, is a good seasoning.

---

* For description of chops see page 55, Frying-Pan.

122. *Plain Veal Chops* are broiled as above. A veal chop, nicely cut from the leg, ought to weigh one pound. I am of opinion that to broil a veal chop by the direct action of the fire is an act of Vandalism. Of course, if there is no time to do it other ways, it must be done so; but that so delicate a kind of food should be subject to such fierce treatment in order to spoil it, is what I do not approve of. It ought to be wrapped up in a sheet of buttered paper, with pepper and salt on it. The sheet of paper ought to be large, thick foolscap; the chop laid on one half, the other brought over, and the edges folded over so that no gravy escapes. They should be placed eight inches above the fire, and broiled for at least twenty minutes, and served in the paper very hot. A little chopped mushroom or parsley may be placed in the paper, and improves the flavour.

123. *Veal Cutlet.*—A pound of veal not more than half an inch thick, from the fillet, will make three cutlets, and should be broiled with some bacon. The same objection exists with this as the former; but both veal and bacon wrapped up in paper, and broiled as above, is very excellent; a little chopped chives, eschalots, or onions, may be added.

124. *Pork Chops.*—These should be cut not quite so thick as mutton, and the skin left on. They will take one third longer to do. Well rubbed with pepper and salt, and an onion, previous to broiling, is an improvement.

These can be served with any sauce, as apple, tomata, horse-radish, mustard, sage and onion, &c. &c.

125. *Calves' Heart* should be cut lengthways, and the pieces not thicker than half an inch; broil with a piece of fat, or bacon, for ten minutes: serve with a little currant jelly and butter in the dish, under the pieces of heart.

It is also excellent (see No. 119) marinaded for a few hours, and the following may be done any way like steak.

Ox, pig's, lamb, and sheep's heart, may be done like it.

Also the livers of the above, cut the same thickness, and broiled with some bacon, a little melted butter with ketchup in it, is a good sauce for broiled heart and liver. Observe, Eloise, that I shall be obliged to send you many similar receipts to these for frying-pan, but the flavour will be very different.

126. *Lamb Chops* should be cut not more than half an inch thick, and broiled before the fire very close and quick; they will

take from eight to ten minutes. Throw some pepper and salt over, and serve very hot, with fried parsley round them, if handy. Lamb chops might be dressed in paper, the same as veal.

127. *Broiled Ham.*—A slice of ham a quarter of an inch thick will take seven or eight minutes, over a sharp fire, turning it often.

Bacon about the same.

128. *Sausages* should be placed high above a slow fire, and done slowly: they will take ten minutes; beef sausages, about eight minutes; prick them first with a fork, or they will burst.

129. *Black Puddings.*—These are often partaken of cold, after having been boiled, but they are best after broiling: they should be at least eight inches above the fire, and the skins pricked, and will take fifteen minutes doing, turning several times.

130. *Cold Meat Broiled.*—The remains of cold meat cut into slices a quarter of an inch thick; season with salt and pepper; when hot through, rub with a little butter, turn it often, and serve with a little ketchup in the dish.

This may be varied with any sauce, or chopped herbs.

131. *Broiled Bones.*—When these have a little meat on them, they should be rubbed over with salt and pepper, and a little butter, broiled some distance above or before the fire, that they may get gradually warm, and should be served very hot, and rather brown.

Remains of poultry, game, &c., should be done the same.

132. *Devilled Bone.*—The remains of the rib of a sirloin of beef, or the blade-bone of a shoulder of mutton, the legs of fowls, turkeys, &c., should be slightly cut all round with a knife, and well rubbed with cayenne and salt, and a teaspoonful of Chili vinegar, or ketchup, or Relish, and broiled gently until hot through and brown. Serve very hot.

133. *Broiled and Devilled Toast.*—Toast a round of bread, cut a quarter of an inch thick; mix in a plate one ounce of butter, half a teaspoonful of cayenne, one teaspoonful of mustard, one teaspoonful of Relish, or Sauce; spread it over the toast, and serve very hot. Broiled kidneys or sausages may be served on it.

134. *Broiled Kidneys.*—Sheep's kidneys should be cut in the middle, so as nearly to divide them, leaving the fat in the middle;

run a skewer through them, that they may remain open; broil gently, five minutes for a common size is sufficient. Season with salt and pepper; rub a piece of butter over, and serve. They can be served on toast, or with any sauce.

Lamb's, pig's, calves', and ox kidneys, may be done the same way, but the two latter will take much longer, and should be better done. You may also egg and bread-crumb them.

135. *Broiled Fowls, Pigeons, &c.*—These, if whole, should be cut in down the back, after being drawn and well skewered to keep them so, or beaten flat with the chopper. Season well with pepper and salt; well grease a double gridiron, and place them a sufficient distance from a moderate fire; turn often. A fowl, if small, will take from twenty-five to thirty minutes; if large, three quarters of an hour; pigeons about ten minutes. Serve either plain, or with any sauce that is liked. They may be egged and bread crumbed.

FRYING-PAN.—INTRODUCTION.

THIS useful utensil, which is so much in vogue in all parts of the world, and even for other purposes besides cookery—for I have before me now a letter, written, at the Ovens' diggings, on the back of a frying-pan, for want of a table; but in your letter you suggest the necessity of paying particular attention to it, as it is the utensil most in vogue in a bachelor's residence. I cannot but admire your constant devotion to the bachelors: you are always in fear that this unsociable class of individuals should be uncomfortable. For my part, I do not pity them, and would not give myself the slightest trouble to comfort them, especially after they have passed the first thirty springs of their life. Let them get married, and enjoy the troubles, pleasures, and comforts of matrimony, and have a wife to manage their home, and attend to more manly pursuits than cooking their supper when they get home at night, because the old housekeeper has gone to bed; or lighting the fire when they get up in the morning, because the old dame has a slight touch of lumbago and should he require something substantial for his breakfast, and want that utensil of all work, the frying-pan, finds it all dirt and fishy, not having been cleaned since he last dined at home.

No, my dear Eloise, I assure you I do not feel at all inclined to add to their comforts, though you may do what you like with the following receipts, which are equally as applicable to them, as to the humble abode of the married fraternity.

You will also find, in these receipts, that the usual complaint of food being greasy by frying, is totally remedied, by sautéing the meat in a small quantity of fat, butter, or oil, which has attained a proper degree of heat, instead of placing it in cold fat and letting it soak while melting.

I will, in as few words as possible, having my frying-pan in one hand and a rough cloth in the other, with which to wipe it (considering that cleanliness is the first lesson in cookery), initiate you in the art of producing an innumerable number of dishes, which can be made with it, quickly, economically, relishing, and wholesome. But I must first tell you, that the word fry, in the English language, is a mistake; according to the mode in which all objects are cooked which are called fried, it would answer to the French word *sauté*, or the old English term *frizzle*; but to fry any object, it should be immersed in very hot fat, oil, or butter, as I have carefully detailed to you in our "Modern Housewife." To frizzle, sauté, or, as I will now designate it, semi-fry, is to place into the pan any oleaginous substance, so that, when melted, it shall cover the bottom of the pan by about two lines; and, when hot, the article to be cooked shall be placed therein. To do it to perfection requires a little attention, so that the pan shall never get too hot. It should be perfectly clean—a great deal depends on this.

I prefer the pan, for many objects, over the gridiron; that is, if the pan is properly used. As regards *economy*, it is preferable, securing all the fat and gravy, which is often lost when the gridiron is used.

All the following receipts can be done with this simple *batterie de cuisine*, equally as well in the cottage as in the palace, or in the bachelor's chamber as in the rooms of the poor.

136. *1st Lesson. To Semi-fry Steak.*—Having procured a steak about three quarters of an inch thick, and weighing about one pound, and two ounces of fat, place the pan on the fire, with one ounce of butter or fat; let it remain until the fat is melted, and rather hot; take hold of the steak at one end by a fork, and dip it in the pan, so that one side is covered with fat; then turn the other side in it, and let it remain for two or three minutes, according to the heat of the fire; then turn it : it will take about ten or twelve minutes, and require to be turned on each side three times, taking care that the pan is not too hot, or it will burn the gravy, and perhaps the meat, and thus lose all the nutriment; in fact, the pan should never be left, but carefully watched; on this depends the advantages of this style and mode of cookery. If the object is not turned often, it will be noticed that the gravy will come out on the upper surface of the meat, which, when turning over, will go into the pan and be lost, instead of remaining in the meat. Season with a tea-

spoonful of salt and a quarter of pepper; then feel with the finger that it is done, remove it with a fork, inserted in the fat, and serve very hot.

So much for the first lesson, the details of which must be learnt as it will then simplify every other receipt.

137. *2nd Lesson.*—Remember that the thickness is never to exceed one inch, nor be less than half an inch, and to be as near as possible the same thickness all over. A good housewife will object to one cut in any other way; but if it cannot be avoided, press it out with the blade of the knife, to give it the proper thickness. When done, wipe the pan clean, and place it on a hook against the wall, with the inside of the pan nearest the wall, to prevent the dust getting in.

Now, dear Eloise, you will perhaps say that the foregoing lessons are too long for so simple a thing as a steak, as everybody think themselves capable of cooking it without tuition, but having now given these directions, I hope those who fancy they can cook without learning will know better for the future, and pay a little attention to so important a subject.

138.—The above lesson may be varied by adding to the pan, with the seasoning, a few chopped onions, or eschalots, parsley, mushrooms, pickles, semi-fried at the same time or after, and poured over the steak; or when the steak is dished up, a little butter, or chopped parsley and butter, or two spoonfuls of either Relish, Harvey's, or any other good sauce that may be handy. Pour the fat of the steak into a basin for future use. Some fried potatoes may be served with it, or the following additions made: after the steak is done, slice a quarter of a pound of onions to each pound of steak, and a little more fat; fry quickly, and when brown place round the steak; pour the gravy over.

Some mushrooms, if small, whole, if large, sliced, put in the pan and fried, are excellent.

Two tablespoonfuls of mixed pickle, put into the pan after the steak is removed, fried a little, then add two tablespoonfuls of the liquor and two of water; when on the point of boiling pour over the steak. The same may be done with pickled walnuts and gherkins, or two ounces of tavern-keepers' butter rubbed over, (see No. 426,) or half a pint of oyster sauce, or mussel sauce, or horseradish sauce; or a little flour dredged over the steak, and a little water added in the pan, when the steak is done, and a little colouring or ketchup, and then poured over the steak.

These .eceipts can be continued and multiplied to any extent, entirely depending on the taste of the cook.

A steak may first be dipped in flour, and well shook; then, when you have semi-fried your meat, it will have acquired a nice brown; this may also be applied to veal cutlets, pork and mutton chops, poultry and game.

139. *Another Way.*—When your steak is partly done, dredge both sides over with a spoonful of flour, dish up, pour out the fat, put a gill of water in the pan; let it simmer a few minutes,—it will make a nice thick sauce.

139A. *Beefsteak, with Semi-fried Potatoes.*—Rub and semi-fry your steak, adding thin slices of potatoes, letting them lie in the pan while the steak is doing; turn them as often as you do the steak, serve round with gravy, to make which pour half a gill of water in the pan under the steak—the moisture of the potatoes will cause some of the gravy to come out of the meat, but it will be found very good.

140. *A Series of Lessons how to Semi-fry Chops of all kinds.* *Lesson* 1.—First select your mutton. Let it not be too fat; if it is, cut some off. Always observe that a mutton chop should be one third fat, and of the same thickness throughout. Have them cut from the loin, let them be about an inch in thickness. Very little attention will accomplish this important point; for I feel convinced, Eloise, that an ill-cut chop never can be but ill-cooked; you can always equalize them by beating them out with a chopper. Have your frying-pan very clean; put in an ounce of butter, or, if you like, dripping or lard; let it get rather hot. As soon as it begins to smoke, take your chop with a fork, by the small end, and dip it in the fat for half a minute; then turn it, let it semi-fry for about three minutes, season the uppermost side with a quarter of a teaspoonful of salt, and half that quantity of pepper; then turn it, and serve the other side the same way. You may then turn it several times while doing, as that equalizes the cooking, as well as carbonizes the meat. Ten minutes will cook it to perfection, and less, if thinner.

Second Lesson.—If the above directions are properly attended to, the chop will present the appearance of a rich brown colour, and the fat a gold colour, cutting extremely white and light, while the meat will look darkish, and give a strong gravy which will almost stick to the knife, instead of running on the plate and partaking of a watery red colour, as is the case when a chop is slowly and badly cooked. This last sort of gravy is called by some people rich, which I am sure, my dear, you will find to be a great mistake;

though the badly-cooked chop will probably weigh more than the other, from not having lost so much of its substance, yet it will not possess half the nutriment and flavour of a chop well done. The above quantity of seasoning will do for a chop weighing about a quarter of a pound, and would, I may safely say, suit the palate of fifteen persons out of twenty; therefore I hope it will diminish the load of salt and pepper every Englishman piles on his plate, previous to tasting the article of food placed before him. The cook ought to season for the guest, not the guest for the cook.

141. *Third Lesson.*—When you can thoroughly cook a chop according to the first lesson, it materially simplifies the second, which is thus done:—Get a chop and cook it as above, but to vary the flavour, when half cooked, sprinkle over it a little chopped chives, or eschalots, or onions, spice, or aromatic herbs; or when done, rub both sides of the chop lightly with a clove of peeled garlic, or a piece of fresh or maître d'hôtel butter. These remarks are applicable to all kinds of semi-fried meat.

The Fourth Lesson is still more simplified, my dear Eloise, namely, cook your chop plainly, as before directed, eat it yourself, and let me know how you relished it.

Chops from the neck, called cutlets, are done in this manner. Pork, veal, and ham chops require the same style of seasoning and cooking. A slow fire is preferable to a sharp one for the above mentioned chops, which, when semi-fried, will take a gold colour, as above-mentioned. You may always ascertain when the chop is done by pressing your finger on the thick part; if the flesh is firm and well set on both sides, it is done and ready to serve. Half a pint of chopped pickled red cabbage put in the pan after the chop is done and warmed through will be found very relishing, especially for pork cutlets.

142. *Mutton Cutlets.*—The chop from the neck is the best to semi-fry; they should be nicely cut, and the bone at the thick part removed, as it prevents the meat from doing; then beat up the yolk and white of an egg, with a pinch of salt; have ready some bread-crumbs, made from stale bread, and sifted, (this may always be kept ready in a canister); beat out the cutlets with a small chopper, dip them or rub them with a brush with the egg, place some of the bread-crumbs on a plate, and lay the cutlet on them; press them; serve both sides the same, and shake off all loose crumbs; have the fat in the pan quite hot, lay them in it; when nicely browned on one side, turn them over, and do the other side the same; take them out, lay them on a cloth, so that no fat remains; serve with any made sauce. For bread-crumb, see No. 452

143. *Veal Cutlets* should be cut round, about three inches in diameter, and a quarter of an inch thick, done very quickly.

144. These may all be *rubbed* previous to bread-crumbing, with either onion or eschalot; by rubbing them there will be no perceptible taste, but a pungent flavour; these can be served with various made sauces, and stewed spinach, greens, peas, and anything, according to taste, remembering that that which pleases the eye will prove agreeable to the palate.

145. *Pork Chops*, semi-fried, without bread-crumbs, are done as the mutton chops; they will require more time, and should be served with a mustard or sharp sauce.

Mutton, veal, pork, and lamb, all look inviting, and are all equally good, when bread-crumbed and semi-fried, as above.

**146. 1st *Lesson.* *Sausages and Kidneys, Semi-fried.*—Peel and chop fine about four small onions, put one ounce of butter in the frying-pan, two ounces of bacon cut in slices, and a tablespoonful of chopped onions; fry for five minutes, stirring it with a spoon; cut half a pound of sausages in half lengthways, place them in the pan, then cut an ox kidney into thin slices, omitting the hard part; put it in the centre of the pan, season with half a teaspoonful of salt and one saltspoonful of pepper; fry gently for five minutes, turning them. Take care they are not done too much, or they will be hard; throw a teaspoonful of flavour over them, add one quartern of water; simmer two minutes; dish with kidneys in the middle and sausages round. Dripping, lard, or oil, may be used instead of butter, and a few small mushrooms is an improvement.

2nd Lesson. Kidneys alone.—Slice thin an ox kidney, put two ounces of butter into a frying-pan; when hot, add two ounces of bacon, cut in thin dice, and the kidney; fry for five minutes, if over a brisk fire; longer, if over a slow fire; add a teaspoonful of flour, salt, and pepper, moisten with half a pint of water, simmer a few minutes, stir round, and serve with or without crisp toasted bread round it: a little lemon is an improvement.

3rd Lesson. Mutton Kidneys, with Ale Sauce.—Cut six kidneys in two, remove the outer skin, cut them into slices; put two ounces of butter into a frying-pan; when very hot, put in the kidneys, and stir continually for about five minutes; sprinkle over a teaspoonful of flour, a little salt and pepper, and, if handy, a little parsley chopped fine; moisten with a little water and four tablespoonfuls of ale; thus it forms a thickish sauce. Lemon is an improvement, or wine in the place of ale, or a little vinegar, if preferred.

147. *Calves' Liver, Semi-fried.*—Cut the liver a quarter of an inch thick, the bacon the same, mix in a plate a tablespoonful of flour, one teaspoonful of salt, and the same of pepper, dip the liver into it; have ready the frying-pan, with sufficient fat or dripping, quite clear, as much as will cover the bottom of the pan a quarter of an inch; when very hot (which try as before directed for fish), put in the liver and bacon; the bacon will be done first, which remove; the liver must be turned in five minutes; when it is done remove it into a dish, and serve.

148. *Another Way.*—Take away nearly all the fat, then put in the pan a teaspoonful of chopped onions, the same of flour, stir till brown, then add some salt and pepper, a tablespoonful of vinegar, and a small teacupful of water, a little curry powder if handy; mix well together, and pour over the liver. *Calves' Hearts,* as well as pig's and sheep's, &c. &c., may be done like liver, cut in slices, with the exception, that either some currant-jelly, port wine, or a little ale or porter, or ketchup, may be added to the sauce; it is also good bread-crumbed.

149. *Lambs' Fry* is sometimes to be had for a trifle; you can purchase it from about threepence or fourpence per pound; wash it in cold water; for every pound put a quart of water; put them in it for ten minutes to set; take them out, lay them on a cloth; then put in a frying-pan two ounces of butter or dripping, letting it get hot, then dip each piece of the fry in the following mixture, and put in the pan, and fry gently: break an egg, beat it well, add a teaspoonful of flour, which mix smooth, half a wineglass of either milk or water, a little salt and pepper may be put in this delicate batter. When your fry has obtained a nice gold colour, turn it; when done, season with a teaspoonful of salt, and a quarter of pepper, to every pound of fry. A few chopped onions put in the pan with the meat is very nice, or a few mushrooms.

Pigs' chitlings, done as above, will be found very good, especially if fried with onions; buy them ready cleaned, then before you fry them let them simmer in a saucepan, in salt and water for thirty minutes, or till tender ; drain them, and fry as above. Tripe may also be done the same.

FOWLS.

150.—THE motive of semi-frying food is to have it done quickly; therefore, to fry a whole fowl, or even half, is useless, as it could be cooked in a different way in the same time; but to semi-fry a fowl with the object of having it quickly placed on the table, in order to satisfy a good, and perhaps fastidious, appetite, it should be done in a similar way to that practised in Egypt some 3000 years since, and of late years for the great Napoleon—that is, cooked in oil.

In France this dish is called " Poulet à la Marengo." It is related that the great conqueror, after having gained that celebrated victory eat three small chickens at one meal done in this way, and his appetite and taste was so good, and he approved of them so highly that he desired that they might always be served in the same way during the campaign.

151.—The fowl should be divided thus ; if just killed it should be plucked and drawn as quick as possible, or cooked whilst still warm ; it will then be tender ; if it has been long killed, the joints and pieces should be well beaten with a piece of wood, not to break the skin and bones, but to loosen the sinews. The legs should be first removed, then the wings, going close up to the breast ; then cut the belly in two ; by this there are eight pieces. They should be seasoned with pepper and salt ; for want of oil, one ounce of either butter, fat, or dripping should be put in the pan. If a young fowl, it will take from twelve to fifteen minutes ; the pieces should be turned several times ; when done serve plain, or put into the fat a glass of wine, some vinegar, or ketchup ; for want of wine add a little vinegar ; give it a boil up till half reduced ; season and pour into the dish, and serve. A few fried mushrooms are excellent with it ; or six oysters, with their liquor, or tomata sauce, &c.

If the fowl is preferred to be done whole, then split it down the back, truss it the same as for broiling ; beat it flat, put two ounces of oil into the pan, lay in the fowl, season it ; it must be done gently, and will take half an hour, if young, but of a good size ; if rather an old bird, it will take one third more than the above time.

152. *Pigeons, whole,* should be cut down the back the same as

'owl; cut off the head, the pinions, and feet; season and fry with an ounce of oil or fat. They will take ten minutes.

153. *Rabbits.*—Cut them in pieces, remove all superfluous bones, beat each piece flat, season them with pepper and salt, place the pan on the fire with two ounces of fat, put in it two onions, sliced, and then the rabbit; they will take twenty minutes or more to do, gently; remove the pieces of rabbit; have the liver, heart, and brains chopped up with a little parsley, and fry with the remaining fat; when done pour off part of the fat; add a gill of water, season it; give it a boil, and pour over the rabbit. A little curry may be added, and boiled rice. served separate.

154. *Poultry of all kinds, Devilled.*—These are best made by poultry previously cooked. The proper way is to do them with the gridiron, but in case the fire is in that state that they cannot be broiled, and the everlasting frying-pan must be made use of, then prepare them as already described for broiling. Place in the pan one ounce only of butter, and fry gently until hot through. A slight improvement may be made in using the frying-pan; it is to rub the bottom with garlic or eschalot before placing the fat in, frying some onions at the same time. A little bacon can also be fried with it.

CURIOUS EFFECTS OF IMAGINATION.

Here, Eloise, I again discuss a subject about which, some little time since, we had an argument; but you will observe that the topic is treated in quite a different manner, and you must use your own discretion whether you will introduce ox liver or not. I can only say that I and three friends dined off it yesterday, and they all declared it excellent. I assure you I am not jesting, they thought they were eating calves' liver, and praised the way it was cooked.

Later in the day I put on a very long face, and asked one of them, a cousin of mine, if he felt well, as the cook had made a great mistake in preparing the dinner? He, knowing my mania for experiments turned very pale, and said, "No! No!" "Do not be frightened, for it is nothing very bad; she used ox liver instead of calves'." The poor fellow was greatly relieved, for he thought himself poisoned; but still the idea of having eaten of the food which is generally given to that domesticated and homely animal, pussy, made him uncomfortable all through the evening.

This is the effect of the imagination, as we have sufficient proof, in China, France, and elsewhere, that many objects which we detest are considered the greatest luxuries.

A curious incident of the force of imagination occurred some years since at a town not a hundred miles from Leicester. A candidate for the borough, as M.P., a noble lord, having been unsuccessful, his supporters proposed giving him a dinner to console him for his loss he, however, could not attend, but sent them a raised pie of game, about the size of a small carriage wheel, which was partaken of by his supporters with great gusto. A few days after a letter arrived to the chairman, as if from the noble lord, stating that he was glad they liked the pie, as he had now got his revenge for their having deceived him in the election—that the pie was composed of polecats, dogs, rats, &c. &c. This letter was shown to the members of the committee; and it soon got noised about, and although four days had elapsed, there was hardly a person that had partaken of it who was not ill. The noble lord having left that part of the country, it was some days before the hoax was found out.

155. 1st Lesson. New Style of Dressing Liver in Frying-pan.

—I dressed it thus: take about two pounds of ox liver; remove the sinew and veins, cut it into long slices, half an inch thick, put in two ounces of dripping in pan; when hot put in three pieces at a time of liver until set; cut a quarter of a pound of bacon in small dice, fry in fat, cut up the liver in small dice, add it to the bacon, then add a tablespoonful of chopped onions, the same of parsley, the same of flour, a teaspoonful of salt and half of pepper, stir round, and then add half a pint of water, or a little more if the flour is strong, till it forms a nice thickish sauce; put all into a dish, cover over with bread-crumbs, put a little fat over, and place in the oven or before the fire for twenty minutes; brown it over with a hot shovel, and serve. A few poached eggs put on the top will give it a nice appearance, and render it more nourishing. Curry may be used.

156. Minced Meat.

—The remains of any kind of cooked meat will be found very good; the meat having been previously done will only require mincing. Cut in thin slices about one pound of meat, put on a dish, sprinkle over about a teaspoonful of salt, third ditto of pepper, one of flour, mix well, put in your frying-pan, add half a pint of water, and a drop of colouring, if handy put on the fire, stir when it commences to boil, then place it on the hob, let it simmer ten minutes, and serve.

N.B.—This is very plain, as you see, and can be made in any

pan or iron pot, but I place it here only for those who possess a frying-pan.

You may now vary this economical dish in twenty different ways; prepare always your meat, flour, salt, and pepper, as above; you may add a teaspoonful of chopped herbs, such as onion, chives, or parsley, or a tablespoonful of sharp pickles, or made sauce, a little cayenne, spices, wine, or vinegar, may also be used, and served on toast if approved of.

157. *Minced Veal.*—Any remains of roast veal may be quickly dressed to good advantage, as follows, by the aid of the frying-pan:—Cut all the meat and fat off the joint into small dice; calculate the amount of fat you put with the lean, say three ounces for every pound; when cut put a pound of it on a dish, add to it a teaspoonful of salt, a little pepper, two spoonfuls of flour, and a chopped onion; put in the pan half a pint of water to boil, two teaspoonfuls of colouring; then put the meat in, stir it, let it simmer gently for twenty minutes, and serve on toast; poached eggs on it are very good; or put the mince into a tin pan, bread-crumb over, drop a little butter or dripping over, then put it in the oven, or before the fire to brown. The mince may be made white by using milk instead of water and colouring.

158. *New Way of Mincing Meat.*—Cut in small dice one pound of either raw beef, mutton, pork, or veal, flesh and fat in proportion; put in the pan two ounces of butter or dripping; when hot, add the meat, stir it occasionally, and season it with two small teaspoonfuls of salt, a little spice, half one of pepper. When the meat is just set, put in a teaspoonful of flour, half a pint of water; let it simmer twenty minutes, or, if tough, a little longer, adding a gill more water, and serve; a little eschalot, chives, or onions, chopped, may be added. If veal, lamb, or pork, the sauce may be kept white, and milk may be used; if beef or mutton, the sauce ought to be brown, and three teaspoonfuls of colouring added; the juice of a lemon, or a drop of vinegar, is very good with it; ox kidneys may be done the same way. This will make a good curry by the addition of half a teaspoonful of that article.

158 A. *Simplified way of Hashing all kinds of Cooked Meat.*—Cut a pound of meat, except salted meat, previously

cooked, into thin slices, put it on a dish, add to it one teaspoonful of flour, one and a half of salt, half a one of pepper, mixing all
together well, then put all in the frying-pan, adding half a pint
of cold water, set it on the fire; let it remain there until it has
simmered ten minutes; take up, and serve.

2nd Lesson. Proceed as above, but vary flavour with either
of the following ingredients: use either a teaspoonful of chopped
onions, eschalot, parsley, a few mushrooms, pickles, sauce, or
ketchup.

The above can be done in either black pot, iron saucepan, or
frying-pan.

159. All the above can be made as curries, and served with
rice, by first frying one onion, cut up small, and half a large
baking-apple, also cut small; then add the meat, give it a fry,
mix with half a pint of water, one teaspoonful of good curry
powder, pour it over the meat, give it a simmer for ten
minutes, and serve with boiled rice separate.

160. *Bubble and Squeak.*—Any remains of salt beef or pork
may be dressed in this old, but good and economical fashion.
Cut your meat, when cold, in thin slices, to the weight of about
a pound, including, if possible, from two to three ounces of fat;
then take one or two Savoy cabbages, according to size, which,
when boiled and chopped, ought to weigh about two pounds; cut
each cabbage in four, throw a few of the green outside leaves away,
as likewise the stalk; put about a gallon of water in an iron saucepan; when boiling add your cabbage, and let it remain about
twenty minutes, or until tender; drain them well, and chop them
up rather fine; then add three ounces of either butter or dripping
in the frying-pan, which put on the fire; when hot put in your
slices of meat, which semi-fry of a nice brownish colour, on
both sides; take them out, put them on a dish, keep them
warm; then put the cabbage in the pan with the fat, add a teaspoonful of salt, the same quantity of pepper; stir round till hot
throughout; put on the dish, lay the meat over, and serve; if no
cabbage, any green will do, first boiled, drained, chopped, and
fried. Boiled carrots and turnips, previously cooked and chopped,
may be added to the cabbage.

161. *Fritters of Meat, Poultry, Fish, and Fruits.*—The fol-

lowing is thirty receipts in one :—Put a pound of the crumb of bread to soak in cold water, take the same quantity of any kind of boiled or roasted meat, a little fat, which chop in dice rather fine, press the water out of the bread; put in the pan two ounces of butter, lard, or dripping, with two teaspoonfuls of chopped onions, fry two minutes, add the bread, stir with a wooden spoon until rather dry, then add the meat, season with a teaspoonful of salt, half of pepper, a little grated nutmeg, if handy; stir till quite hot; then add two eggs, one at a time, mix very quick, and pour on dish to cool.

Then roll it into the shape of small eggs, then in flour, egg them and bread-crumb, fry (as No. 72) a nice yellow colour; serve plain, or with any sharp or any other sauce you fancy.

162. Innumerable are the receipts that can be made in this way; in fact, from everything that is eatable, and at any season of the year,—from the remains of meat, poultry, game, fish, vegetables, using the same amount of seasoning.   Bread soaked in milk is better.

163. The same can be done with chopped dried fruits, and preserved fruits, using a quarter of a pound more bread; fry, and sift powdered sugar and cinnamon over.   Cream may be used for fruits or curds.

They may also be fried in batter, like fritters, instead of bread-crumbs.

There is no end to what may be done with these receipts. They may be fried, and when cold put between paste, cut into nice pieces of any shape, and baked.   They can be ornamented, and made worthy the table of the greatest epicure, if the bread be soaked in cream, and spirits or liquor introduced in them.

164. *Tripe, Lyons fashion.*—Boil two pounds of tripe; when done, drain it, dry with a cloth, cut it in pieces about an inch square, put in the pan four ounces of butter, four middling-sized onions cut in slices, fry for a few minutes, then add the tripe, stir them every four minutes for about a quarter of an hour, then put in a teaspoonful of salt, half ditto of pepper, two tablespoonfuls of vinegar, mixed well, and it will be ready for serving.

Vermicelli, boiled in the water that the tripe has been boiled in, makes good soup.   Rice or bread is nice done this way.   The addition of a teaspoonful of curry, one spoonful of flour, and half a pint of broth or water, will make a good curry with the tripe.

165. *A Fried Toad in the Hole.*—Take *a steak* of the size required, not less in thickness than what I have before stated, and partly fry on both sides; have ready a pint of second-class batter, as No. 462; remove the steak for a minute, add more fat in the pan, put in the batter when it is beginning to become as thick as paste, place the steak in the middle, raise the frying-pan a sufficient height from the fire on a trivet, so as to cook gently; turn it over; or put the pan in the oven; when well set it is done; serve on a dish, the bottom uppermost.

165 A. *Tripe Sautéd.*—Have the tripe already boiled tender; put into the pan two ounces of fat, with two onions in slices; fry them; when brown add the tripe, which must be dry; when they get a little brown add salt, pepper, a pint of second-class batter, No. 462; proceed as above.

The same Curried.—Proceed as above; add one teaspoonful of the curry powder instead of the vinegar.

The same with Pickle.—Proceed as above; adding piccalilly, or gherkins cut small.

166. *The Remains of other kinds of Cold Roast Meats* may be done in this way, and, when eggs are cheap, poach half-a-dozen, which put on the top.

167. *The Remains of Fish*, previously cooked, are very good done in this way. A piece of conger eel or ling, about four inches thick, partly boiled in salt water with onions and parsley, and boned, will make a very economical and also a Lenten dish.

168. *Veal or Mutton*, cut into pieces, about two inches square, and thin, may be fried and added to the batter.

169. *Beef Collops, Fried.*—Take a piece of steak, part and cut thin into pieces of about two inches square, let it be free from sinews, have the frying-pan well greased, add the pieces of meat, do them quickly, sprinkle salt, pepper, and a little flour over them whilst doing; and when nearly done add any flavour you like, either of curry, pickles, tomato or a little vinegar. Serve very hot.

170. *Veal Cutlets for the Aged.*—Cut one pound of veal in eight or ten pieces; season with a teaspoonful of salt, quarter of pepper, little chopped parsley; then take each piece separate, and with the back of the knife beat them well till nearly in a pulp; give them the shape of cutlets with a knife; egg and bread-crumb; beat them nice and smooth, put two ounces of lard in the frying-pan; when rather hot, fry a nice colour; serve plain, or with sharp sauce, No. 420. These may be done, as a general dish, by adding a little fried bacon and chopped onions in the frying-pan. They are extremely tender and full of gravy

Beef, mutton, and lamb, may be done the same way. Sausage-meat of beef or pork may be here introduced, shaped and fried the same.

INTRODUCTION TO BAKING STEW-PAN.

My dear Eloise,—In some of my former letters, I have stated that the principal art of cookery consists in knowing the exact time each object requires to be subjected to the action of the fire; whether it be direct, or by the assistance of either roasting, frying, baking, or boiling. Large quantities of food may be treated in such a manner, that no more nutriment shall be obtained than by smaller quantities; but to learn this requires practice and attention, more than those to whom we wish to dedicate these letters can probably give.

I have been thinking in what way we could obviate the present loss, which either ascends the chimney to disperse in thin air, or pervades the apartments of the house to the inconvenience of its inmates.

I am the more particularly led to the consideration of this subject from having, in my rambles, entered a cottage, the other day, from which an odour proceeded, as if something more than ordinary cookery was going on, when I found a large pot of a kind of Irish stew boiling away on the fire, and the fragrance of the vegetables and meat dispersed over the apartment. Entering into conversation with the occupant, whom I found to be the wife of a carpenter on the adjoining estate, and who was preparing the table for six persons to dine, I soon found she had no mean opinion of her abilities in cooking. I remonstrated with her on the waste she was making, and at once took up a plate, and held it over the pot. so as to intercept the steam, when it was shortly covered by cond used steam and small particles of *fibrine*, which I convinced her would be much better used in giving nutriment to her family than in mingling with the soot in the chimney.

In our superior kitchens there may be plenty of means and utensils to prevent a part of this evil; but in the cottage, the abode of the labourer, whose stock of kitchen utensils consists of an iron pot, frying-pan, and gridiron, these kind of stews could not be done without great waste and difficulty. I have therefore invented a new and simple baking stew-pan, by which all the nutriment and flavour of the various ingredients placed in it are preserved. In order that you may understand it, I will give you a drawing and description of it, feeling confident it will be useful to the million. (See appendix at the end of book.)

It has, likewise, one great advantage over the old method of boiling or stewing, namely, that it gives hardly any trouble in making, retains all the nutriment, cooks in one-third less the time taken by the usual way, and there is not a part of any beast, such as mutton, lamb, beef, pork, veal, or fish, however tough, that may not be cooked tender by this pan. Let whatever you cook in it be sweet, you may, by using this pan and the following receipts, make delicious dishes of fish, flesh, or vegetables; moreover, food prepared in this way will keep much longer than if dressed another way, and must consequently facilitate the way of cooking for a large family, as you can do enough food at once to last for several meals, which you must admit will save an immense deal of time.

This modest pan, as you must perceive, will concentrate all the nutriment and aroma created by any kind of food placed in it; and the object I have in putting a lock and key on it, is to prevent any person raising the lid while cooking, as by so doing the best part of the flavour would immediately escape.

It is so constructed that it may be hung over the fire, or placed on the hob, or steamed or boiled in a stewpan (as you would a pudding boiled in a basin), or in a cottage or baker's oven.

You must agree, my excellent friend, that I have hitherto done all in my power to simplify and economize the food partaken of by the larger part of the people of this country, who, I am sorry to say, are much behind their continental neighbours in the art of cookery, though possessing the best kind of food, and certain I am that huge mountains might be erected with the food daily and hourly wasted, even at the doors of the poor.*

Is it possible, that in a country where the science of political economy has made such progress, that such men as Jeremy Bentham and others have written volumes to benefit their fellow men, and yet

---

* While on my Governmental mission through Ireland, in the year of the famine, 1847, the following conversation took place between Lord Bessborough, then Lord-Lieutenant of Ireland, and myself, after my return from visiting the interior of the country :—

never have given one word on that science which would materially
increase the food partaken of by all classes of society!

Now that I have explained to you my new method of cookery, you
must try the following receipts, and then you will find my assertion
to be correct.

171. *Beef-steak in Baking Pan. First Lesson.*—Take two
pounds of beef steak, which cut in pieces the size of walnuts, but
only half an inch thick ; peel two pounds of potatoes, cut in slices
a quarter of an inch thick, two middling-sized onions sliced ; mix
two teaspoonfuls of salt and one of pepper.

Then lay five or six slices of potatoes on the bottom of the pan,
season them, then add some pieces of beef ; season again, then
potatoes and onions, then beef, until the pan is full, potatoes on

---

" In an interview granted by his excellency, his lordship asked me
if I could account for the generality of the people being so poor ;
when I replied, ' Easily, my lord : why they actually manure the
land with gold to reap copper.' ' How do you make that out ?'
was his excellency's inquiry.   ' Why, my lord, they waste tons of
good fish on the ground to grow a few potatoes.' ' In your opinion,
why do they do it ?' ' Why, my lord ? Because they know how to
cook potatoes to perfection, and are totally ignorant of the way to
cook fish.' ' Well, I believe you are right,' said his lordship ; ' but
how could the evil be remedied ?' ' Easily,' I replied. ' I would
first show them how to cook their food, no matter how simple such
food might be, and prove to them that the maize, or American
flour, now so much in use, if properly prepared, would be a blessing
instead of a curse ; also the necessity of using with their food
other vegetables besides potatoes, as well as instruct them in several
plain ways of cooking fish, which could be had in abundance all the
year round, at a very cheap rate ; it would, at the same time, give
employment on the coast to thousands of indolent people, as well as
circulate an immense deal of money in the interior of the country
and much improve the condition of these poor wretched beings who
only seem to have been born to live between poverty and starvation.

" My plan would be to have public lecturers appointed, whose duty
it should be to go round as often as the agricultural lecturer, and
teach the people how to cook the food which that person now endeavours to make them cultivate.

" Until this is done, this country will never emerge out of the
semi-barbarous state in which it is at present."

His lordship took a note of the conversation, but sudden illness
prevented my ideas being carried out.

F

the top, seasoning each time; pour three quarters of a pint of water, .ock the lid, put in your oven, or send to the baker's, for on hour and a half; when done shake the pot gently, that the gravy may mix with the potatoes and onions, and form a nice thick sauce. Skirt or any other part of beef is excellent done thus.

Observe, Eloise, that this is the plain foundation of every receipt which I am going to send you, on that simple and effective style of cookery. I have omitted all seasoning but salt and pepper; if onions are an objection omit them; therefore take this as a guide for all kinds of meat, poultry, and even fish, which are very good done in this way.

172. Another variety may be made, which gives a change; this is, to mix a quarter of a pound of flour with a little chopped suet, a little salt, a gill of water, to form a paste; roll it out to cover the meat, so that it fits to the sides of the pan; then put the cover on as usual, and bake. A little dripping will do for the paste.

You have often reproached me of liking to give varieties of seasoning; in the above it is according to your own heart; but having done so, let me give one according to my own liking, and though you say the majority of people are not fond of savoury cookery, and do not like any predominant flavour; but I am certain they only require to try it two or three times, and they will like it.

173.—The variation of seasoning is very slight, to the above add only two onions; four will give it a stronger flavour, and six for those fond of onions. These may be varied by the judicious use of the following spices—either two cloves, or one blade of mace, or six peppercorns, or a teaspoonful of powdered ginger. Or with the herbs, two small bay-leaves, two sprigs of fresh thyme, or some winter savory, or lemon thyme; if dried, a little more should be used; two teaspoonfuls of chopped parsley may be employed. A little celery seed is also very good. All these are to be increased in proportion to the size and contents of the pan.

174. *Leg of Beef.*—Take two pounds of the leg—that part which is full of sinew—cut as above, and season the same way; add a pint of water, and give another hour in the oven: meat without bone is preferable; any part of the beef will do for this receipt.

Or, instead of cutting the leg or any other part of the beast, the cheek may be put in whole, letting it weigh about four pounds. This process of cooking will make it very palatable and tender; to vary it, the meat may be larded, and a bunch of herbs (No. 451) added, also cloves, nutmeg, mace, or a little garlic.

175. *Beef with Vegetables.*—Peel two carrots, two turnips, two onions, cut in pieces, put some vegetables at the bottom, then the meat in centre; season, and cover over with remaining vegetables; add a few cloves, a pint of water, or half ale and half water; put in slow oven for three hours, take off the fat, and serve. Four pounds of any inferior part of beef will eat tender done thus.

176. *Ox Tail.*—Cut them at the joint, although I prefer them sawed through the piece; have ready some chopped onions and a little herbs; roll each piece in flour, place them carefully in the pan, with some of the onions and seasoning; add a pint of water, bake three hours, take off the fat, and serve.

177. *Ox Heart and Kidneys.*—The heart does not enjoy a very high reputation. I mean not only with the wealthy, but with the laborious part of the population, in consequence of the difficulty experienced in cooking it properly. It is thus generally left on the hands of the butcher, and consequently sold cheap; but I trust these receipts will occasion a change, and induce them to purchase those provisions which are now despised.

178.—Wash an ox heart in several waters, cut it in six pieces lengthways, like steak, lay a few slices of potatoes at the bottom of the pan, then a few slices of bacon, then the heart, then bacon again, and then potatoes over all; a few slices of beef suet, instead of the bacon, if none handy; it should be cut thin; season as you fill up, add half a pint of water, bake one hour, and serve.

179.—If a small heart, buy half an ox kidney, cut out the hard part, and divide it into small pieces, and mix it with the heart; if you can get a cow-heel already boiled, which is the case in large towns, it may be added in pieces, omitting the bone.

180. *Calves', Sheep's, Pig's, or Ox Heart, stewed whole.*—

Fill a heart, as for roasting, with stuffing, No. 456 . Put in a four quart pan a piece of fat bacon half an inch thick, and on it the heart, the thick part downwards; cut into slices some potatoes, carrots, turnips, and onions, and a piece of bacon cut in dice; season it with three teaspoonfuls of salt and one of pepper: fill up round the heart until the pan is full, put in a pint of water, and bake for two hours. A teaspoonful of sugar and three of browning may be added.

181.—Tongues, brains, and liver, ought to be set before putting in the pot. The tongue should be boiled for ten minutes, and then skinned. These may be done in the same way as the preceding.

182.—But supposing you have all these, and you wish to mix them together, then cut them into thin slices, leaving out the brain; put them on a dish, and for every pound of meat season with one teaspoonful of salt and a quarter ditto of pepper, and two teaspoonfuls of flour; then have one onion and half a pound of potatoes cut in slices to each pound of meat, and place in the pot as before, mixing the brain cut in pieces; add half a pint of water to each pound of meat; bake according to size.

Layers of suet pudding may be used instead of potatoes, and cover it with paste.

183. *Good Plain Family Irish Stew.*—Take about two pounds of scrag or neck of mutton; divide it into ten pieces, lay them in the pan; cut eight large potatoes and four onions in slices, season with one teaspoonful and a half of pepper, and three of salt; cover all with water; put it into a slow oven for two hours, then stir it all up well, and dish up in deep dishes. If you add a little more water at the commencement, you can take out when half done, a nice cup of broth.

The same simplified.—Put in a pan two pounds of meat as before, which lay at the bottom; cover them with eight whole onions, and these with twelve whole potatoes; season as before; cover over with water, and send to the oven for two hours.

Almost any part of the sheep can be used for Irish stew. A gallon pan is required for this and the preceding receipt.

184. *Ox Tongue, Potted and Braized.*—I send you this

receipt as a bonne bouche, it being a dish worthy a first-class picnic or the race-course. Take a tongue from the pickle, and wash it clean; cut off a part of the rough pieces of the root, put a thick slice of bacon at the bottom of the pan, and over that a pound of lean beefsteak or veal, and then the tongue turned round to fit the pan; have a cow-heel, parboiled and ready boned, place it on the tongue, and cover it with another slice of bacon, and a slice of beef or veal; season with two teaspoonfuls of pepper, a little powdered ginger and cloves, one bay-leaf, one carrot sliced, and two onions sliced; add two wineglassfuls of brandy or sherry, four of old ale, and one quart of water; cover well over, and put in a slow oven for three hours take off the cover, and put a piece of board with a weight on the top until cold, then the next day turn it out of the pan, which you can do by placing the pan in hot water. But should you wish to use the tongue hot for dinner, take it out, and when done with it, put the remains in and press, as before described. The vegetables may be also pressed in with the meat or served hot round the tongue.

The remains of pickled ox tongues are very nice, intermixed and placed in a pan, and pressed, when they will turn out like collared head. A tongue boiled in plain water will take about two hours.

185. *Ox Tongues, Fresh and Pickled.*—Put in the pan, as above, add two carrots, four turnips, four cloves, ten small dumplings, (see No. 349,) fill the pan with water, add either a little bay-leaf, thyme, or winter savory; stew in an oven for three hours, trim and dish up with vegetables, and dumplings round, making soup of the broth. For fresh ox tongue, proceed as above, adding three teaspoonfuls of salt.

186. *Veal.*—Take two pounds of the leg of veal, or meat from the shoulder, or the neck or breast, in fact any part, cut in pieces; season it with one teaspoonful and a half of salt, and a half of pepper, and add a quarter of a pound of bacon cut in slices. To vary the seasoning, use herbs, (No. 451 , It will also be very good with some suet pudding, previously boiled in small balls, if you omit either potatoes or stuffing. The pieces of veal should be rolled in flour; add half a pint of water, if with potatoes, and more, if pudding or stuffing; bake one hour and a half, and serve. Mushrooms may be added.

187. Purchase six calves' tails, and after having had them washed, cut them about two inches in length, and cook them as above, with the addition of more vegetables, as carrots turnips, &c. They are excellent and nutritious thus.

188.—*Brown Ragout of Veal.*—Take two pounds of the breast, cut it into rather small pieces, about the size of an egg, roll them well in flour, put some fat in the frying-pan, fry the meat until a nice brown, take it out, and then fry four onions, two turnips cut in large dice, and one carrot the same; when brown take them out, put the veal and vegetables into pan, season with two teaspoonfuls of salt and one of pepper, add a pint of water, to which has been added four teaspoonfuls of browning; put into oven for one hour, skim the fat, shake the pan, and serve. A few herbs and a little ham or bacon is an improvement. Beef, mutton, lamb, and pork may be done the same way. A teaspoonful of sugar is an improvement.

189. *Fillet of Veal for an Extra Dinner.*—A small fillet of veal, boned and stuff with No. 456; tie it up tight, put some fat into a fryingpan, about an inch deep; put in the fillet, fry gently until one side is brown, and then put in the other side until brown; fry in the same pan some large button onions whole, some turnips and carrots, cut in pieces the size of eggs; put the fillet into a pan, with a piece of fat bacon at the bottom; fill up round it with the vegetables; put another piece of bacon on the top, add some seasoning to the vegetables, and a pint of water; put on the cover, so that the steam does not escape; put it into a slow oven, giving a quarter of an hour for each pound weight. When served take out the fillet, put the gravy into a small basin, and skim off the fat; pour the gravy over the veal, and either serve the vegetables round the fillet or separate. A little browning is an improvement.

190. The following is another favourite dish of mine :—It is to lard a calf's liver with about twenty pieces of bacon (see No. 450), put about a quarter of a pound of fat or dripping into a frying pan, fry for twenty minutes until of a nice brown colour, place it in the baking stew-pan, also fry a quarter of a pound of bacon cut in dice. twenty large button onions, twenty pieces of

carrot, twenty of turnip; when a nice colour throw two ounces of flour over them, and stir; three teaspoonfuls of salt, and a small one of pepper, two of sugar; put all this into the pan, add three pints of hot coloured water No. 453 A, and a bunch of sweet herbs; shake the pan well, and place in oven for two hours; skim the fat and serve. These preparations are for a large sized liver. Pig's, lamb's, and sheep's liver, is excellent done thus. You may place all the above ingredients in the baking pan without frying any; it will be very good, though not so savoury in flavour.

191. *Beef-à-la-Mode.*—Take a piece of the thick part of the rump of beef, about four pounds, not too fat; take half a pound of fat bacon and a calf's foot; cut the bacon into pieces about two inches long and half an inch square, lard the beef through with the bacon (see No. 450), place the beef in the pan, and also the foot, divided in two, and a bunch of sweet herbs, two middle-sized carrots, cut into squares, and twenty button onions, or four or six large ones, cut into slices; add half a quartern of brandy, a teaspoonful of salt, half ditto of pepper, one pint of water, put the cover on the pan, to prevent the steam escaping, and send it to the baker's for three hours; should it be done at home, turn the pan so that the heat is equal on all sides; when done remove the fat from the top, put the beef in a dish, with the foot on each side, and the carrots and onions round; throw the gravy over; take away the herbs. This, you may perceive, is a most exquisite dish, will keep good many days in winter, and five or six in summer. It is good cold.

192. *The same plainer.*—Proceed as above, adding half a pint of old ale instead of the brandy, or a wineglass of vinegar and an ox-foot instead of a calf's-foot. Any piece of the fleshy part of the ox is good done so.

193. *The same, to be eaten cold.*—Cut the beef into square pieces, of a quarter of a pound each, cut ten pieces of lean bacon three inches long, have a cowheel already boiled in about two quarts of water, with two onions, pepper and salt, and a little vinegar; take the cowheel and remove all the bones, and place it, with the meat and bacon, in the pan, with the liquor in which the heel was boiled, two carrots cut into small dice, ten gherkins cut into slices, and sent to the oven for three hours; take off the

cover, and place a flat piece of board on the top of the meat, with a heavy weight, so as to make it firm; and when cold use it. It is very good for breakfast. To remove it from the pan place the pan in hot water for a few minutes, and turn it over; it will come out easily, and cut like brawn, or it may be cut from the pan.

194. *Leg, Breast, Scrag, and Head of Lamb.*—These may all be done as follows:—Put it into a gallon pan, with one carrot, two turnips, one leek, cut in thick slices, thirty young button onions whole, three teaspoonfuls of salt and one of pepper, cover with water, and set it on the fire, or in your oven for one hour; at the end of one hour put in one pint of peas, a little green mint, and a teaspoonful of sugar; set it by the side of the fire or in the oven for half an hour longer, and serve. This is for a leg or joint of five pounds weight; for a larger one take a little longer time. A bunch of parsley and sweet-herbs may be added, but should be removed when served. The flavour is exquisite, and may be served with vegetable or without, as liked, but then the broth should be strained, and the vegetables served separate, or the broth made into spring or other soups.

195. *Pork.*—Any part, not too fat, is exceedingly good done in this way: Cut two pounds in slices, rather large and thin, season with salt and pepper, then add a few slices of fat, then some slices of potatoes, then pork and then potatoes, until all is in; add half a pint of water. Bake one hour and a half.

196. *Another way with Apple.*—Cut the pork in thick pieces, peel two baking apples, four onions, and eight potatoes, cut them in slices, season with pepper and salt, and, if liked, a little powdered sage, intermix the vegetables, lay the slices and the vegetables together, half a pint of water, or enough to cover it. Bake two hours and serve.

197. *Another, simpler.*—When in a great hurry proceed thus: —Put in a dish two pounds of pork in slices, one onion, one pound of potatoes, also sliced; two teaspoonfuls of salt, half of pepper, one of flour; mix all well together, put it in the pan with half a pint of water. Bake one hour and a half. A little bone may be used with the meat.

198. *Salt Pork with Peas.*—Take two pounds of the belly

of pork, cut into large dice, wash half a pint of split peas, put them into a three-quart pan, with some pepper, and half a carrot cut in small pieces, fill it up with cold water, send it to the oven for two hours, stir up the peas well before serving. A few vegetables may be introduced. Rice may be used instead of peas.

199. *Salt Pork* may be used thus: Take a four-quart pan, cut up the pork and some greens, remove the stalk, slice them, and also add four onions sliced, four cloves, and one teaspoonful of pepper; press it well down; put over it a quarter of a pound of dripping, add a pint of water, and stew for three hours; a little salt may be added if the pork is not salt enough; it will make an excellent soup if filled up with water half an hour previous to using.

Red cabbage may also be used, but first boiled for ten minutes in plain water; then add half a pint of vinegar and twelve peppercorns, if handy.

200. *Green Peas and Pork.*—Put a piece of salt pork, about two pounds, into pan, with a quart of peas; fill up with water, add two teaspoonfuls of salt, one of pepper, one of sugar, two onions; bake for three hours. Salt beef is also good; a little mint may be added. Three pints of large peas alone, with a little dripping, is good as above.

201. *Cabbage and Pork.*—Cut two good Savoy cabbages in thin slices, wash them, put half in pan, then a piece of pork about two pounds, or either ham, bacon, or salt beef; season as foregoing receipt, add the remainder of the cabbage; season again; add, if you have it, four cloves, or pepper corns, four onions, and a bunch of sweet herbs: do not fill it with water to the brim, or it will boil over. Red cabbage may be used the same way, only adding half a pint of vinegar, and if beef, two ounces of dripping.

202. Haricot beans and other pulse may be done precisely the same way. In fact, all dried pulse may be here used, and I cannot too strongly recommend both the dried haricot beans and lentils. I have also latterly tried the dried green pea, well soaked for twenty hours, and dressed as haricots and lentils. I find that one pint absorbs two quarts of water. It makes an agreeable as well as economical food.

203. *Beef and Pork.—Semi-Carthusian Fashion.*—Sausages, cervelas, savelous, beef sausages, knuckles of ham, and salted pig's feet and tongue, which are daily to be obtained in London, may be dressed in this way: Buy two good savoys or white cabbages, cut them in four, take out the hard stalk, and boil them for ten minutes in water; place them in a dish to drain; cut the quarters again into four, lay some at the bottom of the pan, then a few sausages and saveloys, season with salt and pepper, and then fill up the pan; then add two ounces of dripping or suet, half a pint of water, bake one hour and a half, and serve with cabbage under, and sausages on the top.

Red cabbage with saveloys are preferable; then add one gill of vinegar, a few peppercorns; stew them longer, and serve as above. I have tried with raw cabbage; it is not bad, and saves time.

Two or three onions sliced may be added, or one large Spanish onion.

This receipt will do for pig's feet, knuckles of ham, trimmings of ham or pork, a piece of cooked brisket of beef, which is generally sold underdone, in which case the cabbage should be done first.

Sheeps' and pigs' tongues are very good done in this way, and they make a cheap and wholesome meal.

204. *Large Dutch Rabbits.*—Put into a one gallon pan a rabbit, cut into about eighteen or twenty pieces; peel eight onions, twenty potatoes cut into thin slices; also half a pound of bacon cut into dice, season with salt and pepper, then place the meat and potatoes in layers, add nearly a pint of water; cover over and bake two hours; shake the pan round and serve.

205. *Curry Rabbits.*—Proceed as above; only add to the water two teaspoonfuls of curry powder; let it well mix, or season with it at the same time as the other seasoning.

The same may be done with rice instead of potatoes, but use two quarts of water to every pound of rice. *One pound of good rice* ought to weigh five pounds when boiled.

206. *Plain Rabbit, Chickens, or Pigeons for Invalids.*— The rabbit should be cut into nice pieces; the chicken in quarters; the pigeons into halves; place it in a two-quart pan,

with a quarter of a pound of bacon cut in dice, a little salt and pepper; a few sprigs of parsley, and half a pint of water, if the pan is not quite full; fill up with some small pieces of veal; put a plain paste over all, No. 317; put cover close over, and bake one hour. Skim the fat off, and serve.

HOW TO USE THE PAN FOR SEMI-ROASTING.

The deep tin dish at the bottom of the pan is to contain either pudding, gravy, or vegetables, the grating above is to lay any meat, poultry, fish, or game on, you wish to cook by this process.

207. *Ribs of Beef semi-roasted.*—Purchase two ribs of beef, bone them, then season the interior of the meat with salt and pepper; roll the meat round like a cheese, using a piece of string or a skewer to keep it in that position; make a quart of batter, as No. 462 put it in your pan, which previously well grease; put the grating over, and lay your meat on it, surrounding it with potatoes either whole or cut; allowing from twelve to fifteen minutes for each pound of meat, according to the state of the oven. Dish up the beef with the potatoes round, and serve the pudding in the tin, or turn it out on a dish. The beef may be stuffed with stuffing, No. 456.

Nothing is more objectionable to me than to see salt put on the top of a roast joint, and water poured over to make the gravy. The only way to remedy this is to put a gill of boiling water and a little salt on the hot dish you intend putting the meat on, turning the joint in it once during the interval of a minute; and, whilst carving, the juice from the meat will mingle with it and make a good gravy. Half a teaspoonful of colouring, much improves its appearance. This is applicable to all roasted or semi-roasted joints.

For large ribs of beef or sirloins, you can put the salt on the bones at the back of the joint, and pour half a pint of boiling water over; not however disturbing the meat.

Brown gravy, No. 2, or broth, No. 1, will be found preferable to either of the above.

208. *Mutton semi-roasted.*—Half a leg of mutton, about four pounds, potatoes and pudding, if liked, under, will take about one hour. Shoulder the same.

209. *Pork semi-roasted.*—Place in the bottom four apples, peeled, four onions sliced, and potatoes, and over that a joint of

pork, rubbed with salt and pepper; sprinkle a little sage; add half a pint of water in the pan: bake for two hours.

For a change, pork should be purchased the day before using, covering it all over with salt; and then scrape it well before cooking it, makes it eat short and savoury.

210. *Lamb semi-roasted.*—Boil some spinach in salt and water, drain it well, and chop it up; put it in the pan, seasoned with salt and pepper; put potatoes over the grating, and then the joint of lamb; small ribs or shoulder will take an hour; leg, one hour and thirty minutes. Dish it up with the spinach separate, the fat having been removed from it. Greens of any kind may be done in the same manner, particularly the young leaf of the white beet, which is an excellent substitute for spinach, or even chopped nettles: these are also good under pork, veal, or beef, as also is a Yorkshire pudding, as at ribs of beef, No. 207.

211. *Poultry semi-roasted.*—Almost any kind of vegetables, such as carrots, turnips, onions, potatoes, celery, or mushrooms, may be put raw in the pan and cooked under poultry, as well as cabbage, spinach, or greens, previously boiled and chopped.

1st Lesson.—Pluck, draw, and stuff a middle-sized fowl; peel and cut in middling-sized pieces about half a pound of carrots, the same of turnips; place them in the pan with half a pint of water, half a teaspoonful of salt, one of sugar, and half of pepper; put the grating over, placing the fowl on it, surrounding it with peeled potatoes, season a little more, bake for an hour, and serve; also rub a little butter or fat over the breast, or cover it with a few slices of bacon; a little colouring may be added to the gravy.

This receipt is applicable to all kinds of birds, game, or poultry, allowing about ten minutes baking to every pound of large poultry or game, and the smaller ones in proportion.

212. *Rabbits,* stuffed, put sliced onions in the bottom of the pan, if liked, or boiled rice, previously seasoned, and a bit of butter, &c.; put half a pint of water; bake thirty-five or fifty minutes, according to size, and serve.

If any joint happens to be too fat, it will not do to put a Yorkshire pudding under, as the fat would prevent it setting but if either greens, boiled rice, or potatoes, are added, you will be able to press the fat off with the back of a spoon, or a plate, or the vegetable presser, (see Appendix,) and serve separately.

To semi-roast a Joint with gravy only.—Put in the pan half a pint of water, together with half a teaspoonful of salt, half that of pepper. When done, take off the fat, add a little colouring, pour under the joint, and serve.

USEFUL HINTS ON THE PIG.

Once or twice a year every cottager ought to kill a pig. If a pig is washed and kept clean, it softens the skin and allows it to expand; in fact, a pig thus treated comes much quicker round; it is proved that a pig at fourteen months, kept clean, is equal to one at eighteen which is not attended to. The same day some of the liver may be fried, but the rest can be used in the pan as follows:—

213. Cut it into large dice; put two ounces of fat or dripping into frying-pan, cut up a quarter of a pound of bacon into small dice, fry them for five minutes, and then shake over a teaspoonful of flour, put in the liver, with one teaspoonful of salt, half ditto of pepper, fry it for five minutes, add a gill of water, keep stirring, and put it into pan, with a pound of turnips cut in small dice, four onions cut in four, and half a pint of boiling water; put into a slow oven for fifty minutes, and then serve with toasted sippets round the dish. A bunch of herbs, No. 451, may be added.

Veal, sheeps', lambs', and ox liver, and kidneys, may all be done the same way; less time for lamb and more for ox; any other vegetables may be used, and particularly mushrooms.

214. *Veal.*—Take six pounds of veal usually used for roasting, rub it with salt, put half a pint of water in the tin, and potatoes above, and then the veal; it will take two hours. When it is served, take off the fat from the gravy in the pan, and pour over the veal, reserving the fat for puddings. A piece of bacon and greens should be boiled at home, or a small piece of bacon may be placed with the potatoes; dish the veal with the potatoes, and bacon round it or separate; add a little colouring to gravy.

A piece of veal stuffed may be roasted thus. Or, for gravy, make melted butter No. 410, with four teaspoonfuls of Harvey sauce, or ketchup, and pour it over.

215. *Toad in the Hole.—No.* 1.—May be made in either a baking-dish, pie-dish, or tin. Get about two pounds of trimmings of either beef, mutton, veal, or lamb, not too fat, and cut them

into pieces, each about the size of a small egg; season with salt and pepper, make about two quarts of batter, second class; grease the pan well, put in the meat and batter, and place in a slow oven for nearly two hours, and serve hot.

No. 2, with Potatoes.—Proceed as before. When the pan is ready put about two pounds of previously boiled potatoes, cut in slices, and bake as before.

No. 3, with Peas.—Proceed as before, only adding about one quart of good green peas, previously boiled; broad beans may be used the same way.

No. 4.—Remains of cooked meat may be done the same way, but it will take less time to cook.

No. 5. — Calves', or any brains, previously parboiled in water, and the skin removed, well seasoned with pepper and salt, and a few slices of bacon added to the batter, make a very delicate dish.

No. 6.—Six larks or twelve sparrows, with a slice of bacon skewered round each, with the batter, and put into the oven for two hours.

No. 7.—Ox cheek and sheeps' heads, previously cooked and nicely seasoned, with the addition of a little chopped onions added to the batter, is an economical dish. A few slices of cooked potatoes may be added.

No. 8.—Truss a rabbit for roasting, make a stuffing with the liver, &c., chopped up, bread-crumbs, beef-suet, and seasoning; stuff the rabbit; lay on the bottom of the pan a thick slice of fat bacon, and over that a slice, one inch thick, of beefsteak, and then the rabbit, to which add two quarts of batter; place in the oven for two hours, and serve hot. This is enough for a large family. The rabbit may be cut in pieces; boiled cauliflower may be added.

No. 9.—Remains of previously cooked hare may be done in the same way, with some currant-jelly in the stuffing.

No. 10.—A blade-bone of pork, two onions, cut in slices, and four potatoes sliced, pepper and salt, and one quart of batter put over them; place in the oven one hour, and serve hot.

No. 11.—Remains of salt pork, or any roast meat, may all be done in this way, and varied according to the taste of the partaker.

Remains of any kind of fish may also be done thus, with previously boiled potatoes.

216. *Jugged Hare.*—Cut a small hare into pieces about the size of eggs, cut half a pound of bacon into dice not too small, lay both on a dish, mix together three teaspoonfuls of salt, one of pepper, four of flour, three of chopped onions, one of powdered thyme and bay-leaf, four cloves, and a quarter of a nutmeg, grated; rub the hare and bacon with these; place them in the pan. Having saved the blood, chop up the liver and mix with it, add to it a wineglass of brandy, or two of port or sherry, or one of vinegar, or half a pint of ale, stout, or porter, and a pint of water; put this in the pan, and cover over with pudding-paste No. 319; put on the cover; shake the whole well to make it mix; and bake for three hours, if an old hare; if a young one two hours. It is equally as good cold as hot. If eaten hot, a little currant-jelly should be served with it.

Some stuffing No. 456, made into little balls, can be added with advantage, or even a few suet balls, and two tablespoonfuls of colouring; mix with the water. It can be done plainer, with salt and pepper and water only; or twenty small onions and eight potatoes, cut in slices, may be added, or even mushrooms may be put in.

217. *Jugged Hare, Marinaded.*—It should be cut as above, and put into a bowl, with half water and half vinegar to cover it; four teaspoonfuls of salt and one of pepper, four of brown sugar, two onions cut in slices, a little thyme, a bay-leaf, cloves, peppercorns; turn them now and then for four days, and cook as above, with the marinade in.

218. *How to cook all kinds of Fish in Baking Stew-pan.*—Take six pounds of any fish, cut it crossways, two inches thick, put them in the pan, with salt, pepper, chopped onions; fill it up; well intermix the seasoning; when full, put in a basin four ounces of flour, which mix with a quart of water, which pour over, shake the pot, well cover it, bake two hours in rather a hot oven; seasoning to be four teaspoonfuls of salt, one of pepper, two onions, and chopped parsley; onions may be omitted, but use herbs and mixed spice.

Halibut, hake, ling, conger, cod, pike, carp, tench, perch, and piper may be done the same way.

Rice may be added in the following way :—A pound of previously boiled rice, two quarts of milk, a little sugar and salt, two ounces of butter, a squeeze of lemon, and put into the pan with the fish.

The addition of a few spoonfuls of fish sauce will greatly vary this dish. When done serve, without breaking the piece, if possible.

219. *Pieces of Fish.*—For a two-quart pan, cut four mackerel in three pieces each, which roll in flour, place them in rows in the pan, two teaspoonfuls of salt and a half pepper, two teaspoonfuls of chopped onions ; fennel or parsley may be added ; put in two gills of water, place cover over, bake one hour in a hot oven, and serve, having first taken off the oil from the top.

220. *To Pickle Mackerel and Herrings in the Baking-pan.*—When these fish are plentiful they may be done as follows, and will be found to keep and eat admirably well :—

Cut the mackerel into three pieces, enough to fill the one-gallon pan, lay some at the bottom and season, and continue thus until full ; the seasoning should be four teaspoonfuls of salt, two of pepper, ten peppercorns, four onions sliced, a handful of parsley, chopped ; add over all one quart of vinegar and a pint of water ; place the cover over, and bake slowly for two hours ; some sweet herbs or a bay-leaf may be added.

221. Herrings, pilchards, and sprats can be done as above, only a little variation to the seasoning and the time of cooking, according to the size ; when quite cold pour some oil or lard on the top ; put the cover on, and keep out the air as much as possible, and they will keep a long time.

222. Halibut, hake, ling, conger eel, plaice, gurnet, codlings, sturgeons, and haddock, may all be pickled as above. Cut halibut one inch thick and three inches in length ; place them at the bottom of the pan ; season over as before, and one teaspoonful of ground ginger and sweet herbs.

223. *Baked Eels.*—Cut several eels in pieces of three inches long, roll them in flour, put them in the two-quart pan, season with

salt, pepper, chopped onions, a little thyme; continue until full, add a glass of sherry, half a pint of water, cover over with some crust, either pie or pudding, put on the lid, and bake one hour.

Seasoning, two teaspoonfuls of salt, half of pepper, and two of chopped onions. Take the oil off, and serve.

224. *A Piece of Beef stewed in Baking Pan.*—Get three wing ribs of beef, bone them, season with salt and pepper on each side; to vary the flavour, chopped parsley and a little spice may be added, or even chopped onions; roll it round, and fasten it with string; rub more salt on it, and place it in the pan; send it to the baker's; four pounds will take one hour. This is the best part to bone, but most other pieces may be used. Stuff by making an incision in the lean part, and binding it up with string.

225.—If you wish a Yorkshire pudding and potatoes to be baked at the same time, they may be placed in it, and when it comes home all will be found excellent. Instead of the gratings in the pan, it may be divided in two, one for pudding and the other for potatoes.

All joints may be done the same way.

226. *To Boil Meat in Pan.*—*Spice Beef.*—Take four pound. of the thick ribs of beef, or any part, put in the pan, with a pint of water, a teaspoonful of allspice, two of salt, two bayleaves, two eschalots, or a little garlic; stew three hours, either in oven or on the fire, keeping the cover well closed; half an hour before being done add a teacupful of the raspings of bread, half a pint of vinegar, two teaspoonfuls of sugar, simmer, dish up, and sauce over.

227. *Salt Meat.*—To plain-boil this in the oven, which can be done when no fire is required at home, put six pounds of salt beef into a six-quart pan, with four whole parsnips, two large carrots, and six dumplings; send them to the oven for two hours; dish up the meat with the vegetables, and dumplings round. The liquor can be saved and made into soup; the vegetables can be cut in two.

All kinds of salt meat can be done the same. If the broth be too salt add some water, and use for pea-soup.

ON ROASTING.

My dear Eloise,—My last letter you must have misunderstood.
I did not mean that roasting before the fire should be entirely done away
with, but that, on the score of economy, it should not be practised in
the cottage, but that my new plan of semi-roasting should be followed.
I was the more particularly led to these remarks, from having, last
Sunday, immediately after church, visited several colliers' cottages
belonging to a Mr. Pope, close to this place. My motive for doing so
was to see the economy of the cottage, as well as the kind of food
they had for dinner. The first I went into had a piece of the belly or
flap of beef, just taken down from a dangle, having been roasted. It
was lying in the dripping pan, and was a great deal over done; in
fact, dried. Noticing, in the course of conversation, that the fire
was spoiling it still more, I took a plate from the table, and placed it
against it, so that it should not burn. The old lady noticed my proceeding, and asked me if I was going to have a bit of dinner with
them? "No, thank you, my dear madam," replied I. "Then let
me take away the plate, as it will spoil our dinner." "How do
you make that out?" I asked. "Well, the fat is not yet half
out of the meat, and my Thomas will not eat fat, unless it is
dripping in the crust of pies or puddings." I then perceived that the
meat was, in their estimation, a second consideration, and that they
paid the price of beef for the fat, paying eightpence per pound for the
meat, when they could get the fat at fivepence. There was scarcely
any nutriment left in the meat—that which weighed five pounds
before roasting, weighing hardly three pounds when done. There
were seven to dine off it—the grandmother, the two parents, and
four children. There was, besides, a few potatoes galloping on the
fire—no other vegetable, and no puddings or sweets for the children,
but excellent home-made bread, and not bad small beer. You may
now perceive that some little improvement in this style of cookery
would be an immense saving to these cottagers, and out of the three
shillings and fourpence they paid for the beef, if done in the pan,
with a pudding and potatoes under, and the meat not quite so fat,
they would have got a good dinner and plenty for the next day,
either hot or cold. If they wanted dripping, they could get fat
at four or fivepence, instead of eightpence, and prepare it as No.
464c. It will keep for a long time, without turning sour.

I visited, immediately after, several other of the cottages, in which
I found steaks cooked dry, indeed, some half burnt, chumps of mutton
half done, half legs of mutton neither boiled or baked; in one a
sheep's head baked, and very nicely done, with potatoes round it, which
was very inviting; there was also suet dumplings for the children,

with treacle over. This cottage was cleaner than any of the others, and the children were neatly dressed, and about to change their costume, in order to do full justice to the treacle dumplings. In giving those rosy-cheeked urchins a few pence, I retired much gratified by my visit to these antediluvian workmen, who pass one-third of their life in the bowels of the earth.

You will perceive from what I have said, that to the artisan, labourer, and even the small tradesman, the old mode of roasting, which comes to us from Homeric ages and primitive times, is an extravagant and wasteful mode of cooking, and the sooner it is reformed the better. Though it is preferable to meat done in a baker's oven, if well attended to.

But first let me add one more remark on the experience of that day. Returning to the Normanton Hotel to dinner, we had a beautiful dish of greens; and what do you think those greens were? Green young nettles, which I had asked the gardener to gather for me the day previous, and in less than half an hour we had a basket full. I picked them with gloves, but he made a grasp at a large quantity, and I found that they did not prick him. He got them as fast as a monkey could get chestnuts out of hot cinders. The cook dressed them, according to my directions, exactly like spinach, and most who ate of them thought they were spinach, only rather too hot of pepper, which is their peculiar nature.

I found that they are known in this part of the country as being good and wholesome in the spring; but because the people can have them for nothing, they will not partake of them; like the watercresses, that rot in every clear stream in the neighbourhood. I intend to make another trial or so on the nettles, which I will forward to you.

HOW TO ROAST.

HAVING, thus far, given you some of my experience as regards roasting, I will, in as few words as possible, describe the simple plan of roasting before the fire, which, I must again repeat, is far from being economical. The artisan requires as much nourishment as possible, and should not pay extravagantly for fancy joints, or those called the best, because most in vogue for roasting. Let the wealthy pay for their taste, as they do for their Raphaels, Rubens, and Murillos; it is no reason, because they do so, that a labouring man should imitate them, and because one has a leg of mutton, the other should likewise have one. This very day I have seen, in Nottingham market, all the best joints sold by the butchers, and nothing but the necks of mutton and the coarse pieces of beef left, which, they tell me, hang for days and days, lessening both quality and quantity, and then are sold at twopence or threepence per pound. This causes the joints most in vogue to be dear, whilst there is quite as much nourishment in proportion in those sold at half the price when cooked fresh.

I must here, however, describe the proper system of roasting, either before the fire or by gas (see note). And as an invariable rule, all dark meats, such as beef and mutton, should be put down to a sharp fire for at least fifteen minutes, until the outside has a coating of osmazome or gravy, then remove it back, and let it do gently. Lamb, veal, and pork, if young and tender, should be done at a moderate fire. Veal even should be covered with paper.

Very rich meat, if covered with paper, does not require basting. Fowls, &c., should be placed close to the fire, to set the skin, and in about ten minutes rubbed over with a small piece of butter, pressed in a spoon. Roast meats should be dredged with flour, just at the time when the gravy begins to appear; the flour absorbs it, and forms a coating which prevents any more coming out. Hares and small game the same.

COTTAGE ROASTING.

In the first place, the fire must be made up, and cleared from ashes. Place before it the dripping-pan, and from above the fire, suspend from a hook a piece of worsted thread, sufficiently strong to bear the joint, and a hook suspended at the end. Have a piece of stick forked at one end, which place against the mantle-piece, so that

---

Note.

ON THE COMFORT AND ECONOMY OF ROASTING BY GAS, WHERE IT CAN BE PROCURED.

Experiment made at the Royal Naval School, Greenwich Hospital, by M. Soyer.

Two interesting trials have taken place at the above establishment with an apparatus manufactured by Messrs. Smith and Phillips, patentees, of Skinner-street, Snow-hill, under the superintendence of M. Soyer, which in their results finally determine the question on the merits and economy of roasting by gas.

The result of the first trial, which took place on the 8th inst., was, that 36 legs of mutton, weighing 288 lbs., were roasted at a cost of 1s. 2d.

In order to arrive at more positive results in regard to its economy a second trial was deemed requisite, which took place on the 11th inst., when equal weights of mutton were cooked. Twenty-three joints, weighing 184 lbs., were roasted by gas, at a cost of 10½d., with gas supplied at 4s. per 1000 feet. When cooked, the above weight meat was found to weigh 145 lbs., dripping 19 lbs., and

it keeps the thread at a sufficient distance from the fire. By having two pieces of stick, the distances can be easily managed. Twist the worsted; put on the joint; give it a sufficient distance from the fire. This is quite equal to either a smoke or bottle-jack for cottage use.

Every cottage should have a moveable piece of iron or steel screwed on the mantel-piece, with teeth fixed in it, so as to be able to hang the joint at any distance from the fire. See Appendix, at end of book.

TIME TABLE FOR ROASTING.

228. Ten pounds of beef will take from two hours to two hours and a half roasting, eighteen inches from a good fire.

Six pounds one hour and a quarter to one hour and a half, fourteen inches from the fire.

Three ribs of beef, boned and rolled (see No. 207), well tied round with paper, will take two hours and a half, eighteen inches from the fire, and only baste once.

If beef is very fat, it does not require basting; if very lean, tie it up in greasy paper, and baste well.

229. Eight pounds of veal will take from one hour and a half

---

gravy, or osmazome, $2\frac{1}{2}$ lbs., thus showing the actual loss to be $18\frac{3}{4}$ lbs. Twenty-three joints of mutton were cooked in the usual way, as adopted at the institution, namely, in one of Count Romford's ovens, hitherto considered the most economical way of roasting. When put in they weighed 184 lbs., when done 132 lbs., dripping 18 lbs., gravy none, thus showing a loss of 34 lbs. The coke consumed in this oven was 102 lbs., coal 30 lbs., thus proving the great economy of gas over the oven by a saving of 13 lbs. of meat, 1 lb. of dripping, $2\frac{3}{4}$ lbs. of gravy. The value of the saving is as follows:—
Meat at 6d. per lb., 6s. 6d.; dripping at 5d. per lb., 5d., and gravy at 1s. 6d. per lb., 4s. $1\frac{1}{2}d.$, making a total of 11s. $0\frac{1}{2}d.$

The experiments took place before the governor, Sir C. Adam, and lady, Sir J. Liddle, M.D., Lieut. Rouse, general superintendent, Lieut. Monk, Messrs. Lee and Seville, inspector of works, who expressed their admiration at the cleanliness and simplicity of the apparatus.

In order to show the advantage of the system in all its branches, rump steak was broiled by M. Soyer, before the company present, who partook of it, and who declared it was perfection, and free from all odour.—*Mechanics' Magazine.*

to two hours, eighteen inches from the fire: if stuffed, at least two hours.

Chump, or loin and kidneys, of four pounds, will take one hour and a quarter; baste well.

Six pounds of breast one hour, twelves inches from the fire.

Six pounds of the shoulder or neck the same.

Calf's heart, stuffed and tied up in paper, three quarters of an hour.

230. Mutton (leg of eight pounds), will take one hour and a half, eighteen inches from the fire.

Saddle, ten pounds, one hour and a quarter to one hour and a half, eighteen inches, measuring from the flat surface.

Shoulder, one hour and a half.

Loin, one hour and a half.

Breast, three quarters of an hour.

Neck, one hour.

231. Lamb, according to size, but in the same proportion less than mutton, but ought always to be well done, and placed nearer the fire; if a good fire about fifteen inches from it.

Pork should be well done.

Leg of six pounds, with skin over, two hours, eighteen inches from the fire.

Loin of the same, one hour.

Neck, the same weight, one hour and three-quarters.

Pork rubbed with salt the night previous, and then scraped before roasting, improves the flavour.

In roasting of beef, mutton, lamb, pork, and poultry, place a dripping-pan under the meat, with a little clear dripping or fat, which should be very hot when the meat is basted. A quarter of an hour before serving add half a pint of water to the fat in the dripping-pan; dredge the meat with flour and salt. When the meat is dished up, pour the contents of the pan into a basin, straining it through a gauze sieve kept on purpose; remove all the fat, add a little colouring and salt to the gravy, and pour it into the dish under the meat.

Veal and poultry should have half the quantity of water put in the pan, and that, when strained, added to half a pint of thick melted butter, adding two teaspoonfuls of any sauce for flavour, as Harvey's, Soyer's, or ketchup, &c.

Sage and onions to be served with pork.

Mint sauce with lamb.

Currant-jelly with mutton.

232. *Roasting of Poultry.*—I proceed thus: Hang it up with worsted, about ten inches from the fire, let it hang for ten minutes to set the skin, then press into a wooden spoon a piece of butter or hard dripping; when the skin is very hot rub it over with the fat in the spoon until all is melted, then draw it back to about twelve inches: a good sized fowl will take three quarters of an hour, chicken twenty minutes, middle-sized goose one hour, turkey, fourteen pounds, two hours and a half; hare, large, one hour and a half, if very young three quarters of an hour. Never baste them, but dredge all, after having well rubbed them over with butter, as for fowls.

Small game should be placed nearer the fire.

I always stuff both poultry and game with stuffing No. 456, and make the gravy as for the joints.

Apple sauce with goose.

Currant jelly for hare.

Fried bread-crumbs with grouse.

Bread sauce with partridge and pheasant.

ON MEAT IN BAKER'S OVEN.

THOUGH this system of cooking meat is far from receiving my approbation, especially on the score of economy, still, it would be very ridiculous on our part, Eloise, to think that we should be able entirely to reform this semi-barbarian method of spoiling food. No; it must be a work of time that will prevent small folk from running to the baker's on Sunday with either their legs or shoulders under their arms. The reason why they have recourse to such a process is at once simple and easily explained: first of all, it gives them no trouble, and hardly any of them study economy, so long as the dinner will cook itself, though in company with a score or two of other joints, perhaps no two being of the same size or quality.

How can a baker, even one of the most conscientious of that useful class of individuals, be answerable for the proper cooking of this awkward squad, if such we may term it. How also can he prevent the potatoes galavanting from one dish to another, or even joints changing dishes, and by mistake, going to the wrong home—impossible! Is he to be answerable if an eel crawls out of Mrs. Armstrong's pie (having been put in whole), and, after cooking, being found reposing under one of Mrs. Smith's ribs? or can he prevent Mrs. Jenkins's cod's head staring a neighbouring pig's face out of countenance? No more would he be able to obviate the above evils, than he could disentangle the fragrance which emanates from each homely volcano, forming, as it does, an aerial coating of osmazome under the same roof.

Moral. Is it not more easy for a mother to nurse her own child, than having to take charge of the whole of her neighbours' children? therefore, if every housewife would cook her little family dinner at home, instead of entrusting it to the nursing care of a baker's oven, she would, by so doing, though at the sacrifice of a little time, save both nutriment and money.

A FEW NEW AND USEFUL HINTS ON BAKING MEAT.

IF we, Eloise, cannot entirely reform the evils caused by the above-described system, I feel myself in duty bound to give a few hints on the subject of ameliorating this wasteful method of cooking, which will tend both to economize and vary the flavour, as well as the substance, of any dish that might be doomed to undergo this ordeal.

First of all, I would refer you to such receipts on semi-roasting joints, such as beef, veal, mutton, pork, and lamb, done in the baking-stewing-pan, and proceed in this instance precisely the same. In respect to vegetables, puddings, rice, &c. &c., being anxious that every person should partake of a portion of vegetation with their daily food, independent of potatoes, I have tried all the following receipts, which I beg to forward you, feeling confident they will prove agreeable to our readers' palate, as well as conducive to their health.

AN IMPROVED BAKING-DISH.

(*For drawing of which see Appendix at end of book.*)

I BEG to inform you that I have had made, at a very trifling expense, an improved baking-dish. Its principles are as follows: on the rim of the dish, I have attached a moveable false grating of wire, to the middle of which is fixed a trivet, three inches in height. I then put the pudding at the bottom of the dish, then put in the grating, on which I place the potatoes; then on the trivet I put the meat. By this means the surplus fat, which would otherwise fall in the pudding and prevent its setting, descends on the potatoes, making them delicate and crisp. This is applicable to any joint, and the meat being more elevated than usual when placed in the oven, causes it to partake more of the flavour of a roast joint than it does when put immediately over the pudding or potatoes, the vapours arising from which soddens the meat, instead of leaving it brown and well carbonized.

A SERIES OF RECEIPTS ON BAKED MEATS.

Ribs of Beef baked.—Take three long ribs of beef, bone, season, stuff, and roll as for semi-roasting, No. 207 ; put either Yorkshire pudding or any kind of vegetable in the bottom of the dish, then put on the grating, on which put your potatoes; then fix on the trivet at about three inches above the grating; when done, pour on a hot dish half a pint of boiling water, quarter of a teaspoonful of salt ; pour this under your joint, turn it over ; when hot, turn over twice, and carve ; it will make a rich gravy. Serve the potatoes round, or separate; the pudding to be served on a hot dish.

By chopping the bone small, good broth and soup may be made. If the oven happens to be too hot, cover the joint with a piece or two of plain paper, well greased.

A piece of meat weighing about eight pounds, will take from one hour and twenty to thirty minutes, giving always as a rule from ten to twelve minutes to every pound of meat, for joints of from six to twelve pounds.

Any other piece of beef of an inferior part, requires to be baked slowly, allowing fifteen minutes to every pound, and if too lean, may be larded, as No. 450

2. *For a Leg of Pork.*—Peel six apples, six onions, and twelve potatoes ; put the apples and onions at the bottom of the dish, adding half a pint of coloured water, a teaspoonful of salt, one of sugar, half one of pepper ; lay the potatoes on the grating, the meat over ; give fifteen minutes to every pound of meat. Half a pint of sage and onion sauce may be poured over the apples and onions previous to baking. Any joint of pork may be stuffed with sage and onions.

3. *Fillet of Veal.*—I have also tried the following :—Prepare a fillet, which stuff; oil a sheet or two of clean paper ; cut in slices four ounces of bacon, two onions, one carrot, one turnip, a little celery, if handy, a little thyme and bay leaf; wrap up the veal and the above in the paper, and bake for two hours ; when done, take out the veal and serve with vegetables round it. It will be delicious ; pray let me know your opinion.

Any part of veal may be done the same. Fried bacon may be served with it.

Also half a pint of melted butter, one tablespoonful of ketchup, two of Harvey's sauce, well mixed; pour round and serve.

4. *To bake Mutton.*—Proceed as for beef, time according to size, putting under a Yorkshire pudding, or some rice boiled with curry in it, or boiled French haricot beans, which I have used for a change now and then. I also put a piece of pudding-paste, half way up the knuckle of a leg of mutton, which pre-vents it getting dry, that being so much thinner than the other part.

Loin and shoulder the same; if a piece happens to be lean and dry, butter it over, cover it with paste, and bake as usual. The shoulder, baked, like the leg of pork, is good with apples, potatoes, and onions.

5. *Lamb,* being very delicate, allow only ten minutes per pound for the ribs, the same for the shoulder, twelve minutes for the leg. Spinach, peas, asparagus, and sprouts, are best with lamb.

All kinds of poultry may be done the same, though roast them by all means, if you can; but if wrapped up in paper, as for fillet of veal, No. 3. in this series, it will be excellent baked.

6. *Vegetables with baked Meat.*—My new plan of cooking vegetables with baked meat is as follows:—Scrape, wash, and cut in pieces two pounds of carrots, boil them in salt and water till three parts done, drain them in cullender, then put them at the bottom of your dish, season with half a teaspoonful of salt, half that of pepper, add half a pint of coloured water, then place the potatoes on the grating, the meat on the trevet, and bake as above.*

Any such joints as sirloin, skirt, edgebone, or any other piece of beef, weighing from eight to ten pounds, should have a tea-spoonful of salt sprinkled over, rubbing on also a little fat or

---

* In the way of vegetables for beef, I have tried turnips, Jeru-salem artichokes, parsnips, &c. Also for veal, lamb, and mutton, spinach, greens, cauliflowers, Brussels sprouts, all parboiled and well drained. A pint of second class batter, added to either the parsnips, artichokes, turnips, carrots, peas, asparagus, &c., using only one pound instead of two, but quite boiled, and omitting the gravy, either of these will turn out like a pudding.

butter; roast as above, dish it up with the gravy, taking off the fat, if any, serving the carrots and potatoes with it or separate.

7. *Another Way.*—If an ordinary dish, put the potatoes over the carrots, also a few onions sliced, and the beef on trevet, as usual. When the meat has been too lean, put a piece of fat on the top, and cover the beef with a coating of pudding-paste, No. 319. When done remove the paste, and brown the meat with a shovel, like you would do venison; both meat and paste are excellent, the meat being full of gravy.

MEAT PUDDINGS.

233. *Puddings.*—Although the same word with the same meaning exists in all European languages, yet it may properly be said to be peculiarly English, as pudding has become quite a national dish. The various counties of England have each a particular way of making them, and it is almost impossible to give any method hitherto untried.

The first most important point is never to use any meat that is tainted, for in pudding, above all other dishes, it is least possible to disguise the confined process which the ingredients undergo; the gradual heating of the meat, which alone would accelerate decomposition, will cause the smallest piece of tainted meat to contaminate all the rest. Be particular that the suet and fat are not rancid, ever remembering the grand principle, that everything which gratifies the palate nourishes.

Tainted meat, you will justly say, is bad in whatever way it may be cooked; true, but take a joint which, in the middle of summer, from some trifling cause, has some small part a little tainted, and which is often sold cheap to those who cannot afford to purchase better, this, by the worst part being cut away, rubbed with a piece of charcoal, if for roasting, or a piece of charcoal put into the water, if for boiling, at once renders it sweet; but our great national dish cannot be subjected to this process. Although the tastes of all people differ; some may like the *haut goût* of high venison or the wild fowl, and possibly might like the same in pudding, yet it is our duty here to point out those things which are nourishing, and likewise those that are not; therefore, I here send you some receipts which will please everybody's taste, everybody's palate, and, I hope, everybody's pocket.

234. *Beef Pudding.*—Take about one pound of steak, cut it lengthways in three pieces, and then slantways at each inch, instead of in lumps; but should you buy cuttings of meat from the butchers, then remove all the sinew and over fat, and cut the large pieces slantways, put them in a dish, and sprinkle over with a teaspoonful of salt, a half ditto of pepper, and a tea-spoonful of flour, the same of chopped onions; mix well together, make six or eight ounces of paste as No. 319, roll it to the thickness of a quarter of an inch, or a little more, put pudding-cloth in a basin, sprinkle some flour over it, lay in your paste, and then the meat, together with a few pieces of fat; when full put in three wineglasses of water; turn the paste over the meat, *so as not* to form a lump, but well closed; then tie the cloth, not too close on the paste, or it will not be light; boil it fast in four quarts of water for one hour; take it out, let it stand a few minutes to cool the cloth, cut the string, turn back the cloth, place a dish on the top, and *t*urn it over on it, remove the cloth, and serve.

235.—If you choose to add a kidney it may add to the richness of the gravy, also a few oysters, or even a mushroom. The crust should always be cut with a knife.

If you carefully follow the above instructions you will have a pudding quite perfect, the paste as light and as white as snow, and the meat tender, with a thick gravy.

236.—*Observation.* You will perhaps be surprised that I recommend it to be boiled fast instead of simmering. I do so, because the meat, being enclosed in the paste, and sometimes in a basin, is alone subject to the action of simmering in its own gravy. These puddings lose a less amount of nourishment in cooking than any other kind. In a large pudding a few sliced potatoes is not bad. This may truly be considered as much a national dish as roast beef and plum pudding, and being so, it is surprising that it is so often made badly, and indi-gestible: the pieces of meat and fat often cut two inches square, instead of smaller pieces; the pudding, sometimes left half out of the water, the crust becomes hard and black, and the meat very·dry.

237. *Roast Beef Pudding.*—Any remains of cold roast beef may be done as follows: mince about one pound of cooked meat, cut in dice, put on a dish, add one teaspoonful of salt, half that of pepper, one of flour; fill your paste with it, add a gill of water; cover over as usual, shake it well, tie it up in a cloth,

and boil for half an hour, and serve. A little chopped onions or parsley may be introduced.

238. *Another Way.*—Proceed as above, only add for every pound of meat two ounces of either gherkins, pickled walnuts or mushrooms, chopped fine or sliced.

239. *Mince Beef Pudding with Eggs.*—Proceed as above; omit the pickles, adding boiled ham or fried bacon instead, cut in dice, also add two hard-boiled eggs cut in dice; mix all together, boil as above, white sauce over, or melted butter.

240. *Veal Pudding.*—Cut two pounds of raw veal, four ounces of ham, or lean bacon; season delicately with a teaspoonful of salt, the half of pepper, a little flour and chopped parsley, a gill of water; proceed as for the other puddings, boil two hours, and serve.

241. *Calves' Brain and Tongue of any kind, previously cooked.*—Soak and wash a brain clean, boil it for a quarter of an hour in a quart of water, in which has been added a teaspoonful of salt, a quarter of pepper, and a little vinegar, if handy. Let it get cold, then mould the pudding; cut the brain in half-inch slices, lay thin slices of tongue, previously cooked, on the bottom, then of brain; season with salt, pepper, parsley, and a little chopped onions; continue until full; then mix a teaspoonful of flour with a gill and a half of milk, or water, and pour in; close the pudding, and boil one hour and serve. Cut it with a knife. Two hard-boiled eggs cut in slices, would improve it; also a little gherkin, chopped fine, will vary the flavour.

242. *Sheep's, Lamb's, and Pig's Brains, and Tongue Puddings.*—Proceed as for Calves', but will not take quite so long in cooking.

243. *Calves' Head and Tongue.*—The remains of any from a previous dinner can be used for puddings with or without a little brain: proceed as for brain pudding. A little curry powder added will improve it.

This will produce a better effect on the table as a pudding, than a common hash; for the great principle in cookery is to please the eye, as well as the palate.

244. *Lamb, Veal, or Pork Liver Pudding.*—Cut one pound

of liver in slices, also two ounces of bacon; season with a tea-spoonful of salt, a half of pepper, one chopped onion, one of parsley; mix it well with the bacon, dip each piece of liver in some flour, and lay the liver and bacon in the pudding, with a gill and a half of water; boil one hour. A teaspoonful of colour-ing mixed with the water will give a rich appearance to all pudding gravies.

245. *The same, a plainer Way.*—Cut one pound of liver and two ounces of bacon into dice, a quarter of an inch square; season with only salt, pepper, and onions, a spoonful of flour, and a gill and a half of water; lay it in the pudding, and boil as before. Stuffing No. 456 may be mixed with it.

246. *Liver and Kidney Pudding.*—Put in a frying-pan two ounces of dripping, two ounces of bacon, in dice; put it on the fire; when the liver and kidney are seasoned, place it in the pan, and stir round until it is set; each piece should be firm; then add a tablespoonful of flour, mixed with a gill and a half of coloured water, No. 453A. When nearly boiling, place it in the pudding, tie up, and boil three quarters of an hour. A few herbs is a variation.

247. *Mutton Pudding.*—Chump of mutton is the best part to make into pudding, which cut in slices as for beef pudding; in case it is very fat, add potatoes, and proceed the same.

248. *Sheep's Head, Tongue, and Trotters,* previously cooked, may be made into a very nice pudding, proceeding as usual. A few pickled walnuts, sliced, may be added.

249. *Lamb Pudding.*—Take the breast, and remove the big bones; cut it crossways, season lightly; have some veal stuffing ready, and lay the meat and stuffing in alternate layers in the pudding, with a gill and a half of water to every pound; boil one hour and a half; serve with melted butter over the pudding, and a little chopped parsley on the top; it has an inviting effect.

Any part of the lamb may be done the same way.

250. *Pork Pudding.*—Get about a pound of pork, as lean as possible; any cuttings will do; cut them into slices; season with a little chopped sage, a teaspoonful of salt, half of pepper; roll the pieces up, and put them in the pudding with a few slices

of potatoes, onions, one apple; add a gill and a half of water; cover as usual, and boil for one hour and a half.

251. *Rabbit Pudding.*—A rabbit cut into about sixteen or eighteen pieces, and a quarter of a pound of bacon, sliced; season in proportion to size, as before, and if for a numerous family, add ten potatoes and four onions, sliced, and half a pint of water; boil for two hours, or according to size. Boiled rice may be added instead of potatoes. Well intermix the meat with the vegetables or rice.

252. *Chicken Pudding.*—Cut one into eight pieces, half a pound of bacon, cut into slices; season with one teaspoonful of salt, half of pepper, two of chopped parsley, a little thyme, and one captain's biscuit, well broken; fill the pudding with the meat, add half a pint of milk, boil for one hour and a half; serve with melted butter over, and chopped parsley on the top.

253. *Pigeon Pudding.*—Pluck, draw, and stuff two pigeons with the stuffing No. 456; then cut some large thin slices of beef, and some of the bacon; season well; roll the pigeons in the meat and bacon, lay them in the pudding; boil four eggs hard, cut them into quarters, and fill the cavities with them; mix a teaspoonful of flour with half a pint of milk, or water, close up, and boil for one hour and a half, and serve.

The same in Brown Gravy.—Add a tablespoonful of colouring, a little more salt and pepper.

Young wood-pigeons may be done the same way, but will take half an hour longer doing.

254. *Partridge and Cabbage Pudding.*—Cut a Savoy cabbage into four pieces, removing some of the outside leaves; boil it for ten minutes, let it get cold, press the water out, cut off the thick root. and cut the other in slices; then stuff the partridge as No. 456, place slides of bacon round it, lay some cabbage in the pudding, paste as usual, season the partridge, and lay it in with six or eight button onions, then the remainder of the cabbage, a gill of brown gravy, No. 2, or coloured water, No. 453 A: boil two hours, if an old bird, or one and a half, if young.

255. *Young Rook Pudding.*—If these young inhabitants of the woods and forests are eatable in pies, I do not see why we should not give them, after their wild career, a soft bed of repose

in a pudding crust. Open them by the back, then draw them, divide them into two, and then into quarters; extract the big bones, leaving the flesh only; beat each piece flat, and season with salt, pepper, and a little grated ginger; make a stuffing with the liver, No. 457. Lay on the crust a slice of bacon, then the birds, then a slice of steak; season with any aromatic herbs, or chopped onions, leeks or mushrooms; add a gill of ale, or wine, gravy or water; boil one hour and a half, and serve.

Pigeons may be done in the same way.

256. *Fish Pudding.*—Take two pounds of cod fish, cut in slices about the size of five-shilling pieces, half an inch thick; fill the bowl with the paste, as usual, lay some of the fish on the bottom, season with salt, pepper, a little chopped parsley, onions, a little flour and pieces of the liver, if any, then the fish, and so on until full; add a gill of milk or water, shake it well, tie up, and boil one hour, and serve. A little bay leaf and thyme may be added, if handy.

All fish may be done the same way, varying the flavour according to taste.

257. *Fish Pudding, a plainer Way.*—Cut one pound of any fish in small pieces, season with salt and pepper on a dish, a little flavour; mix well, put in the paste with a gill of water, and if you have a wine-glass full of any fish sauce, add it, cover up, boil one hour, and serve.

258. *Mackerel Pudding.*—Cut off the heads of two mackerel, cut each one in four pieces, keeping the roe in; fill the pudding with the pieces, season with salt, pepper, a little chopped onions and fennel, add a gill of water, boil one hour, and serve with fennel sauce over.

259. *Eel Pudding.*—Cut in long pieces, season with salt, pepper, chopped onions, parsley; add a gill of water; wine or beer is very good, and proceed as for the others.

260. *Baked Puddings.*—My excellent friend, you must be of the same opinion as the rest of the world, namely, that variety is charming in almost every movement of life, therefore you will not object to my new proposal to send it to the baker's; when the oven is at a moderate heat, they will be found excellent, eating different to a pie. The cloth of course is not required.

only grease the basin; lay on the paste when the contents are in; make the paste meet equally on the top, moisten with water, roll out another piece about a quarter of an inch thick, put it over when fit, and cut away the trimmings from the edge of the basin, egg it over, bake in a slow oven, giving about the same time as you would for boiling; when done, shake the basin well, to make the gravy the same thickness throughout, and serve, turning it out on a dish; perforate the top.

261. *Puddings half steamed and boiled.*—Put in a pan a quart of water, when boiling, put your basin in with the pudding in it, boil gently one hour or more, according to what your pudding is made of; add boiling water occasionally, so as always to keep the same quantity in the pot. By having previously well buttered the basin, when done, by passing a knife between the paste and the basin, you may turn or cut it out, and pour over any appropriate sauce you like. They may also be steamed, as now almost every kitchen possesses steam pans, in connexion with the boiler of the range; or put some water in our new baking-pan, put in the pudding, and send to the oven.

IMPORTANT OBSERVATIONS ON THE ABOVE RECEIPTS.

I must not forget to tell you, Eloise, that any of the above sort of puddings, no matter what made of, if sweet or savoury, is preferable made in a basin to being put in a cloth, which is often very dirty in appearance; while, if boiled in a basin, the paste receives all the nutriment of the meat, which, if boiled in a cloth, would evaporate in the water, if by neglect it ceases boiling. If you wish to turn it well out, thoroughly grease the inside of your basin when making.

On Pudding Cloths.—A pudding cloth, however coarse, ought never to be washed with soap; it should be dried as quickly as possible, and kept dry and free from dust, and in a drawer or cupboard free from smell.

MEAT PIES.

PREVIOUS to making any pie do not omit reading the very important remarks I have made at the introduction of fruit pies, see Index.

262. *Beefsteak Pie.* — Cut two pounds of steak into about twenty thin pieces, lengthways, fat included, season them with two teaspoonfuls of salt, one of pepper, and a little chopped herbs. and place them symmetrically on the dish, forming it high

H

in the centre. Add half a pint of water, in which has been put two tablespoonfuls of colouring. Cover over with paste (No. 317) half an inch thick, and bake for one hour in a slow oven. Pudding paste No. 319 may be used. For variety of pie-dishes see appendix.

A little stuffing rolled up in the meat makes a change, and is fit for the best table.

A few spoonfuls of Harvey's sauce is likewise a change.

263. *Family Steak Pie.*—Take and cut two pounds of beef in slices, two pounds of potatoes, a quarter of a pound of onions; season with three teaspoonfuls of salt, one of pepper; mix it well together; put the meat and potatoes into the pie-dish, in alternate layers; add a pint of water; cover over, as above, and bake for one hour and a half.

264. *Veal Pie.*—Delicate veal and ham pies can be made like the above, rolling up the veal and a little ham, or bacon, together, and a little stuffing, if handy. Proceed as for steak, or as for family steak-pies.

Pork pies may be made in the same way.

265. *Rabbit Pie.* — Cut the rabbit up as for pudding (No. 251); roll the pieces in flour, then put them in the pie-dish, with some slices of ham or bacon; season with salt, pepper, chopped onions, nutmeg, (grated, if handy), according to size; add half-a-pint of water; cover, and bake. A teaspoonful of curry may be added, instead of pepper.

For family rabbit pie proceed as for family steak pie.

266. *Fish Pie.*—Proceed in every way as for puddings, and bake one hour. Oysters, muscles, perrywinkles, cockles, &c., may be used.

267. *Hare Pie.*—If it is a large hare it is best to jug it, as No. 216, cut in half crossways. Save the back and legs for roasting, and with the front part, which cut in pieces, make the pie. Put some steak at the bottom of the dish, with salt, pepper, and chopped onions; dip each piece of hare in flour, lay them on the steak, make some small balls of veal stuffing, which place in various places; cover over with more steak; add half-a-pint of water; finish with paste as usual. When baked, shake the dish to mix the gravy. The addition of a glass of wine, a

few herbs, and two teaspoonfuls of currant jelly, is a great improvement.

268. *The Artisan's Pie.*—Any pieces of meat, but not too fat—four ounces of fat to every pound of meat is enough. Take two pounds of meat cut in slices, season it with three teaspoonfuls of salt, one of pepper, four sliced onions; peel four pounds of potatoes, cut in thick slices, which place on the bottom of the dish, then a layer of potatoes, then the meat; season well; add a pint of water, and bake for two hours.

Trimmings of meat of all kinds may be purchased in every large town, especially in London, and are the proper pieces for such economical pies; in buying them, take care there is none tainted, as it will produce the effect as described in introduction of puddings. Cover with crust, as No. 319.

269. *Poor Man's Potatoe Pie.*—Wash and peel six pounds of potatoes, cut them in slices; take half-a-pound of the fat of mutton or beef, or dripping, cut into small dice; season the whole with a teaspoonful of pepper and three of salt; cover with paste, No. 317 and bake one hour and a half.

A bloater, boned and cut up with the fat, makes a nice change of flavour.

VEGETABLES.

As I have before remarked, the food of man, in order to give proper nourishment, should be often varied; in fact, his health depends upon it, and nature seems to have given him those instruments, the teeth, by which he is enabled to masticate both animal and vegetable food, besides having provided him abundantly with vegetable produce, which seems the balance, in point of health, between that and rich animal food. It is to be regretted that the labouring poor of this country do not partake of more vegetables than they do at present. If we travel over the country, we are surprised to find how small a portion of ground is engaged in horticulture; the consequence is that, excepting near large towns, scarcely a vegetable is to be obtained, and the poor are doomed to live almost entirely on bread and cheese and a small portion of animal food, not even a potatoe is to be had during the winter and spring of the year. It is said by some, that the climate being colder than on the continent, the blood requires more heating food, and that in the summer the English are as much vegetable eaters as their neighbours; if such is the case, why not, then, add to the vegetables, in cooking them, those elements which would give all that animal food does.

. The most important of all the produce of the field is wheat, but that we shall treat of hereafter, under the head of bread. The most important of vegetable produce is the potato, a root the failure of whose growth produced a famine in one of the most productive countries in the world. It is a root in universal use, and yet is acknowledged to be by every one the least understood how to be cooked. A writer in a public journal, the other day, speaking of a well-boiled potato, says "that at present it is a thing purely ideal—it has never come out of the pot, in the experience of living man." And why? Because people boil all potatoes alike. If you ask Betty why she boiled the potatoes in such a manner, she answers, "My mother, or my sister, did so, and they were good." And so with everybody, little thinking that almost every potato differs; even the produce of the same seed will often differ in the same field. This is caused by the different soils, and the different manures applied to those soils.

The present potato is quite a different root from its parent one, which grows in the Caribbean islands.

Animal food, although flesh, differs in its nature, and requires different cookery. A Welsh or a Kerry leg of mutton requires to be treated quite different to a Leicestershire or Southdown.

Thus it is with the potato. Some require quick boiling, others slow; some plenty of water, others little; some are best baked in their skins, others peeled; some large ones require to be cut in two, others will spoil if cut; and so on through all the various gradations.

I therefore consider it requisite, that if a potato is found not to be good by one system of boiling or steaming, to try another. Boiling, as I have said before, is the most simple process of cookery, and it is easily tried.

Potato boiled.—Meg Dods says there are great varieties of potatoes, and fully as many ways of cooking them, but recommends boiling in preference to steaming. Mrs. Rundell prefers steaming, or, if boiled, in plenty of water, and when half done, some cold water and salt thrown in, and boil until not quite done, and then left in the pot near the fire.*

---

* This is the Irish peasant's way (if he wishes to fast for six hours), as it leaves the bone or moon in it. The origin of the word in Irish, *au ghealeach*, is that, when a half-cooked potato is cut in two, the centre shows a disk, with a halo around it, like the moon. This does not digest so quick, and allows the person who eats it to go longer without food, which I consider a great detriment to the coating of the stomach.

Mrs. Glasse says, Boil in as little water as possible, without burning the saucepan.

Mrs. Acton gives only the Lancashire way; this is, peeled and boiled slowly; when done, salt thrown over, and then the pot shook violently for some time, so that they are broken. She remarks that this method is not economical.

Having given these, it is only right I should give my ideas. As I have before said, they all, perhaps, require a different system. If steamed, salt should be thrown into the water, and not on the potato, and when done, remove the steamer, and also the cover.

270. *How to choose Potatoes.*—Observe, as a general rule, that the smaller the eye, the better the potato, as when they are too full in the eye they are either of an inferior quality, or are running to seed. To ascertain if they are sound, nip a piece from the thickest end with your finger nail; if good, the inside will either be of a white, yellow, or reddish hue, according to the sort and quality; if, on the contrary, they are spotted, they are bad, or getting so; but though this part may be slightly touched, by cutting a little off the outside they may prove fit for boiling; though they ought to be bought, when in this state, at a cheap rate. Potatoes always get bad in the spring of the year, as then the old ones are going out, and the new ones for some time continue to possess but little flavour, and are watery when boiled. The old ones ought to be peeled and steamed, and mashed, or baked in an oven, under a joint, or fried in fat, as No. 298; for when done whole in their skins, at this time of the year, the slightest spot spoils their flavour. The new ones are tasteless and watery, and, as I described above to you, are much better cooked when put in very hot water, but not boiling, than when put in cold.

271.—If *boiled*, it may be that they require to be put into boiling water, or, may be, in cold, and either boiled quick or slow, but this you must find out. Choose all about the same size, with a smooth skin, and when they are boiled and begin to crack, throw off the water immediately, as it only damages the root. Stand near the fire, with a cloth on, and serve in skin. Salt should be put into the water at the beginning. A watery potato will require quick boiling, and sometimes to be put in boiling water. If very watery, and they will not boil mealy, put them into the pot in their skins, fill up with water, and a piece of lime the size of a nut, and they will turn out mealy. It is unnecessary here to explain scientifically the cause of this.

272. *New Potatoes*—Should be cleaned, and the skin rubbed off with a coarse cloth; add a little salt if the skin is dry. Put them into very hot water, and boil from fifteen to twenty minutes. Take them out of the water and let them drain before sending to table, throwing some salt over them. If very small they will not take above ten minutes.

273. *Baked Potatoes*, with the skin on, should be chosen a large size (regents), placed in a slow oven and so that they do not touch; or if in a Duch or American oven, before the fire, they should be turned often; they will take from one and a half to two hours. If without their skins, they should be done in a brown pan with fat, turning them occasionally.

274. *Baked Potato with Sausage (called Soyer's Potato)*.— Take a large potato and cut out a round piece as big as a shilling, through the potato; put in the scoop and remove some of the inside, fill this with sausage-meat or veal stuffing, cover the hole with a part of what you cut out, and bake with cut part uppermost.

275. *Mashed Potatoes*.—After having boiled twelve middling sized potatoes until mealy, peel them, if with the skins on, and remove the eyes or specks; put them into a bowl, and take two forks in one hand, with the points of the prongs turned outwards; break the potatoes up with them; when breaking, add an ounce of butter and a gill of milk or a little more to them, and half a teaspoonful of salt, to every pound, and a pinch of pepper; they should be beat a great deal, until they become quite light; they should never be hard like paste, as is often the case when stirred with a spoon.

Potatoes, if large, might be peeled, and cut in four pieces, put in boiling water with some salt, boiled rather fast, and well drained when done; let the pan stand near the fire to dry your potatoes—three minutes will do it—and mash them as above.

276. *New Roasted Potato*.—This should be a large potato —the kidney kind preferred—should be half boiled, the skin remove, put into a baking dish, well rubbed with butter or fat,

and dredged with a little flour, salt and pepper, and put into the oven, or before the fire, either in an American or Dutch oven, until done; they ought to be of a nice brown colour, and are very relishing.

277. *Jerusalem Artichoke* should be well washed and peeled, and put into a saucepan of *warm* water, with salt in it; boil till tender, then serve them up; if to be mashed, mash them at once, with salt, pepper, and butter; if whole, keep them covered until served. Melted butter over improves the look.

They may be mashed with a little gravy; put in a dish, bread-crumbed over, and put in the oven, and are very nice.

Or they can be treated in every way like turnips.

278. *Turnips.*—Peel them, and boil in plenty of water, in which has been put some salt; boil till tender, and serve either whole, or mashed. If mashed, they should be put in a saucepan over the fire, with a bit of butter, or some milk, salt, and a little pepper, and a pinch of sugar, mashed up until rather dry, and serve.

A few capers mixed in the mashed turnip, is an improvement for boiled mutton.

279. *Swedes.*—This was a vegetable in very little use for the table until the year of the famine in Ireland, when M. Soyer prepared it for the viceroy's table. It should be treated in every way like turnip, but cut into quarters for boiling. The middle size are only fit to use.

280. *Carrot.*—This root varies quite as much as the potato; some are quickly done, even in twenty minutes, and some require two hours. They should be scraped, and boiled in water and salt; served cut in quarters lengthways.

281. *Parsnip and the White Carrot.*—The same as the carrot.

282. *Red and White Beet.*—These should be washed, but not scraped, and put into the pot with the skin on; when done, which is known by pressing the thick part, to see if it is soft, or by probing it with a skewer; remove the skin, cut it into slices, put it in a pan, with either gravy, butter, or milk, and a little vinegar, salt and pepper, boil it up, and serve. It is also good when cold, for salads.

FIRST AND GENERAL LESSON IN THE COOKING OF ALL KINDS OF VEGETABLES.

283. *Asparagus* is a vegetable between the root and the plant, and requires more cooking, like the latter. It should be well scraped at the bottom part, tie them up in bundles of not more than twelve heads, have ready a pot of water, say three quarts for every hundred heads, in which you have placed one table-spoonful of salt, and if the water is hard half a teaspoonful of carbonate of soda; if they are a good size boil for twenty minutes, and serve with a slice of toasted bread under, and melted butter separate, or cream sauce No. 424.

This, when cold, is very good with oil and vinegar, salt and pepper.

The small, called *sprew*, is very excellent broken small in *clear soup*.

284. *Celery.*—Dress like asparagus, cutting off the green, leaving the branches six inches long; serve on toast, with melted butter or brown gravy over, tying three or four sticks together.

Sea Kale.—Clean the root and boil like asparagus, and serve the same on toast, with either melted butter or cream sauce over.

285. *Green Cabbage and Savoys.*—These close-leaf plants require well washing and soaking in salt and water before boiling; the stems should be removed, and then boiled in half a gallon of water, with two teaspoonfuls of salt and a little soda. These proportions will do for all vegetables. If the plants are large they should be cut in four.

286. *Sprouts, Spring Greens, Turnip Tops, &c.*—These only require washing before boiling, and boil till tender in the same quantity of water as above.

287. *Stewed Cabbage or Savoys.*—Cut in thin slices, wash, drain, and boil till tender; drain them free from water; put into a clean pot two ounces of butter or fat, and a little salt and pepper; when hot add the cabbage, and stir it well until nearly dry, then throw over a tablespoonful of flour, keep stirring, and then add a cupful of either broth, milk, or water let boil ten minutes, and serve.

288. *Spinach* requires to be well washed, and the stalks picked off; boil a quarter of a sieve in the same quantity of water as above for ten minutes; take out, drain, press with the nands or plate to remove the water, and serve it as plain greens; or put it on a clean board, and chop it fine, put it in a stew-pan, with a quarter of a pound of good butter or fat, a teaspoonful of salt, two of flour, half of pepper; place it on the fire, with two gills of milk or broth, for a few minutes, and serve with toast round. More strong *gravy* may be added, or even milk or *cream*.

289. *Green Peas.*—This, of all the pulse vegetables, is the most liked, and the most in use; and perhaps in no country in Europe can they be obtained in the same perfection as in England.

The water should be boiling, and say one quart of peas to two quarts of water, with the same amount of salt as before; put the peas in, leave the cover off, and boil till tender; drain, and serve, with a piece of butter put on the dish. If mint or savory is liked, add it while boiling.

290. *Broad or Windsor Beans.*—The appearance of this vegetable is generally spoiled because it is boiled with a piece of bacon; they ought to be boiled alone like the peas, and very fast, and if young do not take longer. They should be served with parsley and butter. When the skin is wrinkled they are done.

291. *French and Kidney Beans.*—Head, tail, and string them; cut them down in thin strips, or in the middle, throw them into boiling water, in which a little more salt than usual has been put; boil for fifteen minutes, and serve either plain or with parsley and butter, and a little pepper and salt.

These are skins of the pulse, and are considered exceedingly wholesome for persons who take much exercise, and eat freely of animal food; they purify the salt of the blood.

292. *Brocoli and Cauliflower* should be put in salt and water some time before cooking, and require close examination that no insects are inside; cut off the root and the large leaves; they should be boiled in boiling water, and will take about ten minutes. There are a variety of ways of using these vegetables, but in general a little too complicated for our work.

293. *Cauliflower and Brocoli, with Cheese Sauce.*—Boil two or three middle-sized cauliflowers, make half a pint of thick melted butter, adding a little cayenne pepper, if handy, grate four ounces of good cheese, Cheshire preferable; mix this well with the sauce, and when boiling pour over the cauliflower or brocoli; set either in an oven or before the fire for fifteen minutes, until it gets brown; the yolk of an egg may be added; bread-crumb over, and serve. If no grater, cut your cheese fine, it will melt in boiling.

Jerusalem artichokes, Scotch kail, and Brussels sprouts, are also very nice done this way.

PLANT CALLED THE THOUSAND HEADS.

On seeing this plant growing in great abundance in Yorkshire, I inquired of the farmer on whose land they were—if they were a vegetable for the table, and their name? when he informed me that they were intended for spring feeding for sheep, during the lambing season; that he never used them as human food. I asked him to let me have some to try and see how they eat. He did, and I cooked them like greens; and an exceeding nice vegetable they are. They are also good stewed, and cooked with a piece of bacon. As they grow at a time of the year when other green vegetables are scarce, I consider them a valuable article of food. They are sown about April, the small plant put out about October, and planted about three feet apart, and by March or April the whole field will be one luxuriant crop of greens.

Farmers in the vicinity of large towns would do well to undertake their cultivation, as they would find a ready sale in all such places. At that time of year they are in full bloom, and are called by the above singular name in consequence of the thousands of heads continually sprouting from their root. The plant covers nearly one yard in circumference, and bears no resemblance to any other green I recollect seeing, not even to Brussels sprouts.

294. *Haricots and Lentils.*—No receipt is more simple, or easier done, than any of these vegetables; there is hardly a cottage in France but what has them in stock, as they will keep good for years.

Should you be short of potatoes, or supposing they are expensive, or even as a change, some of these are an excellent substitute; one quart will make, when cooked, four pounds of solid food.

Haricots, plain boiled, should be first washed, then put into the black iron pot one quart of them, with four quarts of cold water, one ounce of butter or fat; boil them gently for three hours, or till tender; the water will be nearly absorbed, if the haricots are good; draw off the remainder; mix in a pint of it three teaspoonsful of flour, half ditto of pepper, add it to the haricots; boil for ten minutes, keep stirring, and serve, adding three teaspoonfuls of salt; an ounce of butter is an improvement.

A little meat of any kind may be cooked with them, just the same as dried peas, only these are to be eaten whole, and four onions in slices, fried, may be added with the seasoning, when the haricots or lentils are nearly cooked. The broth, if ample, when strained from them, may be used as soup, with bread in it.

295. *Lentils.*—Wash them as haricots, and cook them as such, putting them in cold water; they will not take so long, but try when tender. Meat is exceedingly good boiled with them, and they make good soup.

These make an excellent salad, both in winter and summer. See Index.

The liquor of either makes a nutritious soup, by adding fried onions, a little flour, pepper, and salt, and poured over bread previously sliced and put in a soup basin.

I herewith send you the receipt I promised you on Nettles, which I tried while in Norfolk.

296. *Nettles.*—Wash them well, drain, put them into plenty of boiling water with a little salt, boil for twenty minutes, or a little longer, drain them, put them on a board and chop them up, and either serve plain, or put them in the pan with a little salt, pepper, and a bit of butter, or a little fat and gravy from a roast; or add to a pound two teapoonsfuls of flour, a gill of skim milk, a teaspoonful of sugar, and serve with or without poached eggs.

This extraordinary spring production, of which few know the value, is at once pleasing to the sight, easy of digestion, and at a time of the year when greens are not to be obtained, invaluable as a purifier of the blood; the only fault is, as I have told you above, Eloise, they are to be had for nothing; it is a pity that children are not employed to pick them, and sell them in market towns.

Another unused vegetable is mangel wurzel. The young leaf of the mangel wurzel, cleaned and cooked as above, is extremely good.

In all my various visits to cottages during this spring, I have found but one where either of the above vegetables were in use, and that belonging to a gardener, who knew their value.

These nettles are good during five months of the year; for even when large, the tops are tender. They make excellent tea, which is very refreshing and wholesome.*

296A.—*Sweet Docks*, also a wild vegetable, or weed, are very good when done as follows, using about two-thirds of sweet dock. and one-third of nettles, boiled with a little carbonate of soda. When done, strain them, and to about one pint basin full, add one onion sliced and fried, a sprig of parsley, a little butter, pepper, and salt; put into a stewpan on the fire, stir, and gradually add a handful of oatmeal; when you think the meal has been sufficiently boiled, dish up and serve as a vegetable.

297. *Large Dry Green Peas.*—One quart of peas, soak for twelve hours; put into a pan with one gallon of water, some fat, six sliced onions, one teaspoonful of carbonate of soda, one of pepper; simmer for two or three hours, or till tender, drain the peas, then add to them half a pound of flour, mixed in a pint of cold water, three teaspoonfuls of salt, a quarter of a pound of butter; boil twenty minutes; serve with bacon over.

Small dumplings may be boiled in it; they will take half an hour.

298. *Fried Potatoes.*—Peel a pound of potatoes, cut them into very thin slices, almost shavings; put some fat into a frying-pan; when very hot, but not burning, throw the slices in, not too many at a time, as they will stick together; move them about with a skimmer, to prevent it. When a nice brown colour, take them out, and sprinkle some salt over; serve them up separate, or over broiled meat. Two inches of fat ought to be in the pan.

299. *Fried Cooked Potatoes.*—Let the fat in your frying-pan be about two inches deep; when smoking hot, add in five or six potatoes, cut crossways in thin slices, letting them be

---

* The best way to pick nettles is to quickly grasp a handful, by doing which you feel no sensation of pain, or by wearing gloves.

previously dried in a cloth; stir with a spoon; it will take about ten minutes to do them crisp; take them out, drain and dish them, sprinkling a little salt over.

EGGS.

THESE, from the earliest records we have, have always been a favourite food, with the exception of a short time in Greece, where a few philosophers endeavoured to make the people refrain from eating them, as they stated that they contained the four elements of the world.*

They are a nutritious food, wholesome in every way, except when boiled too hard; although there are some stomachs which reject them. They can be employed in almost every dish with advantage, and one weighing two ounces contains nearly the same amount of nourishment as an ounce of meat and an ounce of bread; therefore when eggs are eighteen for a shilling, equal to two pounds four ounces, they are not a very dear article of food.

300. To ascertain that they are good and fresh, *candle them*, as it is called; that is, hold them upright between the thumb and finger of the right hand before a candle, and with the left hand shade the eye, by which means you will be enabled to detect any spots that may be in them; if a few white spots only, they will do for puddings, &c.; if a black one, throw it away, as it is perfectly bad. If light and transparent, they are fresh.

301. *Eggs Plain Boiled.*—This is the most simple of all things to cook, and yet is the least attended to; and I am never surprised,

---

* *Singular Ideas of the Ancients in relation to Eggs.*—Orpheus, Pythagoras, and their sectators—good and humane people as ever lived—unceasingly recommended in their discourses to abstain from eggs, in order not to destroy a germ which nature had destined for the production of chicken. Many allowed themselves to be persuaded, and would have believed it an unpardonable crime if they had eaten a tiny *omelette*, or boiled eggs. Many of the most learned philosophers held eggs in a kind of respect approaching to veneration, because they saw in them the emblem of the world and the four elements. The shell, they said, represented the earth; the white, water; the yolk, fire; and air was found under the shell.

The shepherds of Egypt had a singular manner of cooking eggs without the aid of fire: they placed them in a sling, which they turned so rapidly that the friction of the air heated them to the exact point required for use.—*Soyer's Pantropheon.*

when I am travelling, to find the eggs either too much or too little done. They will not take the trouble to distinguish a large one from a small one. Whilst some weigh only an ounce and a half, others weigh two and a half; but as that is a whim of nature, and the servants are so fond of attending to other frolics, they will not see the difference in this; but as all cookery books say three minutes, and the mistress has told them the same, they are right, and she is wrong. From two and a half to four minutes, according to size, is the time they will take. Ten minutes is sufficient to set an egg hard, not thirty, or more, as some persons do by neglect.

You know, my dear Eloise, how fidgety I am about such trifles. I have, therefore, invented a cooking clock, with very distinctly marked time; the hand is pushed back to any time named, and at the time required the bell strikes. I mean to adopt it for general kitchen use for all dishes, from an egg to a heavy joint. See Appendix.

302. *To Boil Eggs.*—Put a pint of water into a small pan; when boiling, put two eggs in, and boil according to size—as I have before said, from two and a half to four minutes. Fresh-laid eggs will not take so long, and if only just set, are excellent for clearing the voice.

303.—To boil them for toast, they require six minutes; take them out, throw them in cold water, remove the shell, and cut them into slices; put them on the buttered toast, a little pepper and salt, and serve. These are excellent with a little ketchup put on the eggs, then bread-crumbed, salamandered over, and serve.

304. *Baked Eggs.*—Put half an ounce of butter into a small tin pan; break four eggs in it, keeping the yolks whole, throw a little pepper and bits of butter and salt over; put in the oven, or before the fire, till set, and serve. They will take about six minutes doing.

305. *Poached Eggs.*—Put in a small pan half a pint of water, half a teaspoonful of salt, three of vinegar; when boiling, break carefully in the pan two nice eggs, simmer for four minutes, or till firm, but not hard; serve either on toast or fried bacon, or ham, or spinach, and on any minced and seasoned vegetable.

306. *Mixed Eggs.*—Break four eggs into a frying-pan, in which you have put two ounces of butter, a little salt and pepper,

set it on the fire, stir round with a wooden spoon very quickly, to prevent sticking to the pan; when all set, serve either on toast or dish. Fried bacon cut in dice, a little chopped onions, or mushrooms, or a little sprew grass, well boiled, may be added to the above.

307. *Eggs and Bacon.*—Cut some bacon very thin, put into a frying-pan half an ounce of butter, or fat, lay the bacon in it; when fried on one side, turn over, and break one egg on each piece; when the eggs are set, put the slice under the bacon, and remove them gently into a dish. Ham may be done the same.

308. *Eggs, Convent Fashion.* — Boil four eggs for ten minutes, put them in cold water, peel and slice thin one onion, put into a frying-pan one ounce of butter; when melted, add the onion, and fry white, then add a teaspoonful of flour, mix it well, add about half a pint of milk, till forming a nice white sauce, half a teaspoonful of salt, and a quarter ditto of pepper; when nicely done, add the eggs, cut into six pieces each, crossways; toss them up; when hot through, serve on toast.

309. *Eggs and Sausages.*—Boil four sausages for five minutes, when half cold cut them in half lengthways, put a little butter or fat in frying-pan, and put the sausages in and fry gently, break four eggs into pan, cook gently, and serve. Raw sausages will do as well, only keep them whole, and cook slowly.

Omelettes or Fraise.

Where is the man or woman cook but says they know how to make an omelette, and that to perfection? But this is rarely the case. It is related of Sarah, the Duchess of Marlborough, that no one could cook a fraise, as it was then called, for the great duke but herself.

The great point is, if in an iron pan, it should be very clean and free from damp, which sometimes comes out of the iron when placed on the fire. The best plan is to put it on the fire, with a little fat, and let it get quite hot, or until the fat burns; remove it, and wipe it clean with a dry cloth, and then you will be able to make the omelette to perfection.

310. *Omelettes.*—Break four eggs into a basin, add half a teaspoonful of salt and a quarter ditto of pepper, beat them up well with a fork, put into the frying-pan one ounce and a half of butter, lard, or oil, which put on the fire until hot; then pour in

the eggs, which keep on mixing quick with a spoon until all is delicately set; then let them slip to the edge of the pan, laying hold by the handle, and raising it slantways, which will give an elongated form to the omelette ; turn in the edges, let it set a moment, and turn it over on to a dish, and serve.

It ought to be a nice yellow colour, done to a nicety, and as light and delicate as possible. It may be served in many ways, but some of the following are the most common :—two tablespoonfuls of milk and an ounce of the crumb of bread cut in thin slices, may be added.

311. *Omelettes with Herbs.*—Proceed as above, adding a teaspoonful of chopped parsley, and half ditto of chopped onions or chives, or a little eschalot; salt and pepper, and semi-fry as above.

312. *Bacon Omelette.*—Cut one ounce of bacon into small dice, fry in a little fat; when done, add the eggs, and proceed as above.

Ham, if raw, do the same as bacon ; if cooked, cut in dice, put in the eggs, and proceed as before.

313. *Omelettes.*—Oysters, mussels, periwinkles, or shrimps. When the omelette is nearly done, add a few tablespoonfuls of either of these sauces in the centre ; turn the omelette, and serve. For the above, see Fish Sauces.

Any cooked vegetables, as peas, sprew, &c. &c., may be used in omelettes.

314. *Sweet Omelettes.*—Beat four eggs into a basin, add a tablespoonful of milk, a teaspoonful of sugar, a pinch of salt, and beat them well up; put some nice butter into pan, put in the eggs, and fry as before described. Serve with sugar sifted over.

314A. *Preserve Omelettes.*—When the omelette is nearly done, put in the middle some preserve of any kind, turn it over on plate, and serve with sugar over.

315. *Omelettes with Spirit.*—These are the above omelettes serve with spirit round them, and set on fire when going to table. Rum is generally preferred.

ON PASTRY.

ONE of the oldest and most current modes of cooking, either by mixing oil or butter with the flour, sweetened, scented, or flavoured, according to the fancy of the cook, is pastry. The Romans had their peculiar cakes of paste, the Egyptians had theirs; in fact, all countries have, during the periods of the greatest prosperity, endeavoured to add to the number of their luxuries new modes of making paste. With none of these have we, at the present moment, anything to do; our task is to show how paste can be made to suit everybody.

My excellent Eloise, I think you are wrong, for once, in proposing that I should give various receipts for sweet pastry. I know you possess a sweet tooth, but let those who require first-class sweet dishes, purchase our "Modern Housewife;" no doubt their pocket is equal to their taste; at any rate, the few I now give will, if properly made by a person of taste, lead them 'o do others that might vie with the most expensive dishes.

The following receipts will be continually referred to, therefore they ought to be made with care.

315A. *Puff Paste.*—Put one pound of flour upon your pastry slab, make a hole in the centre, in which put a teaspoonful of salt, mix it with cold water into a softish flexible paste with the right hand, dry it off a little with flour until you have well cleared the paste from the slab, but do not work it more than you can possibly help; let remain two minutes upon the slab, then have a pound of fresh butter, from which you have squeezed all the buttermilk in a cloth, bringing it to the same consistency as the paste, upon which place it; press it out flat with the hand, then fold over the edges of the paste so as to hide the butter, and roll it with the rolling-pin to the thickness of half an inch, thus making it about two feet in length; fold over one third, over which again pass the rolling-pin; then fold over the other third, thus forming a square, place it with the ends top and bottom before you, shaking a little flour both under and over, and repeat the rolls and turns twice again as before; flour a baking-sheet, upon which lay it, upon ice, if handy, or in some cool place, for half an hour; then roll twice more, turning it as before, place again upon the ice a quarter of an hour, give it two more rolls, making seven in all, and it is ready for use, as directed in the following receipts. You must continually add enough flour while rolling to prevent your paste sticking to the slab.

When I state that upwards of a hundred different kinds of
cakes may be made from this paste and the following, I
am sure it will be quite sufficient to urge upon every cook the
necessity of paying every attention to their fabrication, as it will
well repay for the study and trouble. One fourth of this quantity
may be made.

316. *Half-puff Paste.*—Put on the dresser or table one
pound of flour, half a teaspoonful of salt, two ounces of butter,
mix all together, then add half a pint of water, or little more;
form a softish paste, do not work it too much with the hand, or it
will make it hard and tough; throw some more flour lightly over
and under, roll it out with a rolling-pin half an inch thick, about
a foot long; then have half a pound of fresh butter equally as
stiff as the paste, break it into small pieces, and put it on the
paste; throw a little more flour on it, and fold it over in two
folds, throw some more flour on the slab, roll it out three or
four times, letting it rest between each two rolls, and it is then
ready for use.

It can be made with lard instead of butter.

The yolk of an egg, or the juice of half a lemon, added to the
water, makes it lighter.

316A. Half butter and half lard may be used, or if butter is too
dear, use all lard; if neither, mix well with the flour two
ounces of dripping, *no salt*, lay it on the board, and mix half a
pint of water, till a softish paste; roll it out, then chop a quarter
of a pound of good beef suet very fine, mix with a quarter of a
pound of good dripping, free from water or gravy, roll out the
paste, and add the dripping and suet as preceding receipt.

317. *Plainer Paste, for Meat Pies.*—Put into a pan half a
pound of flour, quarter of a pound of dripping, half a teaspoonful
of salt, rub all well together for about three minutes, add by
degrees half a pint of water, mix the paste well; it requires to be
rather hard; throw some flour on the board, roll, and use it
instead of puff paste; three, or even two ounces, of dripping will
be enough where economy is required, or many children to feed.

Where the cottager has a small garden, in which he can
grow a few herbs, which I have already recommended, then
introduce in the paste a little chopped parsley or eschalot, a very
small piece of winter savory or thyme, or bayleaf chopped fine •
these herbs cost little, and are at once relishing, refreshing, and
wholesome.

By the same rule the same paste will do for fruit pies, mixed with a little grated lemon or orange-peel, with the addition of a teaspoonful of sugar.

318. *Short Paste.*—Put on a slab or board a pound of flour, two ounces of pounded sugar, or whitey-brown, six ounces of butter, one egg, half a teaspoonful of salt, half a pint of water, mix sugar and butter well together, add it with the water by degrees to the flour, and form a nice paste, but firmer than puff-paste; use where described.

In a farm-house, for a treat, they use cream to make this paste.

319. *Pudding Paste.* — 1st Class Paste. Put on a slab, table, board, or basin, one pound of flour, half a pound of beef or mutton suet, chopped rather fine—the first is prefer-able—form a well with your hand in the centre of the flour, add the suet, a teaspoonful of salt, half of pepper; moisten all with water, working the flour in by degrees, till it forms a stiff paste; work it well for two minutes, throw a little flour on the slab, with the paste on it; let it remain five minutes, then roll it out to any thickness you like. This will be referred to very often, therefore pay particular attention to it, and give it an important place in the book. For savoury pudding, I sometimes vary the flavour, by adding a little chopped parsley, or a little onion, or thyme, or mushrooms in it.

2nd Class Paste. Proceed the same way, putting only six ounces of suet.

3rd Class Paste. The same, with four ounces.

4th Class Paste. The same, with four ounces of dripping.

Lamb, veal, and pork fat, may be used; but as they do not chop so floury, the paste is heavier. But they can be used for baked puddings, which I have introduced at page 102 in that series.

320. *Fruit Tart, French fashion.*—This requires a mould or a tin pan; it must be well wiped with a cloth, butter it, then take the remains of half puff paste, and roll it well so as to deaden it, then roll it out a size larger than your mould, and about a quarter of an inch thick; place your mould on a baking-tin, put the paste carefully in the mould and shape it well, to obtain all the form of the mould, without making a hole in the paste; put a piece of paper at the bottom, fill with fruit to the top, and bake

a nice colour; it will take about half an hour baking with any fruit in season; put plenty of sugar over, according to the acidity of the fruit.

321. *Another.*—If you have no mould, make a quarter of a pound of paste (No. 318), roll it round or oval to your fancy, a quarter of an inch thick, wet the edge all round about half an inch, raise that part, and pinch it with your thumb and fingers, making a border all round, put on a baking-sheet, fill it with one row of fruit if large, two rows if small; remove the stones, and sift sugar over according to the acidity of the fruit; it will take less time, too, than if in a mould : You see what variation can be made with very little trouble or expense.

322. *Small Pastry.*—Make a quarter of a pound of half puff paste (No. 318), roll it to a thickness of a quarter of an inch, cut five or six pieces out with the rim of a tumbler; put each piece in a separate tin, shape it well in forming a nice thin rim round the edge with your finger and thumb, three parts fill with either jam, stewed fruit, sweetmeats, custard, pastry, or cream, bake in a very hot oven for twenty minutes; dish up in pyramids, and serve. See Index.

323. *Little Fruit Rissolettes.*—I also make with the trimmings of puff paste the following little cakes : if you have about a quarter of a pound of puff paste left, roll it out very thin, about the thickness of half a crown, put half a spoonful of any marmalade on it, about one inch and a half distance from each other, wet lightly round them with a paste-brush, and place a similar piece of paste over all, take a cutter of the size of a crown piece, and press round the part where the marmalade or jam is with the thick part of the cutter, to make the paste stick, then cut them out with one a size or two larger, lay them on a baking-tin, egg over, place in a nice hot oven for twenty minutes, then sugar over with finely sifted sugar, so as to make it quite white, then put back into the oven to glaze, and serve.

323A. *Plain Puff Paste Cake.*—Make half a pound as No. 315A; when done, roll it about a quarter of an inch thick, cut as many pieces as you can with the cutter, or with the edge of a glass, wet a baking sheet, place them on, egg well over, sift some sugar on each, bake from ten to twelve minutes, and serve.

324. *Orange and Almond Cakes.*—Proceed as above, but lay orange marmalade all over a quarter of an inch thick, four ounces of almonds cut into fillets, mixed with two ounces of sugar, and the white of two egg added to it; lay the almonds all over the marmalade, bake in a moderate oven, and cut in a diamond shape, dish up on a napkin in crown or pyramid; they ought to be of a nice transparent colour. Apple or quince marmalade may be used instead of orange.

325. *Preserve Cake.*—This style of cake is exceedingly simple, and admits of great variation. You must make half a pound of puff paste (No. 315A), take one third of it and roll it out several times so as to deaden it, then mould it round with your hands to the shape of a ball, roll it out flat to the thickness of a crown, lay it on a baking-sheet, put on it marmalade, or any other preserve, a quarter of an inch thick, reserving about one inch all round of paste to fix the cover on, then roll out the remainder of the paste to the same shape, it will of course be thicker; wet the edges of the bottom, and lay the cover on it; press it so that it sticks, cut neatly round the edges, and make a mark with the back of a knife about a quarter of an inch deep and half an inch apart all round; egg over, and lightly mark any fanciful design with the point of a knife on the cover; bake in a very hot oven for twenty minutes; when nearly done, sprinkle some sugar over, frost it with a hot shovel, and serve cold.

326. *Small Cream Cake*—The former one must be made in proportion to the dish you intend to serve on, but the following is simple, and looks as well: Prepare the paste as before, but roll the bottom piece about a foot square, put it on a baking-sheet, cover with half an inch of cream (see Index), leaving one inch round the edge; roll the cover the same size, wet the edges, place it over, trim them, mark it down every three inches, and then crosswise every inch; bake in hot oven, sugar over, and salamander. When nearly cold, cut it where you have marked it; thus, a piece twelve inches square will give you twenty-four pieces; dish as a crown or pyramid. Twelve pieces make a nice dish for a party. They may be made of any puff paste which is left, but will not be so light as if made on purpose; can be cut to any fanciful shape you please. Any jam may be substituted for cream.

327. *Fruit Crusts.*—Cut a French penny roll lengthwise in four slices, put the yolk of one egg with four spoonfuls of milk, mix it in a plate, dip quickly each piece in it, and sauté in a quarter of a pound of butter which you have previously melted in a frying pan ; leave them on the fire until they have obtained a nice gold colour on both sides ; put three spoonfuls of orange marmalade in a stewpan, with two glasses of sherry or brandy and place on the fire ; when on the point of boiling, pour over the bread, which you have previously put in a plate, and serve very hot. Any preserve may be used, also any white wine ; and should you have no French rolls, any fancy roll will do, or even the crumb of common bread. Any kinds of jam may be used.

Nursery Dumplings.

Having, the other evening, been invited to a children's party at Farmer Laurence's, near Oswestry, and the supper being composed, for the most part, of dumplings of various sorts, so as to please the children, I made the following experiment, which proved quite successful.

328.—Greengages being very plentiful, I went and gathered some, and made the following fruit dumplings. I made half a pound of paste (No. 319), rolled it out rather thin, then cut a piece round with the rim of a tumbler, moistened it, and placed a gage in the centre, adding a half teaspoonful of sugar, inclosed all in the paste, thoroughly closing the rim, then placed on the baking-sheet, the smooth part uppermost, and baked them from ten to twelve minutes, serving them up with sugar. They made a beautiful dish.

Gooseberries, rhubarb, cherries, and mulberries, can all be done this way. All kinds of plums can be done the same.

329. *Plain Cheese Cake.*—Put half a pint of milk curds well drained, in a basin, add to it an ounce and a half of butter stir perfectly smooth, put in three teaspoonfuls of sugar, one ounce of washed currants, one egg, half a pint of milk, and any flavour you like, as lemon, orange, &c. &c. Prepare your paste as No. 322, fill up the tins with this, bake the same, and serve.

NATIONAL FRENCH CAKE OR GALETTE.

DEAREST ELOISE,—There is one little and perhaps insignificant French cake, which I feel certain would soon become a favourite in the cottage, more particularly amongst its juvenile inhabitants. It is the famed galette, the melodramatic food of the gamins, galopins, mechanics, and semi-artists of France. Show me one of the above-named citizens who has not tasted this irresistible and famed cake, after having digested the best and most sanguinary melodrama, from the " Courier of Lyons" to the "Corsican Brothers," and from the " Pilules du Diable" to the " Seven Wonders of the World," after having paid their duty to the elegance of the performance and performers, and entirely forgetting, as usual, the author, who is supposed to live in his tomb, whilst the actors and artists are dead in reality. Setting that on one side, observe that the last Seventh Wonder is over, the red-blue-green fire no longer required; the scene-shifter bolts and gets the first cut, smoking hot; then, also, rush the audience, full of melodrama and anything but food, to the galette-shop, where the *Père Coupe-toujours* (Father Cut-and-come-again) is in full activity, taking the money first, and delivering the galette afterwards. Six feet wide by ten long is the galette-shop, and very clean, and above one hundred feet of galette is sold in less than one hour, at a sou or two the cut.

Such is, even in summer, the refreshment of the admirers of the Boulevard du Crime.

Like everything which has its origin with the million, it soon aims to an aristocracy of feeling, and I was not a little surprised, the last time I was in Paris, to see a fashionable crowd round an elegant shop, close to the Gymnase Theatre; on inquiring of a venerable citizen, who was anxiously waiting, with ten sous in his hand, the motive of such a crowd, he informed me that he was waiting his turn to buy ten sous worth of galette du Gymnase, which he told me was the most celebrated in Paris. He passed; and then ladies, beautifully dressed, took their turn; in fact, the crowd brought to my recollection the description of the scene of the bread market at Athens (described in Soyer's "Pantropheon"), where the ladies of fashion or the *petites maitresses* of ancient Greece used to go to select the delicious puff cake, called *placites,* or the sweet *melitutes,* whose exquisite and perfumed flour was delicately kneaded with the precious honey of Mount Hymettus. At all events, I was determined not only to taste, but to procure the receipt if I possibly could ; and as you know, Eloise, I seldom fail, when determined, the following is a copy.

330. *Aristocratic Galette.*—Work lightly in a basin or on a table one pound of flour with three quarters of a pound of fresh

butter; add two eggs, a gill of cream, and a little milk; if too stiff, then add a quarter of a teaspoonful of salt, two of sugar; work all well, to form a good stiff paste, throw some flour on the table, mould the paste round, roll it three quarters of an inch thick, and quite round, over, score it with a knife in diamonds, or any other shape; bake for about half an hour in a rather hot oven, sprinkle sugar over and serve. A pound of either puff, No. 315A, or half puff paste, No. 316, will make a very light galette; sugar over, and bake as above.

331. *Cottage Galette.*—Put one pound of flour, a teaspoonful of salt, six ounces of butter; moisten with milk, and bake as above, adding a teaspoonful of sugar.

332. *Poor Man's Galette.*—One pound of flour, a quarter of a pound of lard, moisten with milk, or water; proceed as above, moisten with a little water on the top, and dredge sugar over. If no lard, use dripping.

INTRODUCTION TO PIES, BOTH SWEET AND SAVOURY.

No matter how ridiculous it may appear to Mrs. Smith, or Mrs. Brown, or Mrs. Any-body-else, do not omit to give room to the following remarks on pies. Never mind how simple these remarks may seem to you, the million will understand them well. For example, where is the little boy or girl in Great Britain who has not eaten pies sweet and savoury? From childhood we eat pies—from girlhood to boyhood we eat pies—from middle age to old age we eat pies—in fact, pies in England may be considered as one of our best companions *du voyage* through life. It is we who leave them behind, not they who leave us; for our children and grandchildren will be as fond of pie as we have been; therefore it is needful that we should learn how to make them, and make them well! Believe me, I am not jesting, but if all the spoilt pies made in London on one single Sunday were to be exhibited in a row beside a railway line, it would take above an hour by special train to pass in review these culinary victims; therefore see the importance of the subject. If we could only rescue to proper standing half a mile of pies and pie-crust, I think we should deserve a piece of plate, or at least a piece of one of our disciple's pies.

How to Make a Pie to Perfection.—When your paste is carefully made (No. 316), or short paste (No. 318), which requires no more time than doing badly, and your pies and tarts properly full—(this is the last and most important process in pie and tart making)—throw a little flour on your paste-board, take about a quarter of a pound of your paste, which roll with your hand, say an inch in circumference; moisten the rim of your pie-dish, and fix the paste equally on it with your thumb. When you have rolled your paste for the covering of an equal thickness, in proportion to the contents of your pie (half an inch is about correct for the above description), fold the cover in two, lay on the half of your pie, turn the other half over, press slightly with your thumb round the rim, cut neatly the rim of your paste, form rather a thick edge, which mark with a knife about every quarter of an inch apart; mark, holding your knife in a slanting direction, which gives it a neat appearance; make two small holes on the top; egg over with a paste-brush; if no egg, use a drop of milk or water; the remaining paste may be shaped to fanciful designs to ornament the top. For meat pies, notice, that if your paste is either too thick or too thin, the covering too narrow or too short, and requires pulling one way or the other, to make it fit, your pie is sure to be imperfect, the covering no longer protecting the contents. It is the same with meat; and if the paste happens to be rather rich, it pulls the rim of the pie to the dish, soddens the paste, makes it heavy, and, therefore, indigestible as well as unpalatable. A little practice and common sense will remedy all those little housewifery tribulations, and probably improve the appearance of this series of dishes.

333. *Plain Apple and other Tart.*—Peel and cut about two pounds of apples, sharp ones being the best for the purpose, cut each in four pieces, removing the cores, then cut each quarter in two or three pieces, according to size; put half of them in a pie-dish, slightly press them, so that they lay compact; put over two ounces of brown sugar, then put in the remaining apples, then add another two ounces of sugar, making the apples form a kind of dome, the centre being two inches higher than the sides, add a small wineglassful of water, cover the top over with paste No. 318; bake in a moderate oven from half to three-quarters of an hour.

All kinds of apples will, of course, make tarts, but if the apples be sweetish or too ripe, you need not put in so much sugar, but add double the quantity of water; in this case the addition of a little juice of a lemon is an improvement to vary the flavour; use also a little grated or chopped lemon or orange-peel, or a quarter of a teaspoonful of cinnamon, or mixed spice, or four cloves,

Green rhubarb and greengages will require a little more sugar, adding nothing else but the fruit; proceed as for apple-tart; pink rhubarb does not require pealing; ripe currants, raspberries, and cherries, also as above; plum, damson, and mulberries the same.

SWEET PUDDINGS.

334. *Plum Pudding.*—Pick and stone half a pound of Malaga raisins, wash and dry the same quantity of currants, chop, not too fine, three-quarters of a pound of beef suet, put it in a convenient basin, with six ounces of sugar, two ounces of mixed candied peel sliced, three ounces of flour, three ditto of bread-crumbs, a little grated nutmeg, four eggs, a gill of water, or perhaps a little more, to form a nice consistence; butter a mould, put a piece of white paper over the top and round the sides, tie it in a cloth, boil for four hours in plenty of water; when done, remove the cloth, turn it out of the mould, take the paper off the sides and top, and serve with sweet sauce round; it may also be boiled in a cloth.

The above is only for Christmas. Now for every day.

Put into a basin one pound of flour, one of chopped suet, half a pound of mixed fruit, a little spice, grated lemon-peel, three ounces of sugar, two eggs, half a pint of milk, or enough to make it a proper thickness, tie it in a cloth, boil four hours, turn it out, and serve with melted butter, or sweet sauce; bread-crumbs instead of flour is good, or half of each.

335. *A Series of Economical Puddings, which can be made either in a mould, basin, tart-dish, or tin cake-pan.*—Well butter either, fill lightly with any of the following ingredients: —Either stale buns, muffins, crumpets, pastry, white or brown bread, sliced and buttered, the remains of sponge-cakes, ma-caroons, ratafias, almond cake, gingerbread, biscuit of any kind, previously soaked. For a change with any of the above, you may intermix with either fresh or dried fruit, or preserves, even plums, grated cocoa nut, &c. When your mould is full of

either of the above, put in a basin a quarter teaspoonful of either ginger, a little mixed spice, or cinnamon, if handy, grated orange, lemon, or a few drops of any essence you choose; put in three eggs, which beat well, add three gills of milk for every quarter mould. When the above is well mixed, fill up nearly to the rim. It can be either baked or boiled, or put into a saucepan one-third full of water, with the lid over, and let simmer for about one hour. Pass a knife round the inside of the basin or mould, turn out your pudding, pour over either melted butter with a little sugar, the juice of a lemon or spirit sauce. It ought to be the pride of each cottager's wife to find out a peculiar and cheap mixture, which would entirely depend on the part of the country in which she lives, that would be liked by the family, and give it as a treat every Sunday.

335A. *Fruit Puddings.*—Such as green gooseberry is best made in a basin, the basin to be buttered and lined with the paste, rolling it round to the thickness of half an inch; then get a pint of gooseberries and three ounces of sugar; after having made your paste, take half the fruit, and lay it at the bottom of your basin, then add half your sugar, then put the remainder of the gooseberries in and the remainder of the sugar; on that draw your paste to the centre, join the edges well together, put the cloth over the whole, tying it at the bottom, and boil in plenty of water. Fruit puddings, such as apples and rhubarb, should be done in this manner; boil for an hour, take out of the saucepan, untie the cloth, turn out on a dish, or let it remain in the basin, and serve with sugar over. A thin cover of the paste may be rolled round and put over the pudding.

Ripe cherries, currants, raspberries, greengage, plums, and such like fruit, will not require so much sugar, or so long boiling.

336. *Curd Milk Pudding.*—Put in a basin three eggs, a little grated lemon-peel, three ounces of currants, one pint of curds, and one pound of bread-crumbs; boil in a cloth half an hour; turn out and serve.

337. *Cocoa Nut Pudding.*—Grate half a nut, add another egg to the milk, mix with the above. An ounce of flour may be added.

338. *Plain Rice Pudding.*—Wash a quarter of a pound of rice, put into a stewpan with a pint and a half of milk, three ounces of butter, three ounces of sugar, lemon-peel, simmer till

the rice is tender, add two eggs, previously well beaten, mix quick, put in pie-dish; bake half an hour, or till set.

339. *Spotted Dick.*—Put three-quarters of a pound of flour into a basin, half a pound of beef suet, half ditto of currants, two ounces of sugar, a little cinnamon, mix with two eggs and two gills of milk; boil in either mould or cloth for one hour and a half; serve with melted butter, and a little sugar over.

340. *Light Dough Dumplings.*—Get one pound of dough, make it into small balls the size of eggs, boil in plenty of water, and use it for roast or boiled meats, or serve with butter and sugar, or with gravy.

Two ounces of chopped suet added to the above, or to vary the flavour, add a few currants, a little sugar, grated nutmeg, or lemon-peel.

341. *Apple and Paste Pudding in Basin.*—Make one pound of paste, No. 319, roll it a quarter of an inch thick, lay some in a bowl, fill it with apples cut in quarters, add two cloves, two ounces of sugar, a little butter, put another piece of paste on the top, and join the edge nicely; tie it in a cloth and boil. It can be served up either in the basin or turned out. Do not open the top to put more sugar in, as it spoils the flavour and makes it heavy.

All fruit puddings may be done the same way.

342. *Suet Pudding.*—Put into a basin half a pound of chopped suet, a pound of flour, two eggs, a teaspoonful of salt, quarter of pepper, nearly half a pint of water; beat all well together, put into a cloth as above; boil one hour and a half.

343. *Bread Pudding.*—An economical one, when eggs are dear. Cut some bread and butter very thin, place it in a pie-dish as lightly as possible, till three-parts full; break into a basin one egg, add two teaspoonfuls of flour, three of brown sugar; mix all well together, add to it by degrees a pint of milk, a little salt; pour over the bread; bake in an oven; it will take about half an hour: this will make a nice size pudding for four or five persons.

This may be done in twenty different ways, by varying the flavour of the ingredients, as lemon-peel, orange-peel, nutmeg, cinnamon, or mixed spice, or essences of any kind.

For children, skim-milk, or half milk and water, dates, or

French plums, or figs, previously soaked and cut, may be added; they are excellent for children.

344. *Brown Bread Puddings*, the same way.

344A. *Broken Biscuit Pudding.*—These may be bought very cheap at a baker's; they should be soaked in milk and sugar the over night, and proceed as above or as No. 335. Stale sponge cake may be used with them.

345. *Rice, Macaroni, and Vermicelli Puddings.*—Wash a quarter of a pound of rice, boil till tender, drain it, place it in the pie-dish with any kind of fruit, and one ounce of butter, in bits; pour custard No. 361 or 343 over, and bake. Vermicelli and macaroni previously boiled, may be done the same.

346. *The Same for a Numerous Family, or School.*—Two pounds of boiled rice, with one pound of chopped suet; mix in a pan with four eggs, ten teaspoonfuls of flour; moisten with five pints of water, or skim-milk; add one pound of sugar and a teaspoonful of salt; bake about one hour. To vary it, a few Smyrna rasins may be added. Apples, or any dry fruit, may be used, previously soaked.

347. *Lemon Dumplings.*—Chop the rind of one lemon fine, add it to the juice; chop up half a pound of suet; mix with half a pound of bread crumbs one egg, enough milk or water to make a stiff paste; add the lemon; sweeten to taste; divide it into five equal parts, and boil in separate cloths for three-quarters of an hour; serve with butter and sugar, or a little honey.

347A. *Apple Dumplings.*—Peel and take out the cores of a large apple, cover it with paste No. 318 or 319, boil in a cloth, or plainly bake for thirty minutes. Serve with butter and sugar.

348. *Another.*—Put into the paste in making it, two ounces of sugar; a few sultans, or plums, may also be added, and served with sweet melted butter or spirit sauce over.

349. *A Simple Suet Dumpling.*—One pound of flour, half a pound of chopped suet, a teaspoonful of salt, quarter ditto of pepper; moisten with water until a stiff paste: use where required. They may be rolled in small balls, and may be used in savoury pies, hash, or stews.

350. *Rice and Preserve.*—Boil half a pound of rice as No. 463; when just done, add one ounce of butter, a tablespoonful of currant jelly, one ounce of sugar; mix all well together with a fork, and serve. Apple marmalade, rhubarb, cherries, currants, and raspberry jam, orange marmalade, &c., may be used, and an immense variation may be made. If it is found too thick, add some milk. Dish up in pyramids, and serve.

351. *Ground Rice Pudding.*—Boil one pint of milk with a little piece of lemon peel; mix a quarter of a pound of ground rice with half a pint of milk, two ounces of sugar, and one of butter; add this to the boiling milk; keep stirring, take it off the fire, break in two eggs, one after the other; keep stirring; butter a pie-dish, pour in the mixture, and bake until set. This is one of the quickest puddings that can be made.

352. *Snow Rice Cream.*—Put in a stewpan four ounces of ground rice, two ounces of sugar, a few drops of the essence of almonds, or any other essence you choose, with two ounces of fresh butter; add a quart of milk, boil from fifteen to twenty minutes, till it forms a smooth substance, though not too thick; then pour in a mould previously oiled, and serve when cold. It will turn out like jelly.

If no mould, put either in cups or a pie-dish. The rice had better be done a little too much, than under.

353. *Handy Pudding.*—Remove the inside of three lemons into a basin, take out the pips, add half a pound of sugar, mix well; roll a long strip of paste, as for rolly-polly pudding, lay the mixture over with a spoon; roll and boil the same as rolly-polly pudding.

Orange can be done the same way, with the addition of the juice of half a lemon.

354. *Young England Pudding.*—Make some paste. No. 319, roll and lay it in a basin; then roll about seven or eight very thin pieces the size of the bason; then get a pound of treacle, or golden syrup, and pour a little on the paste, squeezing a little lemon juice, and chop up the rind of a lemon, and sprinkle a little over; add the other pieces of paste, and then the treacle and lemon until full. Boil in a cloth for one hour, and serve with some treacle over.

I think I remember telling you, my dear Eloise, of the pleasant time I passed at Boulogne two summers since, and of our little trip to the Vallée Heureuse, or Happy Valley, near Marquise, a charming village near Boulogne. In the course of our ramble on that pleasant day, we all gathered a lot of blackberries—but such berries as we do not meet with in England; they are a luscious, ripe fruit. These we took home with us to the hotel, and the next day boiled them up with a lot of sugar, and made them into a pudding like the above, using the fruit and syrup instead of treacle. It was very much liked at dinner, which was a *table d'hôte*, and the colour somewhat resembling Uncle Tom's face, it was at once christened with that name, and is now known as *Uncle Tom's* pudding. A little port wine sauce may be used, and also black currants, boiled to a syrup.

355. *Isinglass and Gelatine for Jellies.*— Dissolve two ounces of isinglass in half a pint of water; boil and reduce to half, pass through a cloth into a basin; use where required.

Gelatine may be used the same way.

The stock of two calf's feet, reduced to half a pint, may be used instead of isinglass; it will make it cheaper.

The stock of cow-heel can also be used.

356. *Bohemian Cream.* — Prepare four ounces of any fruit, as No. 384, which pass through a sieve, and one ounce and a half of *melted* isinglass to half a pint of fruit; mix it well, whip up a pint of cream, and add the fruit and isinglass gradually to it; put it in a mould; let it set on ice or in any cool place, and when ready, dip the mould into warm water, and turn out.

357. *White Cream.*—Put into a bason a quarter of a pound of sugar, a gill of pale brandy, and one and a half ounce of either melted isinglass, gelatine, or calf's foot; stir it well, and add a pint of whipped cream; proceed as before. Rum, noyeau, curaçoa, or other liquors or flavours, may be added. When liquors are used, add less sugar. If you have any ice, use only an ounce of either.

358. *Calf's-foot Jelly.*—It is possible, even in the poorest family, that jelly may be recommended in cases of illness, and they may be at a distance from any place where it could be purchased. I think it right to give the following receipt:—

Cut two calf's feet and put them in three quarts of water; when boiling, remove to the side of the fire, and let it simmer from three to four hours, keeping it skimmed; pass it through a sieve into a bason, where it must remain until quite hard; then remove all the fat, &c., from the top. Put into a pan half a pound of white sugar crushed, the juice of four lemons, the rind of one, the whites and shells of five eggs, two glasses of white wine and a pint and a half of water; stir till the sugar is melted, then add the jelly; place it on the fire and stir well until boiling; then pass it through a flannel bag until clear. Put in a mould with or without fresh fruit. Set in ice or any cool place, till firm. Brandy, rum, or any liqueurs, may be added, or serve plain.

359. *Orange Jelly.*—Procure five oranges and one lemon; take the rind off two of the oranges, and half of the lemon, and remove the pith, put them in a bason, and squeeze the juice of the fruit into it; then put a quarter of a pound of sugar into a stewpan, with half a pint of water, and set it to boil until it becomes a syrup, when take it off, and add the juice and rind of the fruits; cover the stewpan, and place it again on the fire; as soon as boiling commences, skim well, and add a gill of water by degrees, which will assist its clarification; let it boil another minute, when add an ounce and a half of isinglass, dissolved as directed (No. 355), pass it through a jelly-bag, or fine sieve; add a few drops of prepared cochineal to give an orange tint, and then fill a mould and place it on ice; turn out as before. This jelly does not require to look very clear.

360. *Lemon Jelly* is made the same way, only using six lemons and the rind of one.

To those who wish to save trouble, I would recommend them to buy their jellies ready made. They may be purchased at almost every Italian warehouse in town and country, in bottles of about a pint and a quart each, so prepared as to keep fresh and good for years. Many of my friends use these *Bottled Jellies*, of which I find the following are the best kinds: Noyeau, punch, orange, lemon, Madeira, and plain calf's-foot. They are all very excellent and useful in their way.

DEAR ELOISE,—While on the subject of jellies and confectionary I feel I should be wanting in duty to the public were I to refrain from drawing their earnest attention to the recent disclosures in the *Lancet*, which so fearlessly exposed the poisonous adulterations found in the various articles of preserves and confectionary submitted to examination. There is not a doubt these disclosures have had a most beneficial effect in checking the existence of the injurious practices previously adhered to; and I may now look forward with confidence to the day when not only such delicacies, but the whole of the food we eat, may be enjoyed without the slightest fear of injury to our health. Adulteration will then become the *exception,* instead of, as it hitherto has been, the *rule.*

The following paragraph, copied from the *Lancet* of the 4th February, 1854, appears to me not an inapt illustration of my remarks, displaying, as it does, the difference between pure and impure preserves, accompanied by the gratifying intelligence of the possibility of procuring them in a wholesome state.*

361. *Plain Custard.*—Boil a pint of milk, in which place two ounces of sugar, the thin peel of half a lemon; break in a basin four eggs, beat them well with a fork, then pour in the milk by degrees, not too hot; mix it well, pass it through a cullender or sieve, fill cups with it, which place in a stew-pan, on the fire, which contains one inch of water; leave them for about twelve minutes, or till set, which is easily perceived.

362. *Coffee, Cocoa, or Chocolate Custard.*—Make some very strong coffee, beat the eggs as above; put in a pan half a pint

---

* " The practice of imparting to bottled and preserved fruits and vegetables a bright green colour, by means of a poisonous salt of copper, still prevails extensively. Nothing can be more pernicious than this practice; it has, however, received a considerable check by the publication of the reports of the Analytical Sanitary Commission on this subject. One firm, we know, that of Messrs. Crosse and Blackwell, whose establishment is the most extensive of any engaged in this branch of trade, has gone to a very considerable expense in fitting up a large silver vessel, as well as several steam pans, which latter are lined with a thick coating of glass enamel, for the prepara-tion of their various manufactures; thus taking every precaution to guard against the contact with copper. The difference in the appearance of fruits and vegetables which are artificially coloured, and those which have not had any colouring matter added, is very great—so striking, indeed, that a practised eye can readily distinguish the one from the other. The former are of a bright and almost metallic-green hue, much deeper than that of the recent fruit, while the latter are of a pale yellowish-green colour, varying with the nature of the fruit or vegetable preserved. As for the difference in the wholesomeness of the two articles, there can be but a single opinion, while, in our estimation, the appearance in the uncoloured sample is much the most pleasing and natural."

of milk and half a pint of made coffee, with two ounces of sugar, then add the eggs, pass through a sieve, and proceed as above.

Chocolate and cocoa the same, only omitting the lemon-peel in all three.

363. *Custard in Pie Dish.*—Put a border of puff paste round the dish, fill with the above, and bake twenty minutes in a slow oven. Eat whilst cold.

364. *Custard for Puddings.*—The above will be the foundation for any flavour that may be introduced; as orange flower or peel, noyeau, &c. &c. With this mixture an innumerable number of puddings can be made, that in country places, or even towns, will be found as economical an article of food, when eggs are cheap, as can be partaken of, and particularly appreciated by the rising generation.

365. *Farm Custard.*—Put in a small saucepan the yolks of four eggs, four teaspoonfuls of sugar, the peel of half a lemon, or a quarter of that grated, a grain of salt; mix all well, then add half a pint of milk; set the whole on the fire, stir continually with a wooden spoon till it gets thick and smooth; but do not let it boil, or it will curd; then put it in a basin to cool, stirring now and then; if handy, pass it through a sieve, it gives it a nice appearance, and serve either in glasses or cups, with any fresh or stewed fruit, orange peel, or any essence, brandy, or rum, may be used for flavouring.

When at our friend Lindley's house in Yorkshire, I took a gill of cream, whipped it, and mixed it with the custard when cold. It made it very white and delicate. The custard may be whipped while being made.

You wish to know what I did with the white of the eggs, and perfectly right that you should. Well, I put them in a basin with a very little bit of salt, then with a whisk I beat them till firm and as white as snow, then I add four teaspoonfuls of pounded sugar, mix it well; I put a pint of milk to boil in a very clean *sauté*, or frying-pan, and, with the aid of a spoon, I scoop off the white in the shape of eggs, dropping them in the milk, letting them remain till done, turning them occasionally; take them out, and serve when cold, pouring some of the custard over; the remaining milk was used for puddings.

Even now, Eloise, you do not seem satisfied, so I send you a receipt for a soufflé. It seems to you, no doubt, very simple; let me tell you, however, that it is so only in appearance; the great secret is in properly beating the white of the eggs; therefore, if you fail in your attempt, do not blame me, the details of the receipt being quite accurate.

366. *Egg Pudding, or Omelette Soufflé.*—Break four eggs; carefully separate the white from the yolk, put both in different basins; add to the yolk three teaspoonfuls of powdered sugar and one of flour, a little grated orange or lemon peel, or any other flavour you prefer; stir the whole for five minutes, then beat the white of the eggs with a whisk; when firm, mix lightly with the yolk till forming a nice, smooth, light, and rather firm substance; then put it either in a tin pan, cake pan, or a common pan, which can stand the heat of the oven, buttering it well.

If in a tin dish, shape it in pyramids with a knife, put it in a moderate oven from ten to twelve minutes, sugar over and serve.   When nearly done, an incision or two with the point of a knife may be made through the thin crust; it will make it lighter. You may also put two ounces of butter in the frying-pan, and when hot put in your mixture, and toss it round three or four times; put it on a dish, bake as above.   Ten minutes will do it.

367. *How to vary Bread or any Custard Puddings.*—Have some slices of bread cut thin and buttered; lay them in the dish singly; pour in the custard, No. 365, and bake gently, or place in a pan with a little water in it.

These may be altered thus :—
By throwing in some currants.
Or bruised ratafia cakes.
Or sultana rasins.
Or Malaga ditto.
Or French prunes.
Or dried cherries.
Or stewed rhubarb.
Or apple; or, in fact, any fruit according to fancy.
Well boiled rice, macaroni, vermicelli, &c., may be used; the custard always being poured over, and sifted sugar on the top.

New style, as a second-class mixture: two eggs, two tablespoonfuls of flour, and milk enough to make it thickish.

368. *Gooseberry Fool.*—Put in a pan a quart of green gooseberries, with a wineglass of water and half a pound of sugar; stew on a slow fire for twenty minutes, keep stirring; put in basin, and whip a pint of cream; when the fruit is cold; mix

with the cream, and serve in cups or hollow dish, or with pastry round it.

Apple may be done the same way.

Currants and raspberries the same.

Red rhubarb the same.

Cherries may be done the same, having previously been stoned.   If too much syrup, add a little isinglass.

369. *Orange Salad.* — Choose six oranges not too large, cut them in thin slices crossways, remove the pips, lay them flat in a dish, cover over with a quarter of a pound of sugar, a gill of brandy, rum, or Madeira; stir them, and serve.

370. *Strawberry Salad.*—A large pottle of ripe strawberries, picked and put into a basin with two tablespoonfuls of sugar, a pinch of powdered cinnamon, a gill of brandy; stir gently, and serve.

Currants and raspberries the same.

As all fruits and vegetables are destined for the use of man, these should be partaken of by all classes when in season, as they are invaluable for health.

371. *Velvet Cream.*—A very excellent dish is made thus :—Put in a dessert glass a thick layer of strawberry jam or any other preserve, and place over it about a pint of hot snow cream mixture, No. 352; when cold, the top may be ornamented with fresh or preserved fruit.

372. *Rice Croquettes.*—Make some of the above mixture very stiff; when cold, roll it, or serve it in any shape you like.   Egg and bread-crumb, and fry quickly in hot fat in a frying-pan. Sugar over.

373. *Lemon Pudding.*—Put in a basin a quarter of a pound of flour, same of sugar, same of bread crumbs and chopped suet, the juice of one good-sized lemon, and the peel grated, two eggs, and enough milk to make it the consistency of porridge; boil in a basin for one hour; serve with or without sauce.

374. *Dripping Pudding.*—Three eggs and their weight in dripping, two tablespoonfuls of sifted sugar; beat them up until a cream, add a few currants, and the flour gradually, until it forms a stiff paste; bake in cups previously buttered.

375. *Potato Pudding.*—One pound of potatoes boiled and well mashed, a quarter of a pound of butter stirred in whilst warm, two ounces of sugar, the rind of half a lemon chopped fine, with the juice, a teacupful of milk; butter a tin, put in the mixture, and bake in a moderate oven for half an hour; two eggs may be added.

376. *Dough Pudding with Apples.*—Cut four apples into dice, put over two ounces of sugar, half a pound of chopped suet, one pound of flour, and half a pint of water; bake in a pie dish or a mould, or boil in a basin, as a pudding; sweet sauce may be poured over.

377. *First Class Yorkshire Pudding.*—Beat up two eggs in a basin, add to them three good tablespoonfuls of flour, with a pint of milk by degrees, and a little salt; butter the pan, bake half an hour, or bake under the meat, cut it in four, turn it, and when set on both sides it is done. A tin dish one inch and a half deep and eight inches wide, is the most suitable for such proportion.

378. *Second Class.*—Put in a basin four tablespoonfuls of flour, add a quarter of a teaspoonful of salt and a little pepper, beat one egg with a pint of milk, pour over on the flour by degrees till smooth, and proceed as above.

379. *Third Class.*—If no eggs, chop two ounces of beef suet fine, add a little soda, mix as above, and bake the same. A little chopped parsley, chives, or aromatic herbs, may be introduced in either of the above. These receipts are good with any kind of roasted or baked meat, or poultry. To facilitate the turning, when one side is brown and the pudding well set, cut it into several pieces, turning with a knife or a fork. If preferred served whole, put a plate on the top of the baking tin, turn it over, and slip it back; let it remain in the tin ten minutes longer, and serve either round or separate.

380. *Pancakes.*—Put the pan on the fire with a tablespoonful of lard, let it melt, pour off all that is not wanted, then pour in three tablespoonfuls of the following batter:—

Break four eggs in a basin, add four small tablespoonfuls of flour, two teaspoonfuls of sugar, a little salt; beat all well, mixing by degrees half a pint of milk, a little more or less, depending on the size of the eggs and the quality of the flour. It must form a rather thick batter.   A little ginger, cinnamon, or any other flavour you fancy.   Two eggs only may be used, but in this case use a little more flour and milk.   When set, and one side brownish, lay hold of the frying-pan at the extremity of the handle, give it a sudden but slight jerk upwards, and the cake will turn over on the other side; which, when brown, dish up with sifted sugar over.   Serve with lemon.   Chopped apples may be added to the batter; currants and sultanas can be mixed with it.

381. *Apple Fritters.*—Peel and slice crossways, a quarter of an inch thick, some apples, remove the core, and dip them one after the other in the following batter : Put in a basin about two ounces of flour, a little salt, two teaspoonfuls of oil, and the yolk of an egg, moistened by degrees with water, stirring all the while with a spoon, till forming a smooth consistency, to the thickness of cream, then beat the white of the egg till firm, mixing it with the batter; it is then ready to fry; use any fruit as fritters. If no oil, use an ounce of butter previously melted, adding it to the batter before the white of the egg is used.

Apple Fritters Simplified.—When peeled and cut, put sugar over, add a little lemon juice or spirits, let the pieces soak two hours, then dip each piece in flour, and have ready a frying-pan, with at least two inches deep of fat.   When hot, put the apples in one at a time, turn over with a slice as they are doing, and serve with sugar over.   All kinds of ripe pears may be done in the same way.

382. *College Pudding.*—Put half a pound of crumbs into a basin, a quarter of a pound of chopped suet, the same of currants, two eggs, two ounces of sugar, a little nutmeg and salt, and a little milk; mix all together, make round balls, egg-crumb, and fry in hot fat till a nice colour; dish up with sugar over; a glass of brandy or rum in it is exceedingly good.

383. *Buttered Apples.*—Peel, slice, and core one pound of apples, put into a frying-pan about two ounces of butter, add the apple, and cover over with two ounces of pounded sugar; put them in the oven until done.   A very nice dish for children. When done, they may be dished up on a nice crisp piece of toast with sugar over.

384. *Stewed Fruits.*—These, at those periods of the year

when Nature has ordained that they shall come to perfection without artificial means, are as wholesome an article of food as can be partaken of, as they cool the blood and are perfectly harmless.

They are easily done, and are cheap. In the following receipts, which I will mark as lessons, one pound is the quantity named.

Apples. 1st Lesson.—Peel one pound of apples, cut in slices, remove the core, put into a stewpan with three or four ounces of white pounded sugar, one ounce of butter, two tablespoonfuls of water; stir gently on a slow fire until tender; use hot or cold when required. Brown sugar may be used.

2nd Lesson.—To the above add the juice of half a lemon or of one orange, and a little of the peel of either, or a small piece of cinnamon, or in powder.

Red Rhubarb. 1st Lesson.—Cut one pound of rhubarb one inch long, put into a pan with two tablespoonfuls of water and three ounces of white powdered sugar; stir on a slow fire till tender.

2nd Lesson.—Stew with brown sugar: green rhubarb requires peeling. Stir more if old.

3rd Lesson.—Cut a pound of the common rhubarb, put in an iron pot with four ounces of brown sugar; stir well with a spoon until it is quite thick and adheres to it; take it out to cool. It can be used, spread on bread, for tea or supper.

Green Gooseberries, 1st Lesson. — One pound of gooseberries with six ounces of sugar; boil with two tablespoonfuls of water, turning them well; stir, and keep until cold. Or by mixing cream with it, it will make gooseberry fool.

Greengages, Orleans plums, egg plums, cherries, currants, red, white, and black, raspberries, mulberries, and strawberries, may all be done the same way.

The following is another very nice way, and may be used for several fruits in winter. Cherries being the most difficult, we will name that in particular. All the others can be done like it.

Cut the stalk half off of one pound of cherries, put into a pan with eight ounces of sugar; set on the stove for a few minutes, then add half a pound of red currants, and the same of raspberries; stew altogether until getting tender and the juice becomes quite thick; put by until cold. It may be used with pastry or with bread.

Siberian crabs, cranberries, damsons, and all other fruits the same way.

All the above make a very nice light and quick dish for supper done as follows :—

Cut some nice slices of bread half an inch thick, dip them in milk which is sweetened, or sprinkle sugar over, then dip it into some batter of milk and flour, and fry nicely, or put some butter in a tin dish, bread over, and put in an oven. When quite hot and nearly hard, put some of the above fruit over, and serve.

385. *Plum Cake.*—Weigh one pound and a half of flour, one of currants, well washed, one of butter, one of sugar, nine eggs; put into a good-sized basin the butter, which well work, with clean hands, until it is like a cream; in about ten minutes it is ready; then add a little sugar and the eggs by degrees, and then the flour, then add the currants and line a cake-hoop with paper, put the mixture in, set it in a warm place for one hour, and bake it for one hour in a slow oven. Half or even a quarter of the quantity may be made.

386. *Common Sort.*—Put in a basin half a pound of butter, work it well, add half a pound of sugar and four eggs, beat all well together, then add half a pint of milk, two pounds of flour. a quarter of a pound of caraway-seeds or half a pound of plums; put it in a hoop or deep pie-dish, and bake two hours.

To ascertain if the cake is done, take a piece of dry wood or skewer, pass it into the cake, and if it comes out dry, it is done.

387. *Ground Rice Cake.*—Break five eggs into a stewpan, which place in another, containing hot water, whip the eggs for ten minutes till very light, then mix in by degrees half a pound of ground rice, six ounces of powdered sugar, beat it well; any flavour may be introduced; pour into buttered pan and bake half an hour.

387A. *Pastry Cream.*—Break two eggs in a pan, add two tablespoonfuls of flour, a pinch of salt; moisten with a pint and a half of milk; set on the fire, boil twenty minutes, or till it forms thickish smooth consistency; then add two ounces of pounded sugar, one of butter; put in either a little orange flower water, or a drop of any essence you choose, grated orange or lemon peel. One dozen of bruised ratafias will be an improvement, put in at the same time as the sugar. Previous to using, add to the cream one ounce of butter, which you have previously made very hot. This may be used for all kinds of pastry, instead of jam.

388. *Ginger Cake.*—Half a pound of sugar, half a pound of butter, one ounce and a half of ground ginger, six eggs, beat well, stirring one pound and a half of flour, and add as much milk, a little warm, as will make a nice stiff dough for bread; bake in pan; it will take two hours.

388A. *Rock Cakes.*—Put in a basin two pounds of flour, half of sugar, half currants, half of butter, three eggs, beat well, make them into balls or rock, the size of eggs; bake on baking sheets; a little milk may be added.

389. *Common Gingerbread.*—Put on a slab or table a pound of flour, make a ring of it; put half a pint of treacle in, mix well together till forming a stiff paste, working it well. Put some flour in a basin, to which add your dough; it will keep thus for seven or eight weeks. When you want to use it, put in any quantity of ground ginger you require, according to taste; mix well, roll thin, cut any size you like; pieces about the size of a crown are best; then put them on a baking-sheet. bake for a few minutes, till crisp. These cakes will keep a long while if put in an air-tight case. An ounce of butter may be used to every pound of paste.

They are excellent in assisting digestion after dinner.

390. *Rice Cake.*—Wash one pound of rice, put it in a stew-pan, with a pint of water, put it on the fire; when the rice is well soaked add a quart of milk, quarter of a pound of butter, grated lemon-peel or a little nutmeg, or a piece of cinnamon, boil till thick, then add two eggs, well beat, a little salt, and a

quarter of a pound of sugar; place all in a greased pan or tin breadpan; bake one hour, and serve with sugar or jam over.

391. *The same a Cheaper Way.*—Add to one pound of rice, when boiled, two ounces of chopped suet, a spoonful of flour, a quart of skim milk, some brown sugar or treacle; bake in *large pan;* eat cold; and fruit of any kind may be mixed with it.

392. *Apple Cake.*—Butter a pie-dish near a quarter of an inch thick, throw in a large quantity of bread-crumbs, as much as will stick, when pressed well, on the butter; then have some apples already stewed down and sweetened, as No 384, of which nearly fill the dish, put one ounce of butter in bits, cover over with bread-crumbs, also half an inch thick, put into hot oven; when done, pass a knife round and turn it out, sugar over, and glaze with a red-hot shovel.

If used hot, a little rum put round it and lighted is very nice.

393. *Spice Cake.*—To one pound and a half of dough add half a pound of butter, half of currants, half of sugar, half an ounce of spice, beat all well together, and bake in a mould one hour.

394. *Little Milk Cake for Breakfast.*—Place on a table or stab one pound of flour, half a teaspoonful of salt, two of sugar, three of fresh yeast, or a very small piece of German, two ounces of butter and one egg; have some new milk, pour in a gill, mix all together, adding more milk to form a nice dough, then put some flour in a cloth, put the dough in, and lay it in a warm place; let it rise for about two hours, cut it in pieces the size of eggs, roll them even, and mark the top with a sharp knife; egg over and bake quick; serve hot or cold.

A Common Sort.—Only yeast, salt, milk, and butter, and proceed as before.

Cottage Sort.—To one pound of flour, two ounces of lard or dripping, the yeast and skim milk.

Sweet Sort.—To one pound of flour three teaspoonfuls of yeast, two ounces of lard or dripping, quarter of a pound of sugar, a few currants or caraway seeds: bake quick when well risen.

395. *Eccles Cake.*—To a quarter of a pound of currants half a teaspoonful of grated nutmeg, some lemon-peel chopped fine, one ounce of sugar, roll out about a quarter of a pound of puff paste, No. 315, roll it round the size of a small plate, and nearly an inch thick, then put a tablespoonful of the mixture over it, roll another piece of paste over it, and bake a nice delicate colour.

396. *Bread Apple Cake.*—Well butter a tart-dish of any size, about three inches deep, cut some slices of bread quarter of an inch thick, which lay in it so that the bottom and sides are quite covered, stew some apple nearly dry, as No. 384, put them on the bread until the dish is full, cover over with more butter and bread, and bake in a hot oven for half an hour; remove it from the dish; turn over, and dish it up with sugar on the top.

397. *Tipsy Cake.*—Cut a small Savoy cake in slices, put them into a basin, and pour some white wine and a little rum over; let soak for a few hours, put into a dish, and serve with some custard round. It may be decorated with a few blanched almonds or whipt cream and fruit.

These may be made with small sponge cakes, by soaking them in some white wine, in which currant-jelly has been dissolved; take twelve of them stale, which will cost sixpence soak them well, put them in a dish, cover them with jam or jelly, and thus make four layers, decorating the top with cut preserved fruit; dish with custard or whipt cream round.

398. *Plain Cake.*—Mix two pounds of dry flour with four ounces of clean dripping melted in a pint of milk, three tablespoonfuls of yeast, and two well beaten eggs, mix well together, and set aside in a warm place to rise, then knead well and make into cakes; flour a tin, and place it in the oven in a tin ; carraway-seeds or currants may be added, sugar over.

399. *Soda Cake.*—Half a pound of good clean dripping, one pound of flour, half a pound of sugar, not quite half an ounce of soda; beat the dripping well with the sifted sugar, and beat the flour in with the soda; bake in tins in a slow oven for one hour and a half.

Another.—Half a pound of dripping, half a pound of moist sugar, half a pound of currants, one pound of flour, a teaspoonful of carbonate of soda, three eggs, well beaten and mixed with half a pint of warm milk; then mix altogether an bake in a tin lined with writing paper.

400. *Foreign Biscuits.*—A quarter of a pound of butter mix with a pound of flour, dissolve a quarter of a pound of sugar in half a pint of warm new milk, pour gradually to the flour, dissolve half a teaspoonful of salt of tartar in half a tea-cupful of cold water, add it to the flour, and make it into a stiff paste, roll out, and cut in small cakes with a wineglass; bake in a quick oven immediately.

401. *Ground Rice Cake.*—Six ounces of ground rice, six ounces of flour, four eggs, half a pound of sugar, quarter of a pound of clean dripping, a small piece of volatile salts; beat all well together, bake one hour in a pan. A few currants may be added, and also a little milk, if required.

SERIES OF BREAD.

402. The bread which I strongly recommend for the labouring class, or those who shall get their bread "by the sweat of their brow," is that made from unbolted flour, or whole meal. It is only the effeminate and delicate that should partake of fine flour. The mass of bread is increased one fifth, and the price lowered, between the difference of the price of bran as flour, or as fodder for cattle.

Liebig says, "The separation of the bran from the flour by bolting, is a matter of luxury, and injurious rather than beneficial as regards the nutritive power of the bread."

It is only in more modern times the sifted flour has been known and used, and has been followed by the poor, to imitate the luxury of the wealthy, at the expense of their health. Certain it is, that where whole meal is used as bread, the population have better digestive organs than where it is not.

In Ireland, amongst the poor, it is almost a disgrace to eat brown bread. During the year of the famine, being at Malahide, I saw a female, without shoes or stockings, go into a baker's shop, purchase two loaves, one white, and the other brown; the white she carried in her hand, the brown she hid under her everlasting cloak—her pride would not allow it to be seen. These ignorant people should be told that there is hardly a family in England but what have on their table for breakfast and tea a loaf of each kind of bread, white or brown.

If the dough is made and well raised in the pan, if in small quantities, as for buns, &c. throw some flour on the table, put the dough over, and roll it several times to form it solid; then shape the loaf or bun; let them rise twenty minutes in a warm place, and bake according to size.

403. *Cottage Bread, No.* 1.—Put into a large pan fourteen pounds of flour, add to one quart of warm water a quarter of pint of brewer's yeast, or two ounces of German yeast, make a hole in the flour, and pour in the water and the yeast; stir it well up with a wooden spoon till it forms a thickish paste, throw a little flour over, and leave it in a warm room; in about one hour or seventy-five minutes it will have risen and burst through the covering of flour, then add more warm water and four teaspoonfuls of salt, until it forms, when kneaded, a rather stiff dough; it cannot be too much worked; then let it remain covered with a cloth for about another hour, or an hour and a half; the time, as well as the quantity of water it takes, depends greatly on the quality of the flour. Cold water may be used in summer.

Then divide the dough into five pieces; if the flour is old and good they will weigh four pounds each, and take about one hour and forty minutes to bake; the oven should be well heated, and sufficiently large to bake the quantity of dough you make at one time; if the oven is small, make only half the quantity; the door should be well closed. If the bottom of the oven is too hot, a tile placed on it will prevent too much bottom crust; or a baking sheet, kept half an inch above the bottom of the oven, will have the same effect.

In some places they bake in tins, in others in brown pans; if so, the dough may be made softer, and allowed to rise a little longer, though I do not approve of bread being too light, as it is both tasteless and unprofitable.

404. *Milk Bread and Rolls.*—Weigh a pound of flour, put it on the table-dresser, or in a pan, make a hole in the centre, put in a quarter of an ounce of German yeast, one egg, two ounces of butter, quarter of a teaspoonful of salt, one of sugar, have half a pint of warm milk, put a little in, mix all well together, then add by degrees the flour, and also the milk; it may not take the half pint, but depends on the flour; stir all well, work it for a few minutes, until it is a stiff dough; take a little flour and rub off the paste which attaches to the side of the basin, roll it round, throw some flour on the bottom of the basin, put in the dough, keep it in a warm place for two hours or till it has

nicely risen, then throw some flour on the board, cut the paste off in the size of eggs, flatten them with the hand, make them long and pointed, and make a line in the centre with the back of the knife, egg over with a paste-brush, let them rise half an hour longer in a warm place, bake twenty minutes in rather a sharp oven. They ought to be of a nice yellow colour, and light. If the yeast is doubtful, add a little more; brown yeast is preferable.

Another plainer, No. 2.—Put in the centre of the flour two ounces of lard, or good dripping, then add an ounce of German yeast, a little salt, a little tepid water, with which dissolve both yeast and lard; mix it with the flour.

405. *Plainer still, No. 3.*—Put a quarter of an ounce of yeast, salt, sugar as above, add half a pint of tepid water, proceed as above; sugar may be omitted; or make a single loaf of it in a tin pan, or roll it into a lump; make a cross at the top with a sharp knife, egg over, or milk and water; bake in rather sharp oven, which is easily ascertained by placing the hand on it; if you cannot endure it for a quarter of a minute it is fit for bread, but if it burns it is too hot.

406. The brown bread, or that made from whole meal, is done in the same way; the sponge will take a little longer to rise.

Milk used in these breads will occasion it to go a little further, and keep it moist longer; one pint is sufficient, and you get one pound more bread; it also improves bad flour, from the addition of gluten in the milk. A little potato starch or rice starch will improve bad flour, and occasion it to rise better.

The following are two variations for these breads:—Put seven pounds of flour into a pan, mix with three pints of warm milk or water, an ounce of yeast, one ounce of salt, mix well with the flour, set it in a warm place for three hours, form into small loves and bake at once.

407. *Rice Bread.*—To fourteen pounds of dough add one pound of ground rice, boiled in milk until in pulp and cold; bake in small loaves.

408. *Brown Rye Bread.*—To three pounds of flour add one pound of rye flour, the proportions of yeast, salt and water as above, and may be mixed all at once; it will take a little longer to bake.

409. *Good Keeping Bread.*—Mix one quarter of a pound of very light mashed potatoes with four pounds of flour, made into dough for bread, is very good; this kind of bread will keep moist for a long time.

SAUCES.

410. *Melted Butter.*—From whence is this extraordinary word derived? what learned *pundit* could have given it birth?—a word which recalls so many pleasing moments, when the palate has been gratified by its peculiar fragrance and taste. It is, no doubt, an importation at the time of the Conquest, but although having been domesticated amongst us for near 800 years, we are very far behind our allies on the other side of the channel in its numerous adaptations and applications. The great diplomatist, Talleyrand, used to say, that England had 120 religions, but only one sauce, and that melted butter. He was very near the truth, but, at the same time, he should have told how to engraft 119 sauces to the original one, the same as the various sects he mentions, have been offshoots from the primitive one which was first established in this country.

I will now endeavour to prevent his words being any longer a truism, and will point out how that one sauce—melted butter (French *butter sauce*)—can be multiplied *ad infinitum*, according to the ability of the artist.

I must first premise that my melted butter is not for the table of the wealthy, but the simple artizan. It is not to consist of two-thirds butter and one-third cream, warmed gradually with a box spoon, but of two ounces of butter, and two ounces of flour, half a teaspoonful of salt, a quarter that of pepper, mixed together with a spoon, put into a quart pan, with a pint of cold water; place it on the fire, and stir continually, take it out when it begins to simmer, then add one more ounce of butter, stir till melted, and it is ready for use, or as the foundation of the following various sauces.

This melted butter is fit to serve at the best tables, by adding three ounces of butter; take, as a guide, that the back of the spoon, m being removed, should always be covered with the butter or sauce; this is essential, as I find that flour varies very much. If you let it boil, it will immediately get thinner.

Melted Butter, No. 2.—The following is also very good as the foundation of sauces—it is not so rich, and will keep longer: One ounce of butter, one and a half of flour, a little more salt, pepper and a gill more water; simmer, and serve.

These melted butters may be improved slightly by adding half a tablespoonful of vinegar.

With half of the above quantity make the following sauces. Each ingredient to be mixed in the saucepan. Stir and serve when nearly boiling.

411. SERIES OF SAUCES.

Anchovy Sauce.—Add two tablespoonsful of essence of anchovies, and mix well.

Harvey's Sauce.—The same of Harvey's sauce.

Soyer's Relish.—The same of Soyer's relish.

Soyer's Mustard Sauce.—One teaspoonful of Soyer's mustard.

Chili Vinegar.—Three teaspoonsful of Chili vinegar.

Egg Sauce.—Two hard boiled eggs cut in dice and added.

Caper Sauce.—Two tablespoonsful of chopped capers added: if no capers, use pickled gherkins.

Fennell Sauce.—The same of chopped fennel.

Parsley and Butter.—The same of chopped parsley.

Mild Onion Sauce.—Boil four onions in salt and water, take them out, chop them up, and add them to the above with a little more salt, and a teaspoonful of sugar, and a little milk or cream.

Sage and Onion.—To the above, a tablespoonful of chopped green sage and a little more pepper.

White Sauce.—The yolk of one egg, and mix with milk or cream instead of water. A blade of mace is an improvement when boiling, and stir.

Celery Sauce.—Boil in a half-pint of white gravy, if handy, if not, water, one fine head of celery, cut in one inch lengths and well washed,—it will take about twenty minutes,—add it to the melted butter. The yolk of an egg beat up and stirred in is an improvement; it may require a little more salt. Serve with poultry.

Cucumber Sauce.—Cut up two cucumbers lengthways, remove the seeds, cut them in one inch pieces, boil them in a gill of white gravy, with salt and pepper, add it to the melted butter; simmer and serve. Sugar is an improvement.

Vegetable Marrow, when young, the same as above.

412. *Brown Sauce.*—Put a quarter of a pound of butter and eight ounces of flour in a saucepan, and set it on a slow fire; keep stirring

for ten minutes, or till light brown, then take it off and let it get nearly cold, then pour over sufficient brown stock, No. 2, to make it a nice thickness, or like thinnish melted butter; then boil for half an hour, skim, strain it into a basin, and use where and when required. If you have this sauce by you, use it instead of melted butter for brown sauces. To make it darker, a little colouring may be added.

413. *White Sauce.*—Put into a convenient sized stew pan four ounces of butter, and eight ounces of flour; set on fire, keep stirring as above; take the pan from the fire and stir until nearly cool, then pour on sufficient white stock, No. 1, until it is a nice consistency put it on the fire and boil for a quarter of an hour; keep stirring continually; pass it through a sieve, and keep for use.

Half a pint of boiled milk will make it look whiter.

This sauce, when handy, is the foundation of all white sauces, for celery, cauliflower, mushroom, cucumber, vegetable marrow, &c., or any white sauces, instead of using melted butter. Observe, Eloise, that I only send you these two preceding sauces in the event of a little dinner party, as they belong to a higher class of cookery.

FISH SAUCES.

Shrimp Sauce.—Pick half a pint of shrimps, and boil the skins in a gill of water for fifteen minutes; strain the water, and add it, with the flesh of the shrimps, to half a pint of melted butter, and simmer for a few minutes. Add a little anchovy.

Lobster Sauce.—Get the raw eggs, or the inside spawn of the lobster, put them on a plate with a bit of butter, and with the blade of a knife mash them, or pound them in a mortar; this, when put into the hot melted butter, will make it red. Cut the lobster up in small pieces, and add the soft part from the belly with it to the melted butter (a middling sized lobster will make a quart of sauce). A little cayenne or Harvey's sauce is relishing. Boil and serve.

Crab and Crayfish.—The same as lobster.

Mussel and Oyster.—Open twelve oysters or thirty-six mussels, beard, and blanch them lightly in their own liquor; take them out, reduce the liquor, and add them to the half-pint of melted butter; when boiling add a little cayenne, and one ounce of butter. A drop of cream or boiling milk will improve it. Or, when your oysters are raw in the pan, add half a gill of milk and a few peppercorns; blanch lightly, mix half a teaspoonful of flour with half an ounce of butter, put in bit by bit, stir round, boil, and serve. A little cayenne will improve it, also a drop of cream.

Cod-Liver Sauce.—Half a pound of cod-liver, previously boiled, cut in large dice, with a little anchovy sauce, to half a pint of melted butter. Mix the same as No. 410.

Pickle Sauce.—One tablespoonful of chopped pickle or piccallily, one ditto of the vinegar from it; add to half a pint of melted butter, and boil for a few minutes. Good for fish, meat, and poultry.

414. *Apple Sauce.*—Peel six good-sized apples, cut in four pieces, cut out the core, slice them fine, put into a stew pan with one ounce of brown sugar and a gill of water; stew till in pulp, and serve with roast pork, goose, and duck.

415. *Mint Sauce.*—Chop three tablespoonfuls of green mint, put it into a basin with three of brown sugar, half a teaspoonful of salt, a quarter of pepper, and half a pint of vinegar. Use it with roast lamb; also good with cold meat and poultry.

416. *Horseradish Sauce.* — Grate two tablespoonfuls of horseradish, which put into a basin; add to it one teaspoonful of mustard, one of salt, a quarter of pepper, one of sugar, two tablespoonfuls of vinegar; moisten with a little milk or cream until of a thickish appearance. Serve with rumpsteak, cold meat, &c.

417. *Wine and Spirit Sauce.*—Add to half a pint of melted butter, without salt, two teaspoonfuls of white or brown sugar, a glass of brandy, or rum, or sherry, or any liquors.

418. *Hotel Keeper's Sauce.*—Mix in half a pint of melted butter one tablespoonful of hotel keeper's butter, No. 426; warm it and serve.

419. *A White Sauce for boiled Fowls*, &c. &c.—If for two fowls, add to one pint of melted butter (No. 410) two yolks of raw eggs, which mix well with a gill of cream, or milk, and when the melted butter is near boiling mix in and stir very quick, do not let it boil; add a little grated nutmeg and stir in a little more butter, season with a little more white pepper, and the juice of a lemon, and pour over your poultry. This is not an every day sauce, but is exceedingly useful to know.

A little chopped parsley, ham, or tongue sprinkled over the fowl after the sauce is on, gives it a pleasing appearance.

Or parsley chopped fine, or capers, gherkins, mushrooms, or tongue cut into dice, or green peas, may be added to this sauce to change it.

420. *A sharp Brown Sauce for broiled Fowls and Meat.*—Put a tablespoonful of chopped onions into a stew pan with one of Chili vinegar, one of common vinegar, one of colouring, three of water

two of mushroom ketchup, two of Harvey's sauce, one of anchovy, and a pint of melted butter, No. 2; let it simmer until it becomes rather thick to adhere to the back of the spoon, add half a teaspoonful of sugar. This is excellent to almost all kinds of broiled meats, and gives a nice relish to stews, fish, poultry, &c.

421. *The same simplified.*—Put into a pan one tablespoonful of chopped onion, three spoonfuls of vinegar, one of colouring, six of water, three of either Harvey's sauce, or ketchup, a little pepper and salt, a pint of melted butter, boil till thickish; serve for the same as above.

422. *Onion Sauce.*—Peel and cut six onions in slices; put in a stew pan, with two ounces of butter, a teaspoonful of salt, one of sugar, a half one of pepper; place on a slow fire to simmer till in a pulp, stirring them now and then to prevent them getting brown, then add one tablespoonful of flour, a pint of milk, and boil till a proper thickness, which should be a little thicker than melted butter; serve with mutton cutlets, chops, boiled rabbits, or fowl; by not passing it, it will do for roast mutton and boiled rabbit as onion sauce.

423. *Caper Sauce.*—Put twelve tablespoonfuls of melted butter into a stew pan, place it on the fire, and when on the point of boiling, add one ounce of fresh butter and one tablespoonful of capers; shake the stew pan round over the fire until the butter is melted, add a little pepper and salt, and serve where directed.

424. *Cream Sauce.*—Put two yolks of eggs in the bottom of a stew pan, with the juice of a lemon, a quarter of a teaspoonful of salt, a little white pepper, and a quarter of a pound of hard fresh butter; place the stew pan over a moderate fire, and commence stirring with a wooden spoon, (taking it from the fire now and then when getting too hot,) until the butter has gradually melted and thickened with the eggs—(great care must be exercised, for if it should become too hot the eggs would curdle, and render the sauce useless;) then add half a pint of melted butter; stir altogether over the fire, without permitting it to boil. This sauce may be served with any description of boiled fish, poultry, meat, or vegetables.

425. *Mustard Sauce.*—Put in a stew pan four tablespoonfuls of chopped onions (No. 449), with half an ounce of butter, put on the fire and stir till it gets rather hot, add half a teaspoonful of flour, mixed well, also half a pint of milk or broth (No. 1); let the whole boil ten minutes, season with half a teaspoonful of salt, a quarter that of pepper, a little sugar, and two teaspoonfuls of French or English mustard; when it boils it is ready.

425A. *Black Butter.*—Put two ounces of salt butter in a stew pan, set it on the fire; when it gets hot and brown add about twenty parsley leaves, half a teaspoonful of salt, a quarter of that of pepper, and two tablespoonfuls of vinegar, let the whole boil one minute and pour over any article suitable for this kind of sauce.

425B. *Curry Sauce.*—Peel and cut two middling sized onions in slices, one apple cut in dice, and two ounces of bacon; put them into an iron stew pan, with one ounce of butter or fat, put on the fire, stir round for five or six minutes, then add three teaspoonfuls of flour, one of curry powder, mixed well; moisten with a pint of milk, half a teaspoonful of salt, and one of sugar; boil till rather thick, and serve over any article suitable for its use.

If passed through a sieve, put it back into the stew pan, let it boil one minute, and skim it, will be a very great improvement. Curry paste may be used. Broth or water may be used.

425C. *A simpler Manner.*—Apples and onions may both be used, as also a pint of melted butter (No. 410). In this no flour need be used.

425E. *Bread Sauce.*—Put in a stew pan four tablespoonfuls of bread crumbs, a quarter of one of salt, half that of pepper, ten pepper corns, peel a small onion, cut in four, add a pint of milk, half an ounce of butter; boil for ten minutes, when it ought to turn out a thickish sauce.

Important Observation.—It will be seen that in the above sauces there is hardly any but the three first which may not be made with the produce of the cottage garden, or of those articles which are in daily use, and if these directions are followed, many a *bon vivant* in London would often envy the cooking of the cottage, as it would contain the freshness and aroma of fresh gathered vegetables.

426. *Hotel Keeper's Butter.*—This is very simple and good, and will keep potted for a long time. It is excellent with all broiled meats.

Put on a plate a quarter of a pound of fresh butter, a quarter of a spoonful of salt, a quarter ditto of pepper, two of chopped parsley, the juice of a middle sized lemon (if no lemon, use vinegar); a little grated nutmeg may be added.

427. *Anchovy Butter.*—To a quarter of a pound of butter, two tablespoonfuls of anchovy sauce.

ON SALADS.

WHAT is more refreshing than salads when your appetite seems to have deserted you, or even after a capacious dinner—the nice, fresh green, and crisp salad, full of life and health, which seems to invigorate the palate and dispose the masticating powers to a much longer duration. The herbaceous plants which exist fit for food for man, are more numerous than may be imagined, and when we reflect how many of these, for want of knowledge, are allowed to rot and decompose in the fields and gardens, we ought, without loss of time, to make ourselves acquainted with their different natures and forms, and vary our food as the season changes.

Although nature has provided all these different herbs and plants as food for man at various periods of the year, and perhaps at one period more abundant than another, when there are so many ready to assist in purifying and cleansing the blood, yet it would be advisable to grow some at other seasons, in order that the health may be properly nourished.

However, at what period of the year or at what time, these may be partaken of, the following dressing is the one I should always recommend.

In my description of salads, I have advised and described the use of them as plainly dressed, such as they are in many parts of Europe, but perhaps many of our readers will want to know how the sauce is made which is often used with the salad herbs, or such as the Italian count used to make some years since, by which he made a fortune in dressing salads for the tables of the aristocracy. It is as follows:—

PLAIN COSS SALAD.

428. *Coss Lettuce.*—Take two large lettuces, remove the faded leaves and the coarse green ones, then cut the green top off, pull each leaf off separate, cut it *lengthways,* and then in four or six pieces; proceed thus until finished. This is better without washing. Having cut it all up put it into a bowl; sprinkle over with your finger a small teaspoonful of salt, half one of pepper, three of oil, and two of English vinegar, or one of French; with the spoon and fork turn the salad lightly in the bowl till well mixed; the less it is handled the better; a teaspoonful of chopped chervil and one of tarragon is an immense improvement.

The above seasoning is enough for a quarter of a pound of lettuce.

429. *Cabbage Lettuce.*—Proceed the same as above, pull off the outer leaves and throw them away, take off the others one by one, and cut in two, put them in a pan with cold water, then drain them in a cloth, by shaking it to and fro violently with one hand, and extract all the water, put them into a bowl, and season and dress as above.

To vary them, two hard boiled eggs, cut in quarters, may be added; a little eschalot, a few chives, or young onions.

To improve the appearance of these salads, when on the table, before being used, the flower of the nasturtium may be intermixed with taste and care, with a little cut beetroot and slices of radish. These are refreshing to the sight on a table or sideboard at dinner; slices of cucumber may be also introduced.

430. *Endive.*—This ought to be nicely blanched and crisp, and is the most wholesome of all salads. Take two, cut away the root, remove the dark green leaves, and pick off all the rest, wash and drain well, dress as before; a few chives is an improvement.

431. *French Fashion.*—Put in one clove of garlic, or rub a piece of crust of bread slightly with it, or the salad-bowl, mix the salad in the bowl as before; if rubbed slightly on the bread mix it with it. If properly contrived, it gives a flavour, which no one can detect. Tarragon or chervil may be used in these salads.

432. *Marsh Mallow.*—The roots of these should be removed, as likewise the faded leaves; dress as for lettuce No. 428, eggs and beetroot may be introduced in this, being almost a winter salad.

Dandelion, or *dent-de-lion*, should not remain long in water, as they will get too bitter; dress them as endive.

Cow salad the same way.

Watercresses the same, with a little cucumber and celery.

433. *Mustard and Cress.*—These, if eaten alone, make an excellent salad; they should be quickly washed and used, dressed as lettuce. A little tarragon or chervil, or a few chives, may be used.

434. *Salad Sauce.*—Boil one egg hard, when cold remove the yolk, put it into a basin, bruise it to a pulp with a spoon,—do not use iron, prefer wood,—then add a raw yolk and a teaspoonful of

flour, a small teaspoonful of salt, a quarter of pepper, then add half a spoonful of vinegar; stir it round, pour over a tablespoonful of oil by degrees, keep stirring, then a little more vinegar, two more of oil, until eight teaspoonfuls of oil and three of vinegar are used; season with half a teaspoonful of chopped onions, two of parsley, half of tarragon and chervil, a pinch of cayenne and six teaspoonfuls of melted butter cold. The white of the egg may be chopped up and added. It will keep for some time if properly corked, and may be used in proportion with any of the above salads; but still I must say I prefer the simplicity and skill of the Italian count's in preference to this, although this is very palatable. A gill of whipped cream is good in it.

435. *Vegetable for Salads.*—Beetroot, onions, potatoes, celery, cucumbers, lentils, haricots, succory, or barbe-de-capucin, winter cress, burnet, tansey, marigold, peas, French beans, radish, cauliflower; all the above may be used judiciously in salad, if properly seasoned, according to the following directions:—

435A. *Haricot and Lentil Salad.*—To a pint of well-boiled haricots, add a teaspoonful of salt, quarter of pepper, one or chopped onions, two of vinegar, four of oil, two of chopped parsley, stir round, and it is ready; lentils are done the same. A little cold meat, cut in thin slices, may be added as a variety.

436. *Beetroot Salad with Onions.*—Boil four onions in the skin till tender, also a piece of beetroot; let both get cold; remove the skin, cut them in slices, put them in a plate, one slice on the edge of the other alternately; put into a small basin half a teaspoonful of salt, a quarter of pepper, one of good vinegar, three of oil, mix them well; pour over when ready to serve.

Celery, Young Onions, and Radishes may be used in salad with the above dressing, adding a teaspoonful of mustard.

Cucumbers.—Cut in thin slices on a plate, with salt, pepper oil, and vinegar in proportion to the above directions.

Green French Beans.—When cold put into a bowl, with som tarragon, chervil, and chopped chives, dressed as before.

Brussels Sprouts, the same way.

437. *Potatoes.*—If any remaining, cut them into thin slices, and season as before. A few haricots, or cold meat, or a chopped gherkin, may be added.

438. *Meat and Poultry.*—If there are any of the above left, and you require a relishing dish, and not having any fresh salad herbs, proceed as for the other salads, using a little chopped parsley, onions, or pickles. Some cucumber or celery may be used. The meat or poultry should be cut small.

439. *Fish Salad.*—A very nice and elegant dish may be made with all kinds of cold fish, and some kinds of shell-fish but the following way of dressing is for a small *Lobster Salad*, and will do for all fish salads: Have the bowl half filled with any kind of salad herb you like, either endive or lettuce, &c. Then break a lobster in two, open the tail, extract the meat in one piece, break the claws, cut the meat of both in small slices, about a quarter of an inch thick, arrange these tastefully on the salad, take out all the soft part from the belly, mix it in a bason with a teaspoonful of salt, half of pepper, four of vinegar, four of oil; stir it well together, and pour on the salad; then cover it with two hard eggs, cut in slices, a few slices of cucumber, and, to vary, a few capers and some fillets of anchovy; stir lightly, and serve, or use salad sauce, No. 434.

If for a dinner, ornament it with some flowers of the nasturtium and marigold.

440. *Crab Salad.*—The same as the lobster.

Remains of cold cod, fried soles, halibut, brill, turbot, sturgeon cut as lobster, plaice, &c., may be used in the same way.

MA CHÈRE ELOISE,—In the foregoing receipts you will perceive that I have used each salad herb separate, only mixing them with the condiments or with vegetable fruit. I have a strong objection to the almost diabolical mixture of four or five different sorts of salad in one bowl, and then chopping them as fine as possible; the freshness as well as the flavour of each is destroyed; they agree about as well together as would brandy and soda water mixed with gin and gingerbeer, for each salad herb has its own particular flavour, and the condiments, which are onions, chives, parsley, chervil, tarragon, celery, eschalot, garlic, cucumber, beetroot, &c. &c. are only to give it piquancy like the oil and vinegar, salt, and pepper.

Mustard and cress and water cresses may be considered as a slight condiment, but should be used accordingly. It is remarkable that though the inhabitants of this country were for so many centuries (from the nature of the climate) a salad-eating people, yet they seem the least to know how to season them. Until the introduction of the potato, in 1650, and which was first eaten as a sweetmeat, stewed in sack wine and sugar, the various salads were in common use on the tables in Britain, of which country most of the plants are indigenous.

RELISHES.

441. *Herring in Whisky.*—Well wash and clean a red herring, wipe it dry and place it in a pie-dish, having cut off the head, and split it in two up the back; put a gill or two of whisky over the herring, according to size, hold it on one side of the dish, so that it is covered with the spirit, set it alight, and when it goes out the fish is done.

442. *Devilled Bones.*—Take the bones of any remaining joint or poultry, which has still some meat on, which cut across slightly, and then make a mixture of mustard, salt, cayenne, and pepper, and one teaspoonful of mushroom ketchup to two of mustard; rub the bones well with this, and broil rather brownish.

MUSHROOMS, OR THE PEARL OF THE FIELDS.

I HERE send you, Eloise, a most sumptuous relish. There is one dish which the Devonshire cottager can procure and enjoy better than even the most wealthy person. It is the mushroom. After having plucked them, perhaps on the road home for his breakfast, broiled them over a nice bright fire, seasoned with a little pepper and salt, and a small bit of butter placed inside of them; the flavour is then pure and the aroma beautiful, but by accident I discovered a new and excellent way to cook them. Being in Devonshire, at the end of September, and walking across the fields before breakfast to a small farmhouse, I found three very fine mushrooms, which I thought would be a treat, but on arriving at the house I found it had no oven, a bad gridiron, and a smoky coal fire. Necessity, they say, is the mother of Invention, I immediately applied to our grand and universal mamma, how I should dress my precious mushrooms, when a gentle whisper came to my ear, and the following was the result.

443. I first cut two good slices of bread, half an inch thick, large enough to cover the bottom of a plate, toasted them, and spread some Devonshire cream over the toast. I removed all the earthy part from the mushroom, and laid them gently on the toast, head downwards, slightly sprinkled them with salt and pepper, and placed in each a little of the clotted cream; I then put a tumbler over each and placed them on a stand before the fire, and kept turning them so as to prevent the glass breaking, and in ten to fifteen minutes the glass

was filled with vapour, which is the essence of the mushroom; when it is taken up, do not remove the glass for a few minutes, by which time the vapour will have become condensed and gone into the bread, but when it is, the aroma is so powerful as to pervade the whole apartment.

The sight, when the glass is removed, is most inviting, its whiteness rivals the everlasting snows of Mont Blanc, and the taste is worthy of Lucullus. Vitellius would never have dined without it; Apicius would never have gone to Greece to seek for crawfish; and had he only half the fortune left when he committed suicide, he would have preferred to have left proud Rome and retire to some villa or cottage to enjoy such an enticing dish.

Therefore, modern gourmets, never fancy that you have tasted mushrooms until you have tried this simple and new discovery. Remember the month—the end of September or the beginning of October.

As Devonshire cream is not to be obtained everywhere, use butter, or boil some milk till reduced to cream, with a little salt, pepper, and one clove; when warm put in an ounce of butter, mixed with a little flour, stir round, put the mushroom on the toast with this sauce, cover with a basin, and place in the oven for half an hour. In this way all kinds of mushrooms will be excellent. They may be put into baking pans: cover with a tumbler as above, and bake in oven.

444. *Welsh Rabbit.*—Toast a round of bread from a quartern loaf; put about four ounces of cheese into a small saucepan or pipkin with a teaspoonful of mustard, a little pepper and salt, and a wineglass of ale; break the cheese small, set it on the fire, and stir until it is melted, when pour over the toast, and serve quickly.

2nd.—Toast a round of bread, and place on it two pieces of cheese, single Gloucester, a quarter of an inch thick; place it before the fire, and as the cheese melts, spread it over the bread with a knife, also a little cayenne and mustard.

3rd.—Take a penny French roll, cut off a thin slice from one end, and take out some of the crumb and place it in the oven. Melt the cheese as above, and pour it into the roll. It is very good for a journey, or a sportsman, and can be eaten cold.

4th, or Irish Rabbit.—Toast a round of bread; chop up four ounces of cheese, a small piece of butter, one gherkin, some mustard, pepper, and salt, until it is quite a paste; spread it over the toast, and place them in the oven for five minutes, and serve hot.

445.—*Mussels* may be eaten plain. Put a quart of them in a pan, after being well washed, with some onions cut in slices, also a little parsley; put them on a sharp fire for ten minutes, when they will all open; then remove the beard and black part, and eat them plain with some of their juice.

446. *Oysters on Toast.*—Open twelve very large oysters, put them in a pan with their liquor, a quarter of a teaspoonful of pepper, a wineglass of milk, two cloves, and a small piece of mace, if handy; boil a few minutes until set, mix one ounce of butter with half an ounce of flour, put it, in small pieces, in the pan, stir round; when near boiling pour over the toast, and serve. A little sugar and the juice of a lemon, is a great improvement.

447. *Oysters, plain scalloped.*—Butter and bread crumb the scallop shell, put in six oysters, season, and bread crumb, then six more, season again, and bread crumb; if a large shell, six more, with a little cayenne and butter, and some of their liquor; cover thick with bread crumbs, put in oven, or on gridiron, for thirty minutes; brown with salamander, or on a shovel, and serve.

These may also be done in patty pans.

Pieces of the liver of the cod, put into boiling water and set, may be added to any of the above escalops.

448. *Scallops.* — Lobsters, crabs, and crayfish must be first boiled, the flesh removed from the shell, and minced, adding a little chopped onion, pepper, salt, and butter, the scallop shell well greased, the flesh of the fish laid in, well bread crumbed, and put in the oven or on the gridiron for thirty minutes, and serve.

These require a little more pepper or cayenne than other fish, and a little Chili vinegar may be added. Two spoonfuls of melted butter mixed with the flesh of a lobster makes it very delicious.

449. *How to chop Onions.*—Few persons know how to chop onions properly. In the first place, all the dry skin must be removed, then a thin slice off the top and bottom, or they will be bitter, then cut them into thin slices, dividing the onion, and

cut crossways to form dice. If a very slight flavour is required, and the onion is strong, like in the north of England, for it must be remembered that the further north you go, the stronger the flavour of the root, and if French receipt books are exactly copied, it is no wonder that complaints are made of the preponderance of the flavour of the onion; in which case, when chopped, put them in the corner of a napkin or cloth, wash them in water, squeeze them dry, then put them back on the board, and chop finer; or sometimes only rubbing the pan or the meat with the onion is quite sufficient.

450. *Larding.*—The word larding has very often occurred in our receipts; it may be thought to belong to a style of cookery too good for the cottage. On the contrary, it is an economical process, and will make lean meat go much farther than without it.

Get what is called a larding needle, that is, a piece of steel from six to nine inches long, pointed at one end, and having four slits at the other, which will hold a small strip of bacon when put between them. They will perhaps cost tenpence. Cut the pieces of bacon two or three inches long and a quarter to half an inch square, put each one after the other in the pin, insert it in the meat, and leave only half an inch out; eight pieces to each pound.

451. *Bunch of Sweet Herbs.*—In many of the receipts is mentioned a bunch of sweet herbs, which consists, for some stews and soups, of a small bunch of parsley, two sprigs of thyme, and one bayleaf; if no parsley, four sprigs of winter savory, six of thyme, and one bayleaf.

452. *Bread Crumbs.*—Take a piece of the crumb of stale bread not too hard, bruise it with your hand, then pass it through a coarse sieve or cullender, or in cloth; use where required.

453. *Browning for Sauces.*—Put half a pound of brown sugar into an iron saucepan, and melt it over a moderate fire for about twenty-five minutes, stirring it continually, until quite black, but it must become so by degrees, or too sudden a heat will make it bitter, then add two quarts of water, and in ten minutes the sugar will be dissolved. Bottle for use.

453a. *Coloured Water.*—Put in a basin a pint of water and two teaspoonfuls of the above sugar browning; mix well; use where indicated, either for stews, gravies, or sauces.

454. *Pease Pudding.*—Put a pint of split peas into a cloth, leave room for their swelling, boil in a gallon of soft water; if good, they will take an hour, but leave them till tender; pass them through a sieve or cullender, then add a teaspoonful of salt, half of pepper, two ounces of butter, and two eggs, which, if scarce, can be omitted; beat up, tie again in cloth, boil for one hour, and serve with boiled pork. Or when plain boiled, and the peas are done, open the cloth, season, mix well, butter a basin, shape in, and serve.

455. *How to Boil Rice.*—Put one quart of water in a pot, boil it, wash half a pound of rice, and throw it into the boiling water; boil for ten minutes, or until each grain is rather soft, but separate; drain it in a colander, put it back in a pot which you have slightly greased with butter, let it swell slowly near the fire, or in the oven, until wanted. A little butter may be added; each grain will then swell up, and be well separated.

456. *Veal Stuffing.*—Chop half a pound of suet, put it in a basin with three quarters of a pound of bread crumbs, a teaspoonful of salt, a quarter of pepper, a little thyme, or lemon peel chopped, three whole eggs, mix well, and use where directed. A pound of bread crumbs and one more egg may be used: it will make it cut firmer.

457. *Liver Stuffing.*—To the above quantity of stuffing, chop fine four ounces of the liver of either calf, pig, sheep, or lamb, poultry, or game; mix well and use, adding a little more seasoning.

These stuffings are varied by the mixture of a little cooked ham, anchovies, olives, capers, pickles, or even red herring. In fact, a variety of ways, according to fancy, for any dish you please.

458. *Biscuit Balls.*—Put in a basin half a pound of suet, three teaspoonfuls of onions chopped fine, one of parsley, half of salt, quarter of pepper, ten tablespoonfuls of biscuit powder, two passover biscuits soaked in milk or water a few hours before using; two eggs to be added. These are excellent in any thick soups or ragouts, and stews of all sorts : make them in balls the size of a walnut, stew with meat, or boil gently twenty minutes, and use where liked.

459. *Cod Liver Stuffing.*—Half a pound of raw chopped liver, three quarters of a pound of bread crumb or biscuit powder, salt, pepper, and parsley; mix with two whole eggs. Use as stuffing for any kind of fish.

460. *Cod Liver Balls.*—One pound of liver chopped fine, put into a basin with a pound of fine bread crumbs, two tea-spoonfuls of chopped onions, two of parsley, two of salt, half one of pepper, a pinch of ground ginger, three eggs ; mix all well, make into balls, roll them in flour, use them with any kind of stewed fish ; they will take about thirty minutes to cook slowly.

461. *Toad-in-the-Hole Batter.*—Put into a pan six table-spoonfuls of flour, four eggs, one teaspoonful of salt, half of pepper; mix well with a pint of milk; mix very smooth, and use where directed. More milk may be used if liked.
A little nutmeg may be used in it. This is as good as pancake batter.

462. *A Common Batter.*—Put in a basin six good table-spoonfuls of flour, which dilute very slowly with one pint of milk, add one spoonful of salt, quarter that of pepper, beat an egg well in it, if used for a toad-in-the-hole. A little parsley, chopped onions, or a little spice, makes an agreeable change; it will also make nice puddings, if baked alone, or under a joint in a well-greased tin.

A Commoner Sort.—For toad-in-the-hole use water, if you have no milk or eggs handy ; a little suet, or fat chopped fine, is an improvement.

463. *How to Boil and Dress Macaroni.*—Put in an iron pot or stew-pan two quarts of water; let it boil; add two tea-spoonfuls of salt, one ounce of butter; then add one pound of macaroni, boil till tender ; let it be rather firm to the touch ; it is then ready for use, either for soup, pudding, or to be dressed with cheese. Drain it in a cullender; put it back in the pan,

add four ounces of cheese or more, a little butter, salt, and pepper; toss it well together and serve. It will be found light and nutritious, and well worthy the notice of vegetarians.

464. *How to Toast Bread.*—Procure a nice square loaf that has been baked one or two days previously, then with a sharp knife cut off the bottom crust evenly, and then as many slices as you require, about a quarter of an inch in thickness. Contrive to have a clear fire: place a slice of the bread upon a toasting-fork, about an inch from one of the sides, hold it a minute before the fire, then turn it, hold it another minute, by which time the bread will be thoroughly hot, then begin to move it gradually to and fro until the whole surface has assumed a yellowish-brown colour, then turn it again, toasting the other side in the same manner; lay it then upon a hot plate, have some fresh or salt butter, (which must not be too hard, as pressing it upon the toast would make it heavy,) spread a piece, rather less than an ounce, over, and cut the toast into four or six pieces; should you require six such slices for a numerous family, about a quarter of a pound of butter would suffice for the whole. You will then have toast made to perfection.

464A. *Jam of all kinds.*—Almost all small farmers and cottagers have generally some kind of fruit to spare at the end of the season, any of which can be made into jam. Thus, for strawberry jam, pick one pound of strawberries, put them in a pan with three quarters of a pound of white powdered sugar; put the whole on the fire, stir with a wooden spoon, and boil till rather thick; or try a little on a plate, if it sets. When cold, fill your preserve jars, cover over with strong white paper, and let them remain in a rather cold place.

Raspberries and green gooseberries will require a little more boiling, and more sugar. Cranberries, mulberries, cherries, and currants, can all be done the same way.

464B. *Currant Jelly.*—Put in a pan half a sieve of fresh gathered currants, with the talks; add to it a gill of water, put on the fire, and boil till every currant has opened; then pass the juice through a sieve or cullender, and to every quart put one pound of white sugar; boil fast and skim, and when the preserve begins to stick to the spoon, and is quite clear, fill your preserve pots, and cover over when cold; but, to be sure, try some on a plate before potting. If it sets well it is done; a few raspberries added is an improvement.

PICKLES.

465. *Red Cabbage.*—I perceive in most cottages the garden possesses a few of these exceedingly useful productions; at some seasons they grow larger than others, when they should be pickled thus:—Cut them into thin slices, remove the hard stalk, lay them on a slab, cover with salt for twelve hours, turning them now and then, clean off all the salt, and place them in stone jars; boil some vinegar, and to every quart add one ounce of black pepper, and seven button onions, or two large ones sliced, boil for five minutes, and pour over cabbage; cover the jar, and let it remain three weeks before using.

Onions may be omitted, and only cold vinegar used, but I do not approve of it, being hard and indigestible. A bunch of sweet herbs boiled in the vinegar is an improvement.

I send you no other receipts, as mixed pickles can now be bought cheaper than they can be made at home.

A FEW ORIGINAL HINTS ON COFFEE, TEA, &c.

466. *Simplified Mode of Making Coffee.*—Put one ounce of ground coffee in a pan, which place over the fire; keep stirring it until quite hot, but take care it does not burn; then pour over quickly a quart of boiling water, close it immediately, keep it not far from the fire, but not to simmer; then fill your cup without shaking it; or pass it through a cloth into a coffee pot, or it may be made some time previous, and warmed again. The grounds can be kept, and boiled for making the coffee of the next day, by which at least a quarter of an ounce is saved. In country places, where milk is good and cheap, I recommend that half boiled milk should be used with the coffee. The idea of warming coffee is my own, and the economy is full ten per cent.

The following is the result of some of my experiments with this system. But I must first tell you that my exertions in the fashionable quarter of St. Giles's gave great satisfaction to my septuagenarian pupil, whom I taught to cook the ox cheek, and she and several of her neighbours clubbed together to give a fashionable "*tea*," which of course my vanity made me immediately accept. Having but little confidence in what they would provide, I bought a quarter of a pound of ground coffee, intending giving them a lesson how to make coffee. On my arrival, I was received like a princess in a fairy land;

the little parlour was not only clean, but ornamented, at the cost of a few pence, with wall flowers from the neighbouring garden (the best in the world, Covent Garden), generously dispensing their perfume over pyramids of muffins and crumpets. Having cordially shaken hands with my host, I set cheerfully to work, and got hold of an old pitcher, but clean; in it I put the coffee, and placed it close before the fire, begging the old lady to keep turning it round, and stirring it till the powder was hot. I then poured three quarts of boiling water, allowed it to stand for ten minutes, and then poured it out into the cups, with the best milk that could be got, and sugar. The coffee being partaken of, I put into each cup a good teaspoonful of canister cocoa, with half a teaspoonful or sugar, holding the kettle in one hand and a spoon in the other. I poured on the water, and kept stirring all the time, adding a little milk. In the meantime I had put one ounce of tea into a large teapot, which I had placed by the side of the fire, in order that the leaves should get hot, so that when the water was poured on them, that they should immediately give forth their aroma. By the time the cocoa had been partaken of, the tea was ready, and it was declared by all the old dames present that they never had had such a cup of tea, although they bought it at the same shop, and paid the same price; and they could not account for such " legerdemain," but would endeavour to imitate it. I was greatly thanked on my departure; and received the compliment of an old shoe being thrown after me; not a French dancing shoe, but a genuine British bit of solid work, the sole having a very uneven appearance, being studded with several dozen of iron nails.

Thus terminated the entertainment given to me by these poor but grateful people of the black back street of St. Giles's.

I made the cocoa thus, not having sufficient utensils; but I have found it an economical plan to make the ground cocoa hot, adding a little water, and mixing it smooth with either cold milk or water, it gives it a richness which is not got by the usual system. Place it on the fire, keep stirring, and when just on the point of boiling, serve. Chocolate can be made the same way, only stirring it more, with a spoon, if you have no chocolate pot.

In the way of coffee, in my opinion, nothing can be more pure than what I bought the other day from the canister, when walking by chance in the Borough, at the shop of Messrs. White and Fairchild; and I must, while on this subject, be allowed to state that, in my opinion, a good cup of coffee cannot be made without the introduction of a little chicory, although I am aware that some dealers imposed on the public by selling an article composed of chicory at a coffee price. I cannot but admire Messrs. White's plan, which is on no account to sell any ground coffee mixed with chicory, but to sell it to their customers the one separate from the other. They then

M

recommended to me some canister coffee, patented and prepared only
by them.   On opening the canister the aroma was very refreshing.
On asking how it was roasted (rather a bold question on my part,
I admit), he very civilly asked me to follow him to the back of the
premises, where some very extensive rooms are fitted up for the purpose
of roasting; he then put some coffee-berries into a cylinder six feet
in length and twenty inches in circumference; then put them in a
furnace which roasted the berries in a most scientific manner, being
turned during the while by the aid of steam power.   When sufficiently roasted, the coffee was, while hot, put in a steam mill and
ground, being forced from the mill into the canisters and sealed
up as soon as possible, and put into stock.   I beg to forward you one of
the four quarter of a pound packets I bought.   On testing it I
found that an ounce made one quart of excellent coffee.

BEVERAGES.

As far as the food of man goes, I believe, dearest, that our duty is
almost at an end; but here is one important item which supports
the vitality of man as much as food does, I mean beverages; in fact,
one is inseparable from the other : to drink without eating, or to eat
without drinking, would soon send us to an early grave.   True, if too
much is taken of one or the other, it upsets the digestive organs, and
materially affects the functions of that most important part of the
human frame, the stomach, which, acting in accordance with the
wonderful works of nature, refuses any food or drink that does not
accord with its functions.   True, bad food and beverages of all kinds
are sometimes forced on it ; but then, if it does not disturb its functions
immediately, it acts on it gradually, and in course of time entirely
destroys its coating or toilette.   Is it not, then, important, that great
care should be taken in what we eat or drink ?   The best of food is often
spoilt by drinking bad beverages.   Amongst the higher orders of
society, the pride of an " *epicure*" is to select the best of wines, which
he considers one of his greatest treasures, scientifically classing them
to the various courses of his dinner.
You probably will again remark, that I am deviating from the
purport of our present little work, by alluding to the higher class of
living in its pages, while in reality it is intended for the million, and
not for the wealthy few.   My excuse is, that if a rich gourmet take
so much care in selecting his beverages, why should not a poor housewife be as particular in choosing her more humble drinks ?   Is it not
more desirable for the artizan, who cannot afford to drink much beer,
to have with his meal a sound clear glass of pure water, full of health
and life, than to have a muddy one ?   For I have actually seen people
drink the drainings as they drip from the roof of a house—the simple

idea of letting it rest for a minute never entering their heads; or better still, to clarify it by passing it through a clean cloth, or giving it a boil, and letting it get cold before drinking, for any doubtful water will improve and get soft by boiling.

For those in middling circumstances, who can afford their malt liquor at their meals, pale ale, or light table-beer, or ale, is preferable to any heavy stout, as they facilitate digestion.

Since my return from France, there is nothing I miss so much as that light and cooling drink called by our allies " *Vin ordinaire*," though I was in hopes that after the great exertions made by several members of parliament, a reduction of the duty on these simple but generous wines would take place, though probably they would not be partaken of to any great extent by the masses, who would not understand their properties, although there is not one Englishman out of twenty who visits France, but who in time takes a liking to these really harmless wines.

I do not want to deprive you of your sherry or port before or after dinner; however, recollect that nothing assists digestion and refreshes the palate more than a good glass of light wine; and therefore it would be a great boon to the public if they could be imported free of duty.

To our friend Dr. King I am much indebted, after having had a conversation on the above subject, for his sending to me the other day a case of pure French wine, having, as he stated in his letter, been present while it was drawn from the rough French cask. I was more astonished when he informed me that its price was only twenty-eight shillings per dozen, and was purchased from the famous house of Campbell, of Regent Street, London. It appears that this gentleman pays an annual visit to the different vintages and villages which encompass the banks of the *Garonne*, and purchases largely from the peasantry, remaining there all the brewing season, and personally superintending its make. The principal wines are called " La Rose," " St. Julien," " Vin de Grave," " Sauterne," " Barsac," and numerous other kinds, all of which are highly recommended by the faculty. Light Amontillado, Rhenish wine, and Bucellas, are also commendable at meal-times.

For those who cannot afford to buy malt liquors or wines, I have been led to try the following receipts, which will be found extremely useful for people in small circumstances.

A SERIES OF NEW AND CHEAP DRINKS.

467. Put a gallon of water on to boil, cut up one pound of apples, each one into quarters, put them in the water, and boil them until they can be pulped, pass the liquor through a cullender, boil it up again with half a pound of brown sugar, scum, and bottle for use, taking care not to cork the bottle, and keep it in a cool place: the apples may be eaten with sugar.

Another way.—Bake the apples first, then put them in a gallon pan, add the sugar, and pour boiling water over, let it get cold, pass the liquor as above, and bottle.

468. *Apple Toast and Water.*—A piece of bread, slowly toasted till it gets quite black, and added to the above, makes a very nice and refreshing drink for invalids.

469. *Apple Barley Water.*—A quarter of a pound of pearl barley instead of toast added to the above, and boil for one hour, is also a very nice drink.

470. *Apple Rice Water.*—Half a pound of rice, boiled in the above until in pulp, passed through a cullender, and drunk when cold.

All kinds of fruits may be done the same way.

Figs and French plums are excellent; also raisins.

A little ginger, if approved of, may be used.

471. *For Spring Drink.*—Rhubarb, in the same quantities, and done in the same way as apples, adding more sugar, is very cooling.

Also green gooseberries.

471A. *Lemonade.*—Cut in very thin slices three lemons, put them in a basin, add half a pound of sugar, either white or brown; bruise altogether, add a gallon of water, and stir well. It is then ready.

472. *For Summer Drink.*—One pound of red currants, bruised with some raspberry, half a pound of sugar added to a gallon of cold water, well stirred, allowed to settle, and bottled.

473. *Mulberry.*—The same, adding a little lemon-peel.

A little cream of tartar or citric acid added to these renders them more cooling in summer and spring.

ON MARKETING.

MY DEAR FRIEND,—In most cookery books, which are supposed to be written for the middle classes of society, we find at the beginning, and in large type, directions how to market and choose the best joints of meat, poultry, fish, but rarely vegetables, how all the best qualities of each should be known, but nothing is said about the second and third qualities, which two-thirds of the people of England consume; also directions for judging of the finest haunch of mutton, or sirloin of beef, but never of the neck or scrag of mutton, or the skirt of beef, or sheep's head, liver, &c.

If the directions of those works were strictly followed, one-third of the people would be starving, and a population of dogs (as in Turkey) would have to be kept to eat up the supposed offal. At the present moment our soldiers, as well as those of our allies, the French, are feeding excellently off that which is thrown away by the Turks, the head, feet, &c. &c., of the animal, which is by them declared unclean. Such ought never to be the case in a Christian country, for we may be quite certain that, unless the animal is diseased, all those parts which can be digested is good food for man; but, there may be some who, from over-indulgence in luxuries, have so brought the stomach into that state, that there are but certain parts of the animal of which they can partake; these persons must, of course, pay higher prices for that kind of meat, and leave the other parts cheaper for those having healthy and good digestions to feed on. It is, therefore, our duty here to teach the labourer's and cottager's wife how to buy it cheap, sweet, wholesome, and nutritious.

Mutton.—The first quality of mutton ought to be between four or five years old; but at present it is rarely got above three, and often under two years. The flesh ought to be a darkish, clear, red colour, the fat firm and white, the meat short and tender when pinched, and ought not to be too fat.

Second quality.—The fat is rather spongy, the lean close and rough grained, and a deep red, and the fat adheres firmly to the meat.

Third quality.—This is, perhaps, a sheep which has had some disease and recovered; the liver would always show this, but as butchers generally remove it, and do not let it be seen, you cannot judge from it. The flesh will be paler, the fat a faint white, and the flesh loose from the bone; if very bad and diseased the fat will be yellow, and the lean flabby and moist. To ascertain if it is fresh proceed as for pork.

Lamb should be four or five months old, and ought to weigh from thirty to forty pounds; the fat ought to be white and light in appearance, the flesh a faintish white, smooth, and firm to the touch.

The second quality is not so well covered with fat, the flesh rather red, the meat softer, and every joint presents a coarser appearance.

The third quality is flabby, lean, and red, the fat rather yellow, and will keep sweet but a short time.

To ascertain if fresh, place the finger between the loin and kidney, and, if moist, or tainted, will be easily ascertained by the smell.

Beef.—Most towns and counties in the United Kingdom differ in the kind of cattle brought to market. It is not our duty here to mention the breed which we think the best, and on which so many different opinions exist; but the quality of meat depends upon the feeding. The best quality of beef will have an open grain, bright red colour, the fat white, and the bark smooth. Some of the best qualities will have the fat yellow, from being fed on oil-cake; and, unless it has afterwards been fed on turnips, will be wasteful in cooking, although the meat may be tender and rich.

The second quality will be close-grained and rather flabby, paler in colour, and the fat a dead white and the bark rough.

The third quality, the grain is very close, no streaks of fat between the grain, and of deep brickdust red, tough under the finger, the fat hard and skinny. To ascertain the age, look at the bone or horn which runs through the ribs of beef; if a fine four-year old heifer, this horn or bone will be soft or tender, and becomes harder the older the ox. But the best plan to judge of the flavour of the meat before you do it by eating it, is to look at the tongue of the bullock, and if it is plump and has a clean bright appearance, with the fat at the end of a pinkish white, then the meat will turn out good; but if the tongue should look dark, the fat a dead white, then that meat will eat hard and flavourless. The same holds good with sheep.

Veal.—There is more difficulty in the choice of veal than any other meat, although the general opinion is, it is the easiest. I often hear how white it is, how plump it looks: these are often produced artificially.

The preference is usually given to the cow calf, from its being whiter and having the udder; but if a bull calf has been properly fed, and killed at about ten weeks old, nothing can be finer in flavour or closer in grain when cooked, and will be much more juicy than the cow calf. The grain should be close, firm, and white, the fat a pinkish white, not a dead white, and the kidneys well covered with thick white fat; that is the first class veal. The second quality is darker in flesh, may be slaughtered in the country, and equally as nourishing as the first; the third quality will have less fat round the kidney, be coarser grained, and the lean red. It is often more nourishing than the very white veal, but not so delicate or digestible. It is caused by the calf being reared in the open air.

If the suet under the kidney is soft and clammy the meat is not fresh.

The neck is the first joint that becomes tainted. Calves' liver should be firm, and free from gristle or spots; the heart should be surrounded with fat.

When veal has to be kept, it should always be hung up, and never allowed to lay on anything, or it soon becomes tainted.

Pork.—The quality of this entirely depends on the feeding. A friend of mine made various experiments, and more particularly on the same litter of pigs, and the various sizes and different flavour of the meat was extraordinary. There is one thing very certain, that whatever a pig is fed upon, it will be much better in size and quality if kept clean and well washed at least once a week. Those breeds that produce a fine close-grained meat, not too much fat, and that firm, solid, and pinkish white, are the best; if the tongue is clean and full, the animal is well fed and healthy.

The second quality of pork may be very good, but the flesh will be hard and red, and the fat a yellow white.

The third quality, the meat will be coarse-grained, the fat soft, and the tongue and kidneys discoloured. Measly pork may be known by the little kernels in the fat: it is not allowed to be sold by the butchers, and yet, in many large towns in England, it is openly exposed for sale.

If the flesh is clammy and moist, it is not fresh. The best plan to tell the freshness of this, or any meat, is to take with you, in hot weather, to market two wooden skewers, and insert them in the flesh near the bone, and remove them, and the nose will detect it immediately; this is much better than touching the meat. These skewers should be scraped after being used.

Sucking Pigs.—The skin should be clear and fresh, the tongue clean, the flesh of a pinkish hue, and not too large in size.

Poultry.—The means of telling the various qualities of poultry are well known: the age is known by the spur, and the quality by the skin. There is, perhaps, no poultry in the world that comes up to the well-fed Dorking capon. The new breed of Cochin China fowls, of which the best for eating is the grey kind, if fed and treated in the same way as the Dorking capons, might produce a larger fowl, but it is questionable if so tender.

White legged fowls are generally preferred, but there are black ones equally as good. In country places, where chickens are sometimes required to be killed in the morning for that day's dinner, it is best to give each, shortly before killing it, a teaspoonful of vinegar, which will cause them to eat tender. This can be done with all kinds of poultry.

Geese the same.

Ducks should have the feet supple, the breast full and hard, and a clear skin.

Turkeys should have fine, full, and firm legs, skin white, breast full, neck long.

Game may be detected by removing the feathers off the under part of the leg, and if the skin is not discoloured, they are fresh. The age may be known by placing the thumb into the beak, and holding the bird up with the jaw part of the beak: if it breaks, it is young; if not, it is old, and requires keeping longer before cooking to be eatable.

KITCHEN REQUISITES.

As a workman cannot work properly without the requisite tools, or the painter produce the proper shade without the necessary colours, in like manner does every person wishing to economize his food, and to cook it properly, require the proper furniture wherewith to do it. It is to be hoped that these pages, which have cost me both time and trouble, as well as months of travelling, will be read by many above the class to whom it is more especially dedicated; and that hereafter kitchen utensils may be considered proper to give as a wedding present to a couple commencing housekeeping. Nothing, I am certain, could be given that would be a better promoter of peace and happiness in their home.

In a superior cottage, which, should it consist of four rooms, the kitchen should be the back one, and not, as is often the case, the front one, made into a kitchen and sitting-room, and the back one a washhouse and receptacle for dirt, &c. Whilst I am on this subject, I would remark that, in my opinion, all cottages or houses require, in this climate, a porch, or second door; it would prevent the continued draught and blowing in of the rain and dust, and thus avoid a great deal of illness amongst the inmates, and add greatly to the cleanliness and comfort of the dwelling; but if built upon H.R.H. Prince Albert's plan, they do not require it.

The back room should be fitted up with a proper grate, with oven and boiler, and a copper holding at least six gallons. It should have the requisite shelves, and a little sink to hold a tub, and with a tap or pump for water; the latter article I consider the most essential requisite of a cottager's dwelling: it should possess two gridirons, one single, one double, a large and small frying-pan, three black saucepans, holding one gallon, half gallon, one quart, or a three-legged black pot, instead of the gallon one, a large iron spoon, a ladle, two wooden spoons, a wooden bowl, a cullender, a chopper, a large knife, a baking pan, a rolling pin, a paste brush, a stove brush, two tin tart dishes, three brown basins, six bread tins or pans.

A more humble abode, possessing two rooms, or perhaps only one, which latter I disapprove of very much, as there ought to be two in every dwelling, however small, will perhaps not be able to afford so many articles of furniture; in which case I would recommend, as being the most serviceable, the black pot, gridiron, frying-pan, earthen pan, or bowl, or spoon, ladle, cullender, chopper, three basins, two tin tart dishes, baking pan, with oven: with these most of the receipts in these pages may be cooked to perfection.

And with the pan, gridiron, and frying-pan, nearly one half of the receipts may be do   For baking stewing-pan, see Appendix.

ON THE SELECTION OF VEGETABLES

As regards vegetation in general, the eye can soon detect the glowing freshness, which nature deposits upon such delicate articles of food as peas, asparagus, cucumbers, beans, spinach, salads of all kinds; any of the above will not keep fresh after being cut, longer than twenty-four hours, during the summer, and twice that time in winter. All vegetables should be kept in as cool a place as possible; still, when the bloom disappears, it is time to make your bargain, as they then can be had cheaper: do not, however, buy any vegetable on any part of which decomposition has commenced to any extent, as if eaten in this state it will be found injurious to health.

Vegetables such as cabbage, cauliflower, common greens, carrots, turnip-tops, leeks, celery, artichokes, both globe and Jerusalem, will keep much longer.

Another way to ascertain if vegetables are old gathered, is to break a piece off any one with the hand; if it snaps crisply it is fresh; if, on the contrary, it has a flabby appearance, and is of a softish consistency, it is stale, and should be bought accordingly.

SOYER'S AERIAL COOKING STOVE.

My dearest Friend,—Wonders will never cease; and ballooning, I am happy to say, has at last proved itself of some use to humanity, for, no doubt, this ingenious apparatus, which I have now in contemplation before me, must have sprung out of those atmospheric castles so unsafely built in the air; but the superiority of this little aerial pigmy is so much above that of his brother monster balloon, that you can have as many ascents in the course of a day as you choose, even with a parachute, without the slightest danger of getting upset; it is capable also of successfully braving the strongest current of air; and, contrary to all aeronautical notions, its descent is even more agreeable than its ascent, for it actually refreshes and elevates the spirit of the spectators, instead of causing them fear, whilst descending to *terra firma.*

In this unassuming utensil, Eloise, the wealthy epicure and great amateurs of cookery will be able to dress a most *recherché* dinner before the dining or drawing-room fire, without soiling his apartment, apparatus, or even his fingers; the cottager will be able, before his humble fire, to transmogrify his coarse food to a nice stew, roast, or baked pie to perfection.

In every cottage bread will be lighter, and contain more nutriment, than when baked in a large oven, in which considerable evaporation always takes place.

This little oven has not the slightest resemblance to our magic stove, which was made for the wealthy only, and which is now largely fraternizing with our troops and allies, in the war camps in the east.

This little apparatus will be dedicated to all classes, but more particularly to the masses, as I think, from the model which I now have before me, it can be made for a few shillings.

I have already tried many receipts in it, all of which have more than answered my expectations, copies of them will be printed and sold with the apparatus. I have made good soup, and dressed fish and meat of all kinds, as well as vegetables, having also roasted and baked meat, and made sweet and savoury pastry in it.

In fact, I may say, that in reality it is almost a complete kitchen in a very small compass, a real *petit bijoux de famille,* not quite so large as our extensive friend Signor Lablache's favourite hat.

A PLUM PUDDING FOR THE MILLION, OR A LUXURY FOR THE ARTISAN.

Here is a cheap pudding, adapted not for the millionaire but for the million. No eggs are required, and it costs only sixteen pence to make a good-sized one, enough to supply from ten to twelve people :—

Receipt.—Put in a basin a pound of flour, half a pound of stoned raisins, ditto of currants, ditto of chopped suet, two tablespoonsful of treacle, and half a pint of water. Mix all well, put in a cloth or mould, and boil from four and a half to five hours.

Sauce—Melted butter, sugar, and juice of lemon, if handy.

A tablespoonful will well sweeten half a pint. A little spice, or a few drops of any essence, or lemon, or peel chopped; a little brandy, rum, &c. &c., will be an improvement.

CAMP RECEIPTS FOR THE ARMY IN THE EAST.

(*From the Times of the 22nd January,* 1855.)

No. 1. *Camp Soup.*—Put half-a-pound of salt pork in a saucepan, two ounces of rice, two pints and a-half of cold water, and, when boiling, let simmer another hour, stirring once or twice; break in six ounces of biscuit, let soak ten minutes; it is then ready, adding one teaspoonful of sugar, and a quarter one of pepper, if handy.

No. 2. *Beef Soup.*—Proceed as above, boil an hour longer, adding pint more water.

If any flour is handy, make some dumplings thus:—Mix half-a-pound of flour with enough water to form a thick dough, divide it into pieces each the size of a small apple, roll them in flour, flatten with your hands; half an hour will cook them; serve round with the beef. For this receipt half the quantity of biscuit may be used. Soup separate.

Note.—Those who can obtain any of the following vegetables will find them a great improvement to the above soups:—Add four ounces of either onions, carrots, celery, turnips, leeks, greens, cabbage, or potatoes, previously well washed or peeled, or any of these mixed to make up four ounces, putting them in the pot with the meat.

I have used the green tops of leeks and the leaf of celery as well as the stem, and found that for stewing they are preferable to the white part for flavour. The meat being generally salted with rock salt, it ought to be well scraped and washed, or even soaked in water a few hours if convenient; but if the last cannot be done, and the meat is therefore too salt, which would spoil the broth, parboil it for twenty minutes in water, before using for soup, taking care to throw this water away.

No. 3.—For fresh beef proceed, as far as the cooking goes, as for salt beef, adding a teaspoonful of salt to the water.

No. 4. Pea Soup.—Put in your pot half-a-pound of salt pork, half a pint of peas, three pints of water, one teaspoonful of sugar, half one of pepper, four ounces of vegetables, cut in slices, if to be had; boil gently two hours, or until the peas are tender, as some require boiling longer than others, and serve.

No. 5. Stewed Fresh Beef and Rice.—Put an ounce of fat in a pot, cut half-a-pound of meat in large dice, add a teaspoonful of salt, half one of sugar, an onion sliced; put on the fire to stew for fifteen minutes, stirring occasionally, then add two ounces of rice, a pint of water; stew gently till done, and serve. Any savoury herb will improve the flavour. Fresh pork, veal, or mutton, may be done the same way, and half-a-pound of potatoes used instead of the rice, and, as rations are served out for three days, the whole of the provisions may be cooked at once, as it will keep for some days this time of the year, and is easily warmed up again.

Receipts for the Fryingpan.—Those who are fortunate enough to possess a fryingpan will find the following receipts very useful:— Cut in small dice half-a-pound of solid meat, keeping the bones for soup; put your pan, which should be quite clean, on the fire; when hot through, add an ounce of fat, melt it and put in the meat, season with half a teaspoonful of salt; fry for ten minutes, stirring now and then; add a teaspoonful of flour, mix all well, put in half-a pint of water, let simmer for fifteen minutes, pour over a biscuit previously soaked, and serve.

The addition of a little pepper and sugar, if handy, is an improvement, as is also a pinch of cayenne, curry powder, or spice; sauces and pickles used in small quantities would be very relishing, and, as these are articles which will keep for any length of time, they would be the kind of thing to be sent as presents to the camp. As fresh meat is not easily obtained, any of the cold salt meat may be dressed as above, omitting the salt, and only requires warming a short time; or, for a change, boil the meat plainly, or with greens, or cabbage, or dumplings, as for beef; then the next day cut what is left in small dice—say four ounces—put in a pan an ounce of fat; when very hot, pour in the following:—Mix in a basin a tablespoonful of flour, moisten with water to form the consistency of thick melted butter, then pour it in the pan, letting it remain for one or two minutes, or until set; put in the meat, shake the pan to loosen it, turn it over, let it remain a few minutes longer, and serve.

To cook bacon, chops, steaks, slices of any kind of meat, salt or fresh sausages, black puddings, &c.—Make the pan very hot, having wiped it clean, add in fat, dripping, butter, or oil, about an ounce of either; put in the meat, turn three or four times, and season with salt and pepper. A few minutes will do it. If the meat is salt, it must be well soaked previously.

Good Pickling for Beef and Pork.—Put in a pan or tub five pounds of salt, three ounces of saltpetre, half a pound of brown sugar for a joint weighing from ten to twelve pounds, rub it well with the above mixture three or four times, letting it remain in pickle for a week; it is then ready for cooking: half an ounce of peppercorns, or a few aromatic herbs, will vary the flavour.

Round of beef, edgebone, breast, flanks, or ox tongues, are the pieces generally salted; small legs, shoulders, and belly of pork, pig's cheek and feet the same. Time your pickling according to size. For plain pickling, omit the sugar and saltpetre.

NEW WAY OF MAKING BEEF TEA.

Cut a pound of solid beef into small dice, which put into a stew-pan with two small pots of butter, a clove, a small onion sliced, and two saltspoonsful of salt; stir the meat round over the fire for ten minutes, until it produces a thickish gravy, then add a quart of boiling water, and let it simmer at the corner of the fire for half an hour, skimming off every particle of fat; when done pass through a sieve. I have always had a great objection to passing broth through a cloth, as it frequently spoils its flavour.

The same, if wanted plain, is done by merely omitting the vegetables and clove: the butter cannot be objectionable, as it is taken out in skimming; pearl-barley, vermicelli, rice, &c., may be served in it if required. A little leek, celery, or parsley may be added.

APPENDIX.

ON CARVING JOINTS.

DEAR ELOISE,—I insert the following lesson on that culinary accomplishment, carving, knowing what an important item it is in the art and mystery of cookery, and yet, how few there are who understand that apparently simple art.

First, you must truss your joint with taste, and take away any unsightly bone to give it a good shape, more especially the neck, loin, or breast of either veal, mutton, pork, or lamb.

For a shilling or so you can purchase a small saw, and instead of letting the butcher divide the bone of a loin of mutton carelessly, saw the bone through at about a distance of half an inch from each other. Ribs of lamb, and breasts of mutton and veal the same. These being most difficult joints to carve, should be sawn carefully.

Roast ribs of beef, and sirloin, ought to be cut thinnish, following, as near as possible, the grain of the meat, which you can soon learn to do by paying a little attention. A little fat and gravy should be served on each plate.

Salt beef ought to be cut thinner still. If out of a round or a silver side, cut it even. Cold meat requires to be cut thinner than hot.

Roast fillet of veal, cut as round of beef, helping thin slices of bacon or salt boiled pork; a little stuffing and gravy to be added.

Mutton requires to be cut rather thicker than beef or veal; pork the same.

My way of carving a leg of mutton is by putting one prong of the fork in the knuckle-bone, holding it in the left hand, then I cut five or six slices in a slanting manner, towards me, dividing the first two or three cuts equally amongst all the plates. By this method you keep the meat full of gravy, each slice retaining its portion and it is far better, in an economical point of view, than cutting the joint across the centre, as by this means all the gravy runs out, especially if the meat is over done.

Haunch of mutton I carve the same, giving a slice of the loin and one of the leg to each guest.

Saddle of mutton should never be cut across the loin if you study economy. Pass the point of the knife between the back-bone and the meat, then begin at the top and cut as thin chops in a slanting position, each slice about half an inch thick, which will give you a fair proportion of fat and lean. By this method, you can cut enough for ten to twelve persons, whereas by the other way you only get enough for four or five.

For leg of lamb or pork proceed as for mutton, and for loin, ribs, breast, or neck of either, proceed as above, having previously divided it with a saw, which greatly facilitates the carving of these joints.

SOYER'S BAKING STEWING PAN.

DEAR ELOISE,—Since I sent you the receipt for my new pan, I perceive that very little fat is required with any meat done in it.

In the event of stewing fat meat or tripe (which is sometimes unavoidable), I first, before sending it to the table, remove the fat which rises to the top with a spoon.

I must say that the more I use the pan the better I like it. I have had it registered and they are now being manufactured in large quantities by Messrs. Deane and Dray, King William-street, City, and will doubtless be before the public in a few weeks. For description, see page 69.

SEMI-ROASTING IN THE BAKING STEWING PAN.

This cut represents a tin pan in which a pudding is placed, and on the trivet a joint of beef, previously boned; it is suspended from the inside. Potatoes may be baked round the meat, without interfering with the pudding. The pans will consist of three different sizes; namely, one to hold two quarts, one four, and the other six. Lean meat is preferable to fat for semi-roasting in the baking stewing pan.

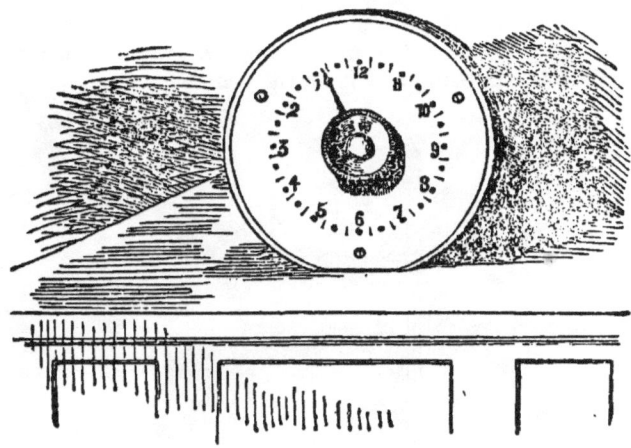

ALARUM, OR COOKING CLOCK.

By the aid of this little alarum the housewife will be able to time her joints, pies, and puddings, to an instant.

By winding it up and setting the hand back, starting from twelve, to the time required for the article to cook. Say it is one, and your joint is to be done at three,—move the hand to ten, wind up the spring, and place the box on the table, giving at the time an impulsion to the pendulum.

N.B. The fire must be of a proper heat, or your joint will be either under or over-done. They are to be purchased at No. 46, King William Street, City.

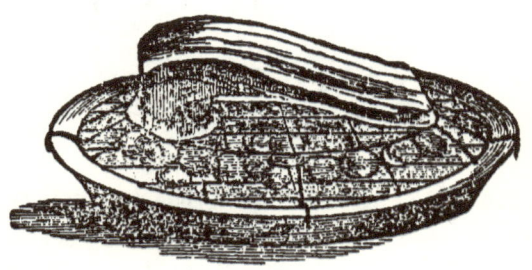

SOYER'S IMPROVED BAKING DISH.

The above is a sketch of my improved Baking-dish, which I have before described at page 94.

If the oven is rather slack, the pudding baked in it will require turning; therefore, when well set, remove the grating containing the meat and potatoes, cut your pudding in four pieces, turn each piece, replace the grating, and bake till done.

VEGETABLE DRAINER.

The above is a sketch of a saucepan, fitted with a perforated pan and a vegetable drainer.

This group, though extremely simple, is perhaps one of the most economical cooking utensils ever put before the public, and ought to have a place in every kitchen.

It possesses two great qualities, inasmuch as it saves time, and supersedes the tedious method of fishing the greens or cabbage out of the saucepan; and prevents the now every-day evil of emptying with the water in which the vegetables have been boiled, a quantity of the material, which by accident might be left in the pot—thereby clogging up the drain, to the annoyance of the household. To be had of Messrs. Deane & Dray, King William Street, City.

DIRECTIONS FOR USE.

Fit the perforated pan inside the saucepan, half fill it with water, add two teaspoonfuls of salt, and when the water boils put in your greens, or whatever else you may cook. Let it boil fast until tender, then lift out the perforator by the handles, and with the crusher press lightly the water out, and serve.

To boil pork, bacon, or salt beef, with greens :—When any of these are half done, put in your greens, using only half the quantity of salt; when ready, dish up the meat, press the broth out, which save for soup for the next day's use. (See Soups.)

This represents a model of a Chimney Screw-jack for suspending joints to. Its cost is very trifling, and may be purchased at any ironmonger's. It will fit on any mantel-shelf; and it enables the joint to be shifted nearer or further from the fire, as occasion requires.

I have ordered a small tin-screen which folds in three, and will occupy only a small space before the fire, which will greatly increase the heat when in use. I cannot give a cut of it in the present edition, as I have not yet received the drawing.

SOYER'S KITCHEN FOR THE ARMY.

DURING the period of the famine in Ireland, I took with me a portable kitchen, and erected it opposite the Royal Barracks in Dublin, and with which I cooked and delivered rations for 26,600 persons daily.

Having last year taken a peep at the camp at Chobham, as well as the camp at Satory in France, and seeing, by the ordinary manner in which the provisions for the different messes were cooked, even in France, that a large amount of nutriment of the food was lost, it occurred to me that, if a moveable kitchen could be made to travel with the army, it would be exceedingly useful, whilst on the march, or when encamped.

The following is an explanation of the above kitchen:

The carriage is made of sheet-iron, weighing, with water, fuel, &c., a little more than one ton. The lower part consists of a circular steam boiler, and the upper part of an oven. Over the oven are placed the various pans containing the rations required to be cooked by steam, and on each side is a hanging shelf, which will also hold steam saucepans in front, and round the driver's seat is a reservoir for water, and a place to hold the condiments, &c.

The plan of working it would be to draw it near to a stream or reservoir of water—if brackish or muddy it does not matter*—there fill the boiler and reservoir, and remove it to any convenient spot. The fuel may consist of wood, coal, turf, &c. &c. Within one hour after the fire is lighted the steam would be up, and the oven hot, and with one six feet long and three feet wide, rations for 1000 men could be cooked by baking and steaming in about two hours, and the apparatus moved on again, or it would cook whilst on the march, if on an even road.

Its advantages are, saving of time, labour, men, and food, and the certainty that the men could get their food properly cooked.

The cost of each apparatus would not exceed 100l.

---

* Any tainted water is made good by first converting it into steam.

OMISSION.

I PERCEIVE, my dear Eloise, that the various receipts for dressing sprats in a plain way, are minus in the previous editions, as far as the 60th thousand of our very successful Uncle Tom's Kitchen, as our publisher, Mr. Routledge, calls it,—nearly sixty thousand books having been sold in less than six weeks. Let us, therefore, be grateful to the public, and give them the omitted receipts, which I assure you I had in my original manuscript, but which I have in vain endeavoured to fish out of the book. Being food, and good food for the million, when properly dressed, it is most important that these simple receipts should be immediately introduced in this, the 70th thousand, and more especially as those silvery stars of the ocean are daily expected to pay their annual visit to "terra firma," and that on the next Lord Mayor's Day everybody probably will be in a good "moon" to partake of them. And most heartily do I join the opinion of the numerous friends of the late celebrated alderman, when I say that the Citizen Kingship of London has never, and never will be, *eclipsed* by a better subject of Her Most Gracious Majesty, Queen Victoria.

1st Lesson. Sprats, Semi-fried.—Wipe gently with a cloth a dozen of sprats or more, according to the size of your frying-pan, which requires to be very clean; place it for a minute or two on the fire, to get hot through; sprinkle in it about half a teaspoonful of salt to every dozen of middle-size fish, which place immediately in the pan: leave them for two minutes, turn carefully with the blade of a knife, leave them three or four minutes longer, and serve very hot. To serve them on a napkin is preferable.

Addition.—About a quarter of a teaspoonful of pepper, or a little Cayenne; also the juice of lemon, or a drop of vinegar, is a pleasing variation.

2nd.—Dip each sprat in flour, put in the pan a little fat, or oil; when very hot, put in the fish, which semi-fry as above. They may also be lightly covered with egg and bread-crumbs—or use sifted biscuit, which is a very agreeable variety of dressing them.

Another way.—Put them in a tin, with a little lard, oil, or butter, salt and pepper, into the oven. They will take about double the time doing, and will not require turning, which is important. Serve in the tin. You may add chopped parsley and a little lemon, &c.

To broil.—Take a skewer long enough to hold a dozen sprats; dip them lightly in flour; put the gridiron on as clear a fire as possible, and when hot lay them on for two minutes; turn them carefully, leave them till done, sprinkle with salt and pepper, and serve.

Sprat Toast just strikes me.—Take a piece of bread nice and crisp, butter it over; add salt, pepper, and a little mustard, and dish the sprats on it.

Sandwich.—Put another similar slice over, cut in four, and serve. You may add to any of the above receipts a little Harvey's sauce, Chili vinegar, Soyer's relish, or any mild sauce. A little Anchovy paste on the toast would be an improvement.

DEAREST ELOISE,—

WE have remarked before, and must now repeat it, with Hippocrates, that that which pleases the palate nourishes the most.

Nothing can be more applicable than these words of far famed antiquity; and rightly do they apply to a new discovery I made whilst in London, about a month back, which I regard as a blessing to the sufferer who is obliged to seek relief from cod-liver oil. I am pleased to tell you that, in lieu of the generally rancid quality of this preparation, I have found it palatable and rather agreeable, in comparison with the other, and far superior to what I tasted at the Hull Infirmary, during a visit there (see pages 41, 42, and 43), which caused me to think of those dishes in which fresh cod-liver is used: but, as these cannot supply the "mass," I must make you acquainted with this "boon for the million:" and I certainly prefer Dr. De Jongh's Light Brown Cod-liver Oil, which approaches in taste as near to that delicacy, the sturgeon "Caviare," as anything I ever tasted, leaving its medicinal properties in the hands of such eminent authorities as Professor Liebig, Wöhler, Berzelius, Fouquier, Dr. Jonathan Pereira, &c., and the Analytical Commissioner of the "Lancet," who so highly speak in its favour.

I will in a few days forward, as you requested, the receipt of the celebrated Lancashire Pepper Pot.

SOYER'S

NEW CHRISTMAS RECEIPTS.

SOYER'S NEW CHRISTMAS PUDDING.

You are right, dearest Hortense, this is by far the most delicate and best plum-pudding I ever tasted, without being, at the same time, too rich; the combination of ingredients is perfect, and although there is hardly any difference in the materials used in this to an ordinary plum-pudding, it tasted to me like one made of entirely new ingredients, and I consider it a great acquisition to this, the hundredth thousand of our Shilling Cookery.

This receipt, if closely followed, would, at this festive season of the year, save tons of fruit and other expensive ingredients, which are partly wasted for want of knowing how to turn them to the best advantage.

Carefully prepare the following previous to mixing the pudding:—

Christmas Pudding.—Four ounces of stoned raisins, four ounces of sultanas, half-a-pound of well-cleaned currants, half-a-pound of beef suet chopped fine, two ounces of powdered white sugar, two ounces of flour, half-a-pound of bread crumbs, twelve bitter almonds blanched chopped small, half a nutmeg grated, two ounces of candied citron, the peel of half a small lemon chopped fine. When all is prepared separately, put in a basin, break over four eggs, and add half a gill of brandy. Mix these all well the evening before wanted, cover over till the morning, then add half a gill of milk, and well stir your pudding; slightly butter a cloth, sprinkle a little flour over, put it in a basin, pour in the mixture, tie your cloth in the usual way, not too tight; put in half a gallon of boiling water, adding a little more now and then to keep it to half a gallon, let simmer two hours and thirty minutes, turn out of cloth, and serve on a hot dish.

After which, when at the dining-room door, pour round a gill of either brandy or rum, which set on fire with a piece of paper; place the dish on the table, let burn half a minute, and pour the following sauce over from the saucer. Cut seven or eight slices from the pudding crossways, or according to number, when help, and serve very hot.

The sauce I prefer with it is as follows: Make half-a-pint of melted butter, as No. 410, or ordinary plain melted butter, rather thick, add to it two teaspoonfuls of sugar, a small glassful of noyeau, the juice of half a lemon, and a pat of butter; stir quick, pour over your pudding when very hot, or serve separate in a sauce-boat.

You beg of me a simplified receipt of my Christmas pudding. You cannot expect that it will be as good as the above; and if I consent to give it you, it is upon the sensible remark that you make to me on this subject, that though it cannot be expected to be as good as the above, yet in its way it will far excel thousands of puddings with richer ingredients, which are made at this festive season of the year for want of judgment in the proportion.

The above Pudding simplified.—Stone half a pound of common raisins, wash and clean half a pound of currants, half a pound of beef suet chopped fine, two ounces of brown sugar, three ounces of flour, three eggs, half a pound of bread crumbs, half a gill of rum, and a gill of milk. Mix all well the night previous, put in a cloth as above, boil three hours, and serve. Pour over melted butter in which you have put one tablespoonful of sugar and the juice of half a lemon, if handy.

How to vary and improve the Pudding at a trifling expense.— The addition of a little mixed spice or pounded cinnamon, lemon, or orange peel, chopped fine, or a drop or two of any essence, a couple of sharp apples cut in dice, and a few dates or French prunes. Cut the same, using only half the raisins or currants.

Observe, Eloise, that I send you this receipt as a dainty dish, or *bonne bouche*, therefore, if you find it a little complicated in its details, it will at the same time well repay the extra time and trouble, and hardly increase the expense, as I perceive it only costs two shillings and fourpence, and that by buying everything in small quantities. But for those who require plainer puddings, I refer them to receipts No. 334 and the following one, which is still plainer, simpler in its details.

As, no doubt, our readers will fix all their attention on the new receipts for Christmas, it is important to know that some excellent ones are to be found in the body of the book, as being well adapted for this festive season. Some are very economical, to suit persons in such circumstances. For instance, see receipts Nos. 335, 336, 338, 339, 340, 342, 343, 346, 348, 349, and 350.

DEAR ELOISE,—You are aware that any great event in every nation has almost always left behind some national culinary reminiscence of the circumstance, and many a sanguinary battle is kept alive in our memories, both in youth and age, from our eating either puddings or cakes to commemorate it. For instance, the French have their poulet à la Marengo, from that great battle. We have our Michaelmas goose from Queen Elizabeth's victory over the Spanish

Armada. Mince pies, pancakes, &c., all have their data. It would not be attempting too much on our part to add another of these everlasting delicacies to the above many, under the glorious title of the "*Alma Allied Pudding.*" And may the palate of the future generation be as gratified with the excellence of this concoction as the ears of the present one has been with the announcement of the grand victory which took birth, under the united flags of two of these great nations;—which will, it is to be hoped, form the rainbow of union and liberty, and illuminate for ever as a mighty meteor the darkness of despotism.

The Alma Pudding.—Make half a pound of bread crumbs, which put in a basin; add two ounces of sago, six ounces of fine chopped suet, five ounces of sugar, four ounces of sultana raisins, six eggs, half a gill of rum, and one tablespoonful of apricot jam. Well butter the interior of a pudding basin; add the mixture. Put some water in a sauce-pan, set it on the fire; when beginning to boil, put in your basin, which ought to be a little more than half immersed in the water. Boil gently on a slow fire for two hours; take it out, pass the knife between the basin and pudding, and serve.

The Sauce.—Put in a small pan two tablespoonsful of apricot jam and two glasses of sherry; warm gently, when boiling pour over.

How to Ornament the above.—The interior of the basin or mould may be nicely ornamented with currants, green angelica, sultana and Malaga raisins, candied peel, almonds, ginger, &c., &c., which will firmly adhere to the pudding. The first I made I ornamented with a sugar drum fixed on the top, the three allied flags passed through, forming a trophy, surrounding it with brandy balls; a gill of French brandy round it, set on fire, and serve. All the above ornaments may be obtained at a confectioner's.

New Christmas Dish.—A most delicious and cheap dish, easily made.—Buy sixpenny worth of light sponge-cake and raspberry rolls, which cut across in slices about half-an-inch thick; lay them on a small dish in a circle, one lying half over the other; put in an oven for ten minutes, add in a small stew-pan two tablespoonsful of currant-jelly, two glasses of sherry, put on the fire, and when boiling pour over and serve. Any jam, jelly, or marmalade, will do.

Pancake à la De la Pole.—Break four fresh eggs, separate the yolk from the white, which put in two different basins, add to the yoke two tablespoonsful of white pounded sugar, half a one of flour, half the rind of either an orange or lemon, chopped very fine, or a drop of any good essence; beat the whole together, and then with a whisk whip the white of the eggs as you would for a sponge-cake. This requires some practice. When hard and white as snow, mix lightly with the yolk, then have ready a very clean frying-pan, which put on a slow fire, add an ounce of butter, when melted put in two tablespoonsful of the batter, let it fry half a minute, then toss it up on the other side, as a pancake, turn it on a dish, use all the batter thus, and when done put them one on the other. Sugar over, bake ten minutes, and serve. While paying a visit in Devonshire, where I invented this dish, I introduced a gill of cream, previously whipped, which made it very delicate. Ordinary cream may be used instead.

How to make Mincemeat.—Chop fine one pound of beef suet, four ounces of lean beef previously roasted, half a pound of apples, four ounces of raisins previously stoned; the above articles must be chopped separately; put them all in a basin, add to it two ounces of candied lemon and orange peel and citron; cut these small, then put in a quarter ounce of mixed spice, four ounces of sugar, mix the whole well together, add in the juice of a lemon, a quarter of a pint of brandy, stir it, put it in a jar, and use when required. Stewed tripe (cold) may be used instead of beef, and half an ounce of bitter almonds and lemon peel. The above, if made one week before Christmas, will answer every purpose, as I wholly object to fermentation. Line your patty-pan with puff-paste, No. 315A, fill thee-parts full with mincemeat, cover over with paste, egg over, sugar, and bake.

Royal Christmas Fare.—The mince-meat as made at Windsor-Castle every year, the ingredients being mixed one month before wanted, is as follows: 240 lbs. of raisins, 400 lbs. of currants, 200 lbs. of lump sugar, 3 lbs. of cinnamon, 3 lbs. of nutmeg, 3 lbs. of cloves, 3 lbs. of ground allspice, 2 lbs. of ginger, 300 lbs. of beef, 350 lbs. of suet, 24 bushels of apples, 240 lemons, 30 lbs. of cedret, 72 bottles of brandy, 3 lbs. of mace, 60 lbs. of lemon-peel, and 60 lbs. of orange-peel.

New Style of Mince Pies.—Have ready some mince-pie pans, take some firm butter, cover the inside of each pan with it to the depth of an eighth of an inch, lay on this half an inch of bread crumb, made as No. 452, let it all be of the same depth, then fill your pans with stewed apples, as above, till quite full, then lay on some more bread crumbs, on which put a small piece of butter, and bake for half an hour in an oven, then turn out on a dish. They will be found excellent. You may use any kind of small baking-dish.

Apple Toast.—Cut six apples in four quarters each, take the core out, peel and cut them in slices; put in a saucepan an ounce of butter, then throw over the apples about two ounces of white pounded sugar and two tablespoonfuls of water; put the saucepan on the fire, let it stew quickly, toss them up, or stir with a spoon: a few minutes will do them. When tender, cut two or three slices of bread half an inch thick, put in a frying-pan two ounces of butter, put on the fire; when the butter is melted, put in your bread, which fry of a nice yellowish colour; when nice and crisp, take them out, place them on a dish, a little white sugar over, the apples about an inch thick. Serve hot.

2nd Lesson, with Improvements.—Egg the top of the apples, bread-crumb, and put a little butter over; put them in the oven for half an hour, sprinkle over with sugar, and serve. They are also good cold. A tablespoonful of currant jelly, or any nice jam, or a glass of port, sherry, or brandy poured over is excellent. The bread may be well toasted, buttered, and sugared over, the bread being cut in any shape you may fancy, either round or in dice; they will dish well in crown shape. A glass of rum or brandy may be placed in the centre and set on fire when sent to table.

If served cold, whipped cream may be put over.

Amongst my Christmas gifts I must not omit one of the simplest and nicest that I ever concocted. It is at once simple and economical, and should follow the immortal plum-pudding.

New Manner of Stewing Pears.—Take six large pears, well ripe, which at this season of the year can be bought for about two pence each, cut each in two lengthways, peel them slightly, put them in a very clean stewpan, cover them over with three ounces of white sugar powdered, slightly peel a lemon, cut the rind into small strips, press the juice on top of the sugar, gently shake the pan, it will dissolve the sugar, then put it on a very slow fire for ten or fifteen minutes, shake it gently once or twice, turn each piece with a fork put it on the fire, and let it stew again for ten minutes. When done, put them on a dish to cool, then dress them on a flat dish, pour the syrup over, and serve. They may also be done in a slow oven.

The above varied.—Two teaspoonfuls of currant jelly or jam, marmalade, or orange may be mixed with syrup, or half a glass of either maraschino or brandy. Any kind of pear, if ripe, will do. The core, if large, must be removed.

OMISSION.

Goose Stuffing.—For a middling sized bird, peel and cut in two, crossways, four large-sized onions, weighing altogether about one pound; slice these rather fine, chop them up with some green sage, or bruise with both hands some dry; then put in a black pot or pan two ounces of butter, lard, or dripping; add in the chopped onions two teaspoonsful of sage if green, three if dry, one of salt, one of brown sugar, half one of pepper. Set this on a slow fire, letting it stew for fifteen to twenty minutes; then with a spoon stuff your bird while the onions are quite hot. This may be done in winter a few days before it is put to the spit, as it imparts to the goose a nice savoury flavour.

How to vary the Stuffing.—Four tablespoonsful of bread crumb may be added, or two of broken biscuit, or four of chopped apples, or four of rice, or four of cold boiled potatoes, or a little chopped lemon, or a little herbs of almost any kind, or chopped boiled beetroot.

INDEX.

. *In the following Index, the figures with the letter* p. *refer to pages;*
the other numbers refer to receipts.

www.ingramcontent.com/pod-product-compliance
Lightning Source LLC
Chambersburg PA
CBHW020625030726
47497CB00007B/2412